FRANCE AND BRITAIN 1900–1940:
ENTENTE AND ESTRANGEMENT

FRANCE AND BRITAIN 1900–1940:

Entente and Estrangement

P. M. H. Bell

Longman
London and New York

Longman Group Limited,
Edinburgh Gate, Harlow,
Essex CM20 2JE, England
and Associated Companies throughout the world.

*Published in the United States of America
by Longman Publishing, New York*

First published 1996

ISBN 0 582 22954 5 CSD
ISBN 0 582 22953 7 PPR

British Library Cataloguing-in-Publication Data

A catalogue record for this book is
available from the British Library

Library of Congress Cataloging-in-Publication Data

Bell, P. M. H. (Philip Michael Hett). 1930–
    France and Britain, 1900–1940 : entente and estrangement /
P.M.H. Bell.
      p.   cm.
    Includes bibliographical references and index.
    ISBN 0-582-22954-5 (csd). -- ISBN 0-582-22953-7 (ppr)
    1. France--Foreign relations--1870–1940. 2. France--Foreign
relations--Great Britain. 3. Great Britain--Foreign relations--
France. I. Title.
DC59.8.G7B45   1996
327.44041--dc20   95-41012
                                           CIP

Set by 7r
Produced by Longman Singapore Publishers (Pte) Ltd.
Printed in Singapore

Contents

Preface and Acknowledgements   vii

Introduction: Attitudes and Landmarks   1

 1 **The Remembrance of Things Past**   6

 2 **Entente Cordiale, 1902–1905**   23

 3 **Entente or Alliance? 1906–1914**   38

 4 **Comrades in Arms: (i) The High Command**   60

 5 **Comrades in Arms: (ii) Economics and War Aims**   78

 6 **The Shock of War**   92

 7 **Peace-making, 1919–1920**   113

 8 **The German Question, 1920–1926**   132

 9 **'Providence has made us an island'**   154

10 **Things Fall Apart, 1929–1934**   167

11 **Storm Cone, 1935**   184

12 **Appeasement and War, 1936–April 1940**   204

13 **Their Finest Hour – L'Heure Tragique, 1940**   232

Contents

Conclusion 251

Bibliographical Essay 255
Index 266

Preface and Acknowledgements

The subject of this book has been near the centre of my intellectual life for many years, ever since I first embarked on university teaching and research. In this I am far from alone: relations between France and Britain, and their views of one another across the Channel, impinge on many aspects of academic work, and (far more widely) engage the interest of many Britons who live, work or take their holidays in France. The book has also been a labour of love. I write as a devoted and patriotic Englishman with a deep and abiding affection for France, and I hope this book will appeal to all those who share these attributes. After all, it has been wisely said that every civilised man has two countries: his own and France.

In writing this book, I have incurred many obligations. Most of the personal ones I prefer to acknowledge privately; but I owe a special debt to those friends who have read drafts, with keen eyes and careful judgement, and usually in the midst of heavy work of their own. I am deeply grateful to David Dutton, John Lukacs, Ralph White and Charles Williams for all their comments and advice. Among institutions, the University of Liverpool allowed me a year's study leave to work on this book; the British Academy and the Association for the Study of Modern and Contemporary France awarded me research grants which assisted that work. To these bodies I am most grateful.

Much of the research, reading and writing has been accomplished during long residence in Paris. I was made most welcome by French historians, and learned much in seminars and even more from conversation.

From a life-time's enthusiasm and activity, there is much archival research behind this book; but even so, by its very nature, it is primarily a work of synthesis. My main intellectual debts are to those who have worked in the field before me, and I gladly offer my recognition in the bibliographical essay. Reference notes are mostly used to give sources for quotations and statistics. Quotations from French sources have been translated, usually by my wife. Much more important, it was my wife who introduced me to France many years ago; and she has shared the work and the delight of this book from start to finish.

Another book, already well advanced, will take the story of relations between France and Britain, and their views of one another, from 1940 to as near the present day as can be managed.

P. M. H. Bell
Paris and Kew
1994–95

Introduction

ATTITUDES AND LANDMARKS

Nations reveal much about themselves in their relations with one
another. Jules Michelet, that great patriotic French historian, wrote in
his *Tableau de la France*:

> The struggle against England has done France a very great service by
> confirming and clarifying her sense of nationhood. Through coming together
> against the enemy the provinces discovered that they were a single people.
> It is by seeing the English close to, that they felt that they were France. It
> is the same with nations as with the individual; he gets to know and
> defines his personality through resistance to what is different from himself.
> He becomes conscious of what he is through what he is not.[1]

The main thread of this book is relations between France and Britain
as states – political, military and economic; but always intertwined
with that thread there runs the theme of each country's understanding
of the other, and of itself in relation to the other.

The period from 1900 to 1940 was one of close relations between
France and Britain as states. It was marked near the beginning by the
conclusion of the agreement of April 1904 which is always known as
the *Entente cordiale*, a name which has entered the vocabulary of both
countries, and whose persistence is a tribute to the power of words.

---

1. Jules Michelet, *Tableau de la France* (Paris, reprint by Société d'Edition 'Les
Belles Lettres', 1947), pp. 82–93. This *Tableau* originally formed about one-half of Vol.
II of Michelet's *Histoire de France*, first published in 1833 and substantially revised in
another edition in 1861. It was the 1861 edition which was re-issued in 1947 and is
quoted here.

There followed the common struggle and immense sacrifice of the Great War of 1914–18. Thereafter, despite much friction, each country continued to believe that in the last resort it could count on the support of the other in a war against Germany; and indeed the conflict was renewed in 1939.

In the nature of things, this was not the whole story. Relations with Germany were not clear-cut or static. It was again Michelet, reflecting on the influence of geography, who wrote that: 'Germany is not opposed to France, rather is she parallel to her.'[2] There was truth in this, even in the period marked by great Franco-German wars; and there were significant signs of understanding between the two countries, particularly in economic affairs. Equally there were times when Britain sought to act as mediator between France and Germany, or even took the side of Germany against France. At the same time, another triangular relationship took shape, between Britain, France and the United States. Here, the usual alignment tended to be one of Britain and the USA over against France. Despite much friction between the British and Americans, the French certainly believed in an Anglo-Saxon combination against them, in politics, economics and not least cultural matters. The French language was constantly losing ground to the growing influence of English – a cause of lasting chagrin to many Frenchmen.

Relations between France and Britain as states were thus close but complicated. The attitudes which the two peoples held towards one another were also deep-rooted and ambiguous. In both countries there were elite groups – travellers, businessmen, intellectuals, journalists – who took a close interest in affairs across the Channel. At the turn of the nineteenth and twentieth centuries there were strong common sentiments, amounting sometimes to mutual admiration, among these elites. Cultivated Englishmen were fascinated by French art and literature. Many among the upper and middle classes found the French way of life (and French prices) so agreeable that they settled on the Riviera, in Normandy or in Paris. The French capital during the *belle époque* was a magnet of culture, elegance and *joie de vivre*. In France, political writers admired the stability of British institutions, which stood in marked contrast to France's frequent changes of regime and the fleeting ministries of the Third Republic. Queen Victoria's long reign and the genial yet shrewd personality of Edward VII impressed many Frenchmen with the virtues and utility of the British monarchy.

British and French elites thus each admired something different in

2. Ibid., p. 5.

the other country; but they shared a sense of belonging to a common civilisation, a cultured and liberal society, believing in progress and humanity. The two countries had developed different forms of parliamentary democracy, but they were conscious of the common ground between them, especially in contrast to authoritarian traditions elsewhere in Europe. At a deeper level, they both still drew heavily on their roots in the legacy of ancient Greece, Rome and Christianity.

Outside the elites there prevailed other stereotypes and persistent ideas, mainly of a sombre hue. The antagonism between the two countries had been long and bitter, and had left its mark on the history books (not least those used in schools), and also often on popular opinion and folk-memory. Napoleon may serve as a case in point. To many – probably most – Frenchmen around the turn of the century he was a hero, whom the British had prevented from uniting Europe and then imprisoned on St Helena. To most of the British to whom his name meant anything, he was a tyrant, who had got his come-uppance at the hands of Nelson and the Duke of Wellington. However vague the history might be in either case, the images were strong and enduring. Such memories had a life of their own, and came to the surface from time to time, even when political circumstances or official propaganda encouraged a quite different view.

Within the period examined in this book, it sometimes happened that the two countries and peoples took utterly different views of the same events – landmarks which assumed very dissimilar shapes when viewed from opposite sides of the Channel. At the end of the nineteenth century there occurred the Fashoda crisis, when two military expeditions, one French and the other British, encountered one another at Fashoda on the White Nile in September 1898. On the ground, no shots were fired or casualties incurred. Between the two governments there was a brief battle of wills, with the British insisting on immediate and unconditional French withdrawal from Fashoda. The French had to accept these terms, amounting to a public humiliation. There was a great outcry in the French press, and emotions ran strong and deep in the officer corps of the armed services. Fashoda was long remembered in France as an example of British brutality and injustice. De Gaulle referred to it near the beginning of his memoirs of the Second World War. During that war, over forty years after the event, the British War Cabinet's Minister-Resident in the Middle East, Richard Casey, remarked despairingly that the French General Catroux was talking to him about Fashoda, of which he had never heard. As recently as February 1994 the London correspondent of *Le Figaro* mentioned Fashoda in an article, and claimed that the British too still remembered it. In this he was certainly mistaken. In Britain the episode was forgotten almost as soon as it was over. From the British point of view, nothing had actually happened, and within a year the Boer War gave people something much more serious to think about. By the time of the Second World War, never mind 1994, the affair had entirely vanished from memory, except among a few historians. Fashoda forms a striking example of a landmark which long remained prominent from a French point of view, but rapidly became almost invisible to the British. The consequences gave ample scope for bitterness on the French side and incomprehension on the British.

A more recent and conspicuous landmark is found in the evacuation from Dunkirk at the end of May and beginning of June 1940. Within some ten days, about 220,000 British troops and rather over 100,000 French, surrounded by German forces, were taken off from the port and beaches of Dunkirk by a host of ships, mostly British. In Britain this was seen at the time as a deliverance, almost a victory. The word miracle was used without any sense of incongruity. The event was remembered with pride for years afterwards, and it became a commonplace for British Prime Ministers to invoke 'the spirit of Dunkirk' as a rallying-cry in adversity. In France the impression was, and has largely remained, utterly different. At the time, the French troops involved were painfully conscious that the British were getting away first; and some 30–40,000 French soldiers were in fact left behind to form the rearguard and finally to surrender. There rapidly developed the belief that the whole operation had involved a deliberate and cynical betrayal of the French by the British. In a longer perspective, even the most favourable French interpretation has been that Dunkirk was an operation in which the two armies made drastically unequal sacrifices. Any conception of deliverance or miracle is completely out of the question. This landmark long remained visible from each side of the Channel (and probably has still not completely faded from view), but its appearance in the eyes of the two peoples has been completely different, and these contrasts have had a lasting effect on national outlooks.

In this book, the foreground is occupied by the relations between France and Britain as states, geographically close neighbours and with many shared political and strategic interests. But these relations were constantly affected by the background: long histories, much intertwined; shared cultural roots; similar liberal-democratic institutions and values; and the perceptions which each country had of the other – sometimes admiring, sometimes hostile, rarely indifferent. The story is a complex one, and deals with both the relations of states and views across the Channel. For clarity of exposition, the two aspects are sometimes separated out into different chapters.

In discussing all these matters, there is a pervasive problem of nomenclature. France and the French are relatively straightforward words, to be used with confidence and little fear of misunderstanding. Britain, on the other hand, is a short-hand expression generally used to denote the state whose proper title is the United Kingdom of Great Britain and Northern Ireland (Ireland *tout court* at the beginning of our period); and British describes a nationality which has developed since the Act of Union between England and Scotland in 1707. In practice, English, Welsh, Scots and Northern Irish have retained separate identities; and attitudes towards France can vary a good deal among these different peoples. For example, English nationality and identity were originally formed in conflict with France during the Hundred Years' War; but the Scots long cherished the 'auld alliance' *with* France against England. Such memories have not entirely disappeared.

The French usually tend to deal with these problems by ignoring them, referring indiscriminately to England and the English, even when they mean Britain and the British. Writers in English have often fallen into the same habit, and used 'Anglo-French relations' as an all-embracing term. Richard Faber took as his title for an admirable book on relations between the two peoples *French and English*, referring to a game played in his boyhood.[3] Denis Brogan, that good Scot and lifelong Francophile, often wrote about French relations with England, even long after the Act of Union.[4] I have tried to deal with this tricky problem by referring always to Britain and Franco-British relations whenever that is proper, reserving England for its own precise meaning.

3. Richard Faber, *French and English* (London, 1975).
4. See, e.g. D.W. Brogan, *The French Nation from Napoleon to Pétain, 1814–1940* (London, 1957), p. 205 and elsewhere.

5

CHAPTER 1

The Remembrance of Things Past

France and Britain entered the twentieth century bearing a heavy burden from the past. Both peoples lived with their history, the French perhaps more deliberately so than the British. The French tended to invoke the past with a set purpose, in anniversaries and other commemorations (as they still do), and in the patriotic aspirations of school textbooks. The British evocation of their history was less formal, but perhaps even more deep-rooted in stories and folk-memory.

Much of this mental baggage concerned relations between England (later Britain) and France, and some of it had been carried from as long ago as the Hundred Years' War. The archers of Crécy and Agincourt were familiar in the Britain of 1900. (They were supposedly to appear in ghostly form to support the hard-pressed British infantry at Mons in 1914.) In France, Joan of Arc was a universally recognised symbol of French nationalism, and the enemy she fought was of course the English. The Hundred Years' War set England and France on a course not simply of separation but of antagonism. The later wars between the France of Louis XIV and the England of William III and the Duke of Marlborough left memories in both countries, as did their Atlantic and Indian wars in the eighteenth century. Clive in India and Wolfe at Quebec figured in popular boys' stories by G. A. Henty. For the French, the long struggle in America ended badly at Quebec, leaving an outpost of France cut off from the motherland. But there was revenge in the War of American Independence, when the French helped the Americans to win their freedom from the British. Then came the Revolutionary and Napoleonic Wars, lasting over twenty years and leaving lively memories. In Britain, the Duke of Wellington held a Waterloo dinner annually as long as he lived, which was until

1852. The Royal Navy marked Trafalgar Day with due ceremony, and Nelson's Column in Trafalgar Square was one of London's best-known landmarks. In France, the remains of Napoleon were brought back from St Helena (by courtesy of Palmerston, it should be added) and interred with great ceremony in the church of the Invalides. The Arc de Triomphe was restored, inscribed with a long list of all Napoleon's victories, and became the nation's military shrine. These memories were not far beneath the surface as the twentieth century began. In 1913 the British were discussing how to mark the centenary of Waterloo when it came round in 1915. At the French Embassy in London it had already been decided that no representative should attend.

Yet it was also true that in 1900, for the first time since the invention of gunpowder, there was no-one living in either country who had fired a shot in a war between Britain and France – a remarkable and hopeful condition. Moreover, the years since Waterloo had witnessed distinct improvements in Anglo-French relations. The process began in the 1820s, and continued in the 1830s during Talleyrand's years as Ambassador in London. In the 1840s Peel in Britain and Guizot in France, two sober, shrewd and conservative statesmen, did much to develop good relations between the two countries. It was in the early 1840s that the phrase *entente cordiale* came to be applied to Anglo-French relations. When King Louis-Philippe visited London in October 1844, he said in a speech: 'France asks nothing from England. England asks nothing from France. We only desire *entente cordiale*.' In 1846 the Duke of Wellington wrote that 'There is no individual more convinced than I am of the necessity for peace, and indeed good understanding, possibly even *entente cordiale* with France. . . .'[1] In 1854 Victor Hugo treated it as a familiar phrase, though he was aggrieved by its practical consequences. He found it difficult to get to London, 'for, since the *entente cordiale*, the Bonaparte–Palmerston police is lying in wait for us'.[2] The popularity and longevity of the phrase are striking. It is rare for such a term to enter current speech in two countries, and even less common for it to keep its place for 150 years.

1. Louis Philippe quoted in M. Ressy, ed., *Dictionnaire des citations de l'histoire de France* (Paris, 1990), p. 418; Wellington quoted in Richard Faber, *French and English* (London, 1975), p. 40.

2. CNRS, *Trésor de la langue française* (Paris, 1979), vol. VII. This entry also includes a reference by François Mauriac in 1961: 'The *entente cordiale* was a masterpiece of diplomacy, completely artificial.' This was only partially true: the phrase acquired a life of its own.

The new Anglo-French cordiality was displayed in an exchange of royal visits in 1855, setting an example for what was to become a long series of similar state occasions. Napoleon III and the Empress Eugénie were invited to England, and then Queen Victoria, Prince Albert and the fourteen-year-old Prince of Wales (later Edward VII) went to Paris. In a dramatic gesture the Prince, at his mother's behest, knelt before the tomb of Napoleon. At the same time, far away in the Crimea, the British and French armies were fighting side by side against the Russians. In 1860 the Cobden commercial treaty between the two countries was intended to promote friendship as well as trade. Cobden wrote optimistically that 'The people of the two nations must be brought into mutual dependence by the supply of each other's wants. . . . It is God's own method of producing an *entente cordiale*.'[3] The actual consequences were not quite so rosy, especially for French manufacturers exposed to competition from across the Channel; but the hope of concord through commerce was not easily extinguished.

The *entente cordiale* went on, but even in the 1850s there was an uneasy accompaniment of friction. In 1852 the funeral of the Duke of Wellington on 18 November, evoking memories of the war against Napoleon, was followed almost at once by the proclamation on 2 December of the Second Empire, under Napoleon III. The British at once drew alarming parallels, and set about strengthening the Channel defences with Martello towers. The scare quickly died away (though the Martello towers are there to this day), to be followed by the honeymoon of 1855. But soon there was a renewed crisis, sparked off by naval rivalry. In 1859 the French launched *La Gloire*, the first steam-powered ironclad battleship, and the British replied the next year with HMS *Warrior*. There was a sudden fear of a French invasion, and the British raised a volunteer Rifle Corps. Tennyson published his poem, 'Form, Riflemen, Form!' in *The Times* in May 1859. In June Queen Victoria herself reviewed detachments of the volunteers. In July a member of the House of Lords told his fellow peers that 'the French eagles might stream from every steeple from Acton to Ealing and from Ealing to Harrow; the very prospect was enough to throw every Frenchman into a transport of joy . . .'[4] The precision of this route is remarkable, and the whole invasion scare now seems far-fetched. Yet at the time there was a nerve in England ready to be jangled by such an alarm. There were similar nerves on the other side of the Channel. Even during the Crimean War, when France and Britain were fighting

3. Faber, *French and English*, p. 43.
4. Hansard, *Parliamentary Debates*, 3rd series, vol. 154, cols. 517–18. The speaker was Lord Howden.

on the same side, the sight of sails off Camaret Bay in Brittany raised an alarm of an English invasion. After all, they had landed there twice before.

These scares passed, but they left a mark. Naval rivalry continued for the remainder of the nineteenth century, and was by no means dead in the twentieth. The Franco-Prussian War of 1870 left another and a deeper scar on French attitudes to Britain. At the start of the war the British government (with Gladstone as Prime Minister) quickly declared its neutrality, an action bitterly condemned by the French, who held that Britain stood aloof while Germany seized the mastery of Europe. Over forty years later, in 1915, Jacques Bainville (the intellectual mentor of the Action Française and a gifted historian) saw in the press that one of Gladstone's grandsons had been killed in action. 'There', he wrote, 'is a grandson whom his grandfather killed as surely as if he had loaded the Boche's rifle himself.'[5] Such a judgement is a shock to an English reader, yet Bainville was only expressing with a particular sharpness a resentment which was widely shared.

The 1880s and 1890s were the time of the so-called scramble for Africa, and of Anglo-French colonial rivalry in West Africa and the Nile valley, as well as even further afield in Burma, Siam and the Pacific islands. This rivalry produced much skirmishing in the press of both countries, and some danger of actual conflict. It was always possible, for example, that French and British expeditions in disputed areas of Africa might stumble against one another. In the event, the sharpest crisis arose in the Nile valley, in a confrontation between a force commanded by Kitchener and a French expedition led by Marchand at Fashoda in 1898. The circumstances were hazardous, but the actual danger of war was probably slight. On the spot, the British superiority in numbers was so great as to render a conflict pointless. In Paris, the French naval staff was consulted, but reported that the fleet could not sustain a war at sea. In any case, Delcassé, the French Foreign Minister, was well aware that for France the Nile valley was not worth a large-scale war. His best course was to find a way out of the crisis that would save face. The trouble was that the British offered no such route. The tone of the press was strident, and Lord Salisbury was immovable, insisting on unconditional withdrawal by the French expedition.

This left the French with no real choice. Delcassé agreed to withdraw from Fashoda. As far as the British were concerned, this

5. Jacques Bainville, *Journal 1901–1918* (Paris, 1948), p. 167.

took all the steam out of the crisis, even for the press, and the event was quickly forgotten. But on the French side deep scars remained. It was doubtless true, as Paul Mantoux wrote a few years later, that hardly anyone in France knew where Fashoda was or whether it really mattered. But the newspapers voiced a resentment and sense of humiliation which was deeply felt by many of their readers. The nationalist papers in particular pulled no punches: the British were arrogant, bullying, hypocritical – charges in which there was much truth. A cartoon in *Le Rire*, a leading humorous political journal, depicted Albion as a bird of prey. Another cartoon, on the cover of *L'Illustration* (a popular weekly) showed France as Little Red Riding Hood, carrying fruit labelled 'Fashoda', and Britannia as the wolf. The resentment thus expressed bit deep and lasted long in some parts of French society, not least among the officers of both the army and the navy.

At quite another level – intellectual, not emotional – Fashoda raised a fundamental problem in French foreign policy. Her European and colonial policies pulled in different directions. In Europe, Germany was the enemy; in Africa, Britain. Clemenceau put the matter forcibly: France could not go to war over marshland in Africa while the Germans held Strasbourg. But not everyone agreed. Parts of the nationalist press claimed that Germany was merely a temporary opponent, while England was the permanent enemy. At the time, this argument found few supporters, but it was stored away in the collective memory of the nationalist Right, to re-emerge after the defeat of 1940.

Within a year, Fashoda was followed by the Boer War. At the end of 1899 Britain went to war with the Republics of the Transvaal and the Orange Free State. For the French, this was another display of British arrogance and brutality against a tiny opponent. The opening Boer victories were greeted by the French press. When the British won the war in the field and turned to what were called at the time 'concentration camps' to finish off the guerrilla campaign, the French invoked the Rights of Man against them. In November 1900 President Kruger of the Transvaal visited Europe to seek support. He was welcomed at Marseilles by enthusiastic crowds, and the Senate and Chamber of Deputies passed resolutions of sympathy. He was received by the President of the Republic and the Foreign Minister, though what they actually said was cautious and noncommittal. In the event, the war passed without the French government taking any action against Britain; but the importance of the episode lay not in diplomacy but in public feeling.

Fashoda and the Boer War, coming closely one after the other, meant that the old century ended and the new began on a very sour note. The French had been given much cause to revive that loaded phrase 'perfide Albion.' It was Bossuet, the great bishop and orator, who in the late seventeenth century attached the adjective 'perfidious' to England, in the unlikely context of a sermon on the Feast of the Circumcision. It was while lamenting the English lapse into Protestantism that he exclaimed 'L'Angleterre, ah! la perfide Angleterre.' Much later, Napoleon quoted Bossuet's phrase when he was about to depart for exile on St Helena. As Richard Faber commented: 'Levelled by two such authorities, with whatever enormities in view, the charge of perfidy could not fail to stick.'[6] With the romantic substitution of 'Albion' for the straightforward 'Angleterre', Anglophobia in France gained its distinctive slogan. At the turn of the nineteenth century, it was back in vogue.

The French and British carried plenty of mental baggage from the past, from the time of the Hundred Years' War onwards. At the start of the twentieth century, the two countries were also being forced into fresh calculations about their respective positions in terms of power. In the past, these had undergone some drastic changes. In the late seventeenth century, in the reign of Louis XIV, France was by far the leading power in Europe, in wealth, armed strength, culture and reputation. During the eighteenth century Britain moved forward, as her wealth, population and power grew. In the nineteenth century the balance tilted very much in Britain's favour as she became the first modern industrial nation and developed an empire greater than that of France. Moreover, the long reign of Queen Victoria saw the growth of a massive self-confidence and pride in British institutions which outlived the Queen and left a profound mark on the British character. France on the other hand slipped from her position of predominance in Europe. From about the middle of the nineteenth century her population increased only very slowly. The performance of French industry over the century, in terms of per capita product, may not have been very far behind the British, but the sense of dynamism and vitality was lacking. The British economy thrived on free trade, the French needed protection. The most terrible verdict on France was that of battle. The Franco-Prussian War of 1870–71 ended in crushing defeat and the loss of Alsace and Lorraine. The new German Empire (the Second Reich) was actually inaugurated in the Hall of Mirrors at Versailles.

6. Faber, *French and English*, pp. 60–1.

In the course of the century, Britain had become the leading power in the world, and Germany the predominant power in Europe. France had fallen behind in both spheres. Britain was at the height of her wealth, power and confidence, displayed to the world in the celebrations of Queen Victoria's diamond jubilee in 1897. France was in relative decline. Her internal divisions were reflected in frequent changes of regime: since 1815, the French had lived under two different monarchies, an Empire and two Republics. The Third Republic had lasted nearly thirty years, but its foundations still seemed shaky, and it was governed by old men – the French themselves had a joke that their country was ruled by men in their seventies only because those over eighty were dead. In the 1890s the Dreyfus Affair exacerbated existing divisions in French society.

But this was not the whole story. Not far beneath the surface of British self-confidence lay gnawing anxieties. The British were conscious that their economic performance was not what it had been. Industrial production was still rising, but at a much slower rate than earlier in the nineteenth century. The industries of Germany and the United States were developing fast, and possessed greater resources, better technology and more dynamism. Moreover, Britain's strategic security was in doubt. Even the Royal Navy, the largest fleet in the world as well as the proudest, could not be strong everywhere. Already the government had concluded that they would have to accept American control of the Caribbean. In the Mediterranean, British predominance was threatened by the Franco-Russian alliance. A large Far Eastern squadron could only be maintained at the cost of other stations. On land, the small professional Army was tightly stretched to defend a diverse and widespread empire. Kipling marked the Queen's diamond jubilee with his poem 'Recessional', published in *The Times*:

> Far-called, our navies melt away,
> On dune and headland sinks the pyre;
> Lo, all our pomp of yesterday
> Is one with Nineveh and Tyre.

It was, of course, a warning against thoughtless over-confidence, not a strategic analysis; but in fact the strategic warning was also just.

These economic and strategic problems were bound to have repercussions on foreign policy. British policy towards the end of the nineteenth century was often described by the term 'isolation', sometimes dignified as 'splendid isolation'. The term was somewhat misleading. Complete isolation was never attempted or desired. Lord Salisbury, who was Foreign Secretary for most of the 1880s and 90s, was well aware that Britain had to co-operate with other powers from time to time, making particular agreements to deal with particular problems. What he insisted on avoiding was any binding commitment which might draw Britain into a European war in circumstances which were not of her choosing or which did not affect her vital interests. The policy was not so much one of isolation as of a free hand, and the avoidance of commitments at a time when every other great power in Europe was building up alliances.

The Boer War threw this policy into doubt. In South Africa, the British Army suffered humiliating defeats at the hands of a few Boer farmers. In Europe, Britain faced almost universal condemnation. Deep anxieties were raised at home by the poor physical state of recruits for the army. Medical examinations revealed cases so appalling as to set off a wave of concern about living conditions in the cities, the health of the nation, and even the whole future of the British race. What was to be done? Did British security now demand the making of alliances? The answer was by no means clear. Given time, the British Army recovered from its defeats and won the war in South Africa, with help from Australian and Canadian volunteers which induced a warm imperial glow. The Navy moved squadrons about ostentatiously, to demonstrate the fact of British control of the sea-lanes to the Cape. The European powers were critical of Britain and wondered about joint diplomatic action, but did nothing. Not for the first time, the British muddled through and won the last battle.

The Boer War thus raised questions without producing clear answers. The British knew they must remedy their own weaknesses. They reformed and redeployed the Army and the Navy. But was it necessary to look for outside help, and seek an alliance with a European power? They were by no means certain. What they looked for was a half-way house: reassurance against the dangers of isolation without the commitment of an alliance. But the key point was that they felt the need for reassurance. If the British had retained all their old self-confidence there would have been no basis for an entente with France at all.

French governments were more clearly conscious of their difficulties. The French population (not quite 39 millions in 1901) had been almost static since 1880. French industry was mainly small-scale, with many small firms and very few giants. Foreign trade (imports and exports together) was almost static in value between 1880 and 1900, while German foreign trade increased by 80.9 per cent over the same period.[7] Only in banking did the French outdo the Germans, France being the second banking power in the world, with large-scale foreign investments, notably in Russia. In general, however, the facts of population and economics made it increasingly difficult for France to maintain her status as a great power.

In foreign policy France faced two problems. In Europe her enmity against Germany, with Alsace and Lorraine at its root, seemed irreconcilable. In the Place de la Concorde in the centre of Paris, a number of statues represent the great cities of France, and after 1871 the statue of Strasbourg was draped in black as a sign of mourning for the lost provinces. With the passage of time the emotional force of the gesture diminished, but even so no French politician dared to say in public that he would renounce Alsace-Lorraine. Outside Europe, on the other hand, France was in frequent dispute with Britain, at points which lay scattered across the world from the Newfoundland Banks to West Africa, the Nile valley, Siam and the South Pacific.

France therefore confronted two major enemies: Germany across the Rhine, Britain across the world. To assist her she had an alliance with Russia, concluded in 1894. This was primarily anti-German, facing the Germans with the threat of war on two fronts; but it could also function against the British in Central Asia. But even with Russian support, France could not afford to fight both Germany and Britain. Indeed it was doubtful whether she could fight either singly. French policy increasingly faced the question of whether both these feuds could be continued, or whether one should be abandoned to pursue the other more effectively. During the Fashoda crisis and the Boer War, the French speculated about some agreement with Germany to free their hands against the British, but nothing came of it. Alsace-Lorraine stood in the way. That left the possibility of a reconciliation with Britain to strengthen France's position against Germany.

In terms of diplomacy and strategy, therefore, Britain and France had begun to eye one another with a guarded but hopeful surmise. Both were considering changes in the pattern of their foreign policies. Britain was wondering whether it was necessary to seek a European ally. She was far from convinced, but if the necessity arose France was a possible candidate. France was much nearer to the point of decision. To continue the long-standing enmities against both Germany and Britain was to have one enemy too many. The need to seek reconciliation with one or the other was becoming pressing. The territorial and emotional wound inflicted by Germany in 1871 was

---

7. M. Tacel, *La France et le Monde au XXe siècle* (Paris, 1989), pp. 19–21, 43.

deeper than anything left by colonial disputes with the British, and an approach to Britain looked the better prospect.

CURRENTS OF OPINION: FRANCE

At this stage the remembrance of things past – the mental baggage of the two countries – and the calculation of national interest had to become compatible. France and Britain were both parliamentary democracies, with vigorous and vigilant newspapers and a small but keenly interested public opinion on questions of foreign policy. For any reconciliation between France and Britain to be practical and durable, it would have to satisfy the needs of both policy and opinion. What could happen when these were in conflict was shown by the Anglo-Russian agreement of 1907. The reasons of policy which lay behind it were sound, but liberal opinion in Britain could never see Russia as anything but a backward tyranny, and imperialist opinion still feared the Russian threat to India. The agreement was therefore constantly dogged by criticism, and never worked well.

How did France and Britain stand with regard to such a concurrence of interest and opinion?

French opinions of Britain about the turn of the century showed some favourable trends, less dramatic than the bitterness engendered by Fashoda or the Boer War but none the less real. It was a striking fact that many French exiles, from the time of the Huguenots onwards, chose to go to England when fortune turned against them in their own country. They still did so under the Third Republic. Revolutionaries who escaped after the suppression of the Paris Commune took refuge in London. Later, when a number of religious orders were expelled from France under the Law on Associations, the monks from the abbey of Solesmes settled in the Isle of Wight, where they continued to sing their Gregorian chant in what was not an unduly strange land. These exiles, whatever their politics, recognised the virtues of British tolerance and generosity. At home, French liberals throughout the nineteenth century admired British political institutions. So did Tocqueville, who was not a liberal. (Tocqueville in his turn had influential British admirers, and when he visited England a warship of the Royal Navy took him back to Cherbourg.) Parisian society cultivated the idea of the 'gentleman'. In popular fiction, Jules Verne made a hero of the phlegmatic English clubman Phineas Fogg in *Around the World in Eighty Days*.

In addition, a number of French observers were taking a serious interest in their northern neighbour. It is true that most of them did not travel far. The cross-Channel links of the time meant that French visitors almost invariably landed at one of the south-eastern ports and took the train to London, where many of them stayed. Some ventured to Oxford or Cambridge (the ancient English universities were much admired), or to Windsor (so was the monarchy). But for the most part, as a learned French writer on these matters concluded: 'For a Frenchman, Great Britain is England and England is London.' Oddly enough in view of the 'auld alliance', there seem to have been few French descriptions of Scotland. Jacques Bardoux, whom we shall shortly meet as one of the best-informed French commentators on British affairs, visited Scotland in 1895 and vowed never to return. He admired the grandeur of the scenery, but was oppressed by the solitude and poverty of the countryside. 'I am full of admiration, but cannot bear for more than a single day the dreadful dreariness of the Highlands.'[8]

Social horizons were also limited. Louis Cazamian, a distinguished French authority on English literature, wrote in the 1920s, 'we retain our fathers' old idea that an Englishman is nearly always a lord.'[9] That was certainly true at the turn of the century. In 1895 Bardoux spent some months at Oxford University, where his circle included John Simon, Leo Amery and Charles Osborne – in later life two Cabinet ministers and a senior official in the Indian Civil Service. Paul Morand, later a diplomat and a prolific writer about England, also went to Oxford in 1908–9, and wrote English verses for the undergraduate magazine *Isis*. Later, when he was posted to the Embassy in London, he lived in Belgravia, where his circle of acquaintances included Margot Asquith and Lady Cunard. André Siegfried, destined to become over many years the most widely respected French interpreter of British affairs, was at first at home, through family friends, in the world of the Stock Exchange and Manchester businessmen. Of course there were others who ventured outside these limited circles. Elie Halévy, for example, was one of the best and most widely informed historians of nineteenth-century Britain, and taught the British much about their own country. But for the most part the world of French observers of Britain about the turn of the century was that of the aristocracy and country houses, the ancient English universities, the

8. Marius-François Guyard, *L'image de la Grande-Bretagne dans le roman français, 1914–1940* (Paris, 1954), p. 47; Felix Bonafé, *Jacques Bardoux. Une vocation politique* (Tulle, 1977), p. 45.

9. Quoted in Faber, *French and English*, p. 81.

London clubs and – at the furthest – the upper middle class. At that time, and in terms of political contacts and information, there was much advantage in this. It is hard to see how Bardoux, as a young man of 21, could have improved on his Oxford friends. (Leo Amery was still calling on him for lunch in Paris in 1938.) There was doubtless some danger of misjudging the wider context of British opinion, or of being too much enmeshed in an old England which was soon to pass away. But for most purposes this limited field of vision served very well.

Among French observers of England, Jacques Bardoux stood out in the early 1900s as a rising young journalist and writer. Born in 1874 into a conservative Republican bourgeois family, Bardoux was a student at Oxford, where he was impressed by two things: the small number of undergraduates who did any serious work, and the sense of social and civic duty which none the less prevailed in the university. He attributed this strange contrast to the pervading influence of religion. He met few practising Christians, but was conscious of the constant presence of the religious ethos. This impression proved lasting, and Bardoux long continued to emphasise the importance of religion in British life and politics. In 1901, at the age of 27, he became foreign policy editor for the *Journal des Débats*, a serious and influential newspaper which had close contacts with Delcassé, the Foreign Minister and architect of the *entente cordiale*. In 1903 Bardoux published in that paper a number of articles on British affairs, which became the starting-point for a massive book entitled *Essai d'une psychologie de l'Angleterre contemporaine: Les crises belliqueuses.*[10] It was a sign of his self-confidence that he proclaimed that this was to be the first volume of a series, and a proof of his tenacity that he made good his claim.

In his first volume, published in 1906, Bardoux set out to explain the English character and cast of mind to his fellow-countrymen. According to his analysis, the British people possessed a civic solidarity which was the basis of political liberty, a religious faith which was the foundation of social order, and an immense energy which was the mainspring of economic growth and colonial expansion. They lacked aesthetic sensibility and were weak in critical intelligence, but made up in will-power. Workers stuck persistently at their tasks, however monotonous. Soldiers fought with steady courage – Bardoux actually used the English world 'pluck'. Yet through this stolid tenacity (which

10. Jacques Bardoux, *Essai d'une psychologie de l'Angleterre contemporaine*, vol. 1, *Les crises belliqueuses* (Paris, 1906). The book was 563 pages long.

Bardoux believed reflected the weather, with its damps and mists) there sometimes broke a streak of violence, berserker-like in its intensity. The British could then be pitiless in conflict, as they showed during the Boer War; but the outburst would die away and they were not cruel in victory. (Bardoux may well have recalled this diagnosis in 1919, when he was a member of Marshal Foch's staff and tried to persuade the British to be more severe towards the defeated Germans.) The English mind lay at the opposite pole from the French, in that it could neither formulate nor respect general principles. English books, wrote Bardoux, displayed neither order nor clarity because their readers were not interested in structure but required only that each page should contain its ration of information. Englishmen were interested in facts, and they could neither distinguish a principle nor believe in its beauty.

Strikingly, Bardoux insisted that the British were a people apt for war, and sustained by an ordered discipline which enabled them to wage it successfully. Their religious inheritance had convinced them of divine favour; and if they entered into a war in what they believed to be a just cause they would fight to the end, with a formidable tenacity. British patriotism was a sturdy, confident growth, with no room for self-doubt. Bardoux believed that the old Cobdenite dream of peace through commerce was over, and liberal pacifism in decline. The British were now conscious that their safety and prosperity depended on armed force, and above all on sea-power; and they would use force to protect their interests and especially their commerce.

Bardoux's book appeared in 1906, two years after the conclusion of the *entente* in 1904, but much of its content was based on articles written earlier. It bridged the period of improvement in Franco–British relations, and its main message was that Britain was a suitable friend for France, and potentially a solid ally in war. The British mind held many mysteries, and the British character had its defects, but Bardoux's emphasis lay on British virtues: will-power, steadfastness, patriotism and warlike qualities. It was a striking portrait, and within a few years the British record in the Great War was to demonstrate its accuracy.

In contrast to Bardoux's comparative youth stands the maturity of Paul Cambon, who became French Ambassador in London in 1898, at the age of 55. On his appointment, Cambon wrote to Delcassé that London was unknown territory for him. He stayed for twenty-two years, and came to know it well – or at least those parts which he judged useful for his purposes. He read and understood English, but declined to speak it in diplomatic conversations through a scrupulous desire for precision.

Cambon's impression of Britain and the British placed trade at the centre. This British concentration on commercial interests was a constant source of dispute with France because of the very different approaches of the two countries to questions of trade. In the simplest terms, British free trade was opposed to French protectionism, and some parts of Cambon's analysis are prophetic of the problems which were later to haunt Anglo-French relations in the European Economic Community. He wrote to his brother Jules in 1899:

> It is understandable that England, a trading and industrial nation, should always and everywhere be for free trade. It must be understood that France, an agricultural nation, is obliged to resort to certain protectionist measures to safeguard her agriculture, and agricultural protection entails industrial protection.[11]

Nearly a century later France is still obliged to take certain measures to protect her agriculture, and still comes into conflict with Britain by so doing.

Like Bardoux, Cambon believed that Britain would fight for her commercial interests. The true cause of wars, he maintained, was the need to eat. France could live without her colonies and her overseas links, but Britain could not. She must maintain her fleets, her maritime communications, and her bonds with her colonies. Again like Bardoux, Cambon was struck by the British concern for facts and their empirical approach to problems. He thought that this led the British to be short-sighted in their diplomacy, because they were reluctant to arrange anything in advance of events. Empiricism, in his view, led to short-term views – 'this lack of foresight which is the true characteristic of this people'.[12]

Cambon knew perfectly well that there were problems in dealing with the British, but equally he believed that with patience and care these could be overcome. France would then find a sturdy and a reliable friend. Bardoux thought the same.

CURRENTS OF OPINION: BRITAIN

What was the British view of the French as they looked across the Channel about the turn of the nineteenth and twentieth centuries?

11. Paul Cambon to Jules, 19 June 1899: Paul Cambon, *Correspondance 1870–1924* (3 vols, Paris, 1940–46), vol. II, pp. 17–18.
12. Paul Cambon to Jules, 29 March, 8 April 1900: ibid., pp. 43–5.

The roots of dislike and distrust of France ran deep, nourished by centuries of warfare and an insular suspicion of foreigners, of whom the French were the nearest. It is true that the British never coined a slogan like 'perfidious Albion' to express their dislike of the French, which remained more diffuse than French Anglophobia. Dislike was also partially tempered by the tendency of minorities to admire some aspects of French politics and much of French culture. There were always Englishmen who admired Napoleon – some while he was alive, and more when he was dead. Progressives, liberals and socialists found inspiration in the French revolutionary tradition and the Declaration of the Rights of Man. Love of French culture was particularly strong at the turn of the century, when Parisian art, literature and fashion captured the mind of the English intellectual elite.

These admirers of French culture came from an intellectual elite which had limited influence in the country as a whole. Equally, admirers of French politics, however ardent, were few. In general, the British took a poor view of French politics. Some commentators held that the French were revolutionary by temperament, emotional and excitable, changing their form of government at the merest whim. *Punch* in 1848 published a mock French constitution, in which one article declared that the date of the next revolution was left entirely to the wish of the French people. Others believed that the periodical revolutions merely served to disguise the fact the French were fundamentally conservative. The *Quarterly Review* in 1890 argued that the conservatism of the French would preserve the Third Republic – as indeed for a long time it did. In any case, no-one could deny that the French changed their form of government (monarchy, republic, empire) with disconcerting frequency, and that under the Third Republic French politics was a sort of kaleidoscope, a complete contrast to the steady alternation of Liberal and Conservative. The stereotype of France became a capricious woman – the flighty Marianne as against the solid John Bull.

Looking at the English, Bardoux and Cambon had found them excessively devoted to facts and uninterested in principles. British observers of French politics often reversed these views, finding the French too theoretical and over-concerned with principles rather than practice. The French were prone to pursue some theory to its logical conclusion, irrespective of practicality or commonsense. In the early 1870s it was scarcely credible to any sensible Englishman that the Pretender to the French throne, with the situation apparently ripe for a restoration of the monarchy, should throw away his chances because he insisted that the national flag must be the white banner of the

Bourbons, not the tricolour. The French, in fact, were altogether too sharply and bitterly divided over politics, as distinct from the British, who liked to congratulate themselves on the courtesies observed in the House of Commons, and on the fact that political leaders subscribed to statues of their late opponents.

In a remarkable book on France, published in 1898, J. E. C. Bodley wrote that the British liked to think that every people got the government it deserved, and that they deserved – and had secured – the best. He transferred to the English the Pharisee's prayer: 'Lord, I thank thee that I am not as other men, or even as this Frenchman.'[13] The normal British attitude to French politics was scorn for those who changed both their governments and their regimes far too often. At best, this was modulated into a patronising condescension towards a people who were trying to attain a parliamentary form of government which the British had produced by instinct and continued by tradition.

Beneath such views lay a fundamental problem in British attitudes towards France and the French. The British were convinced that the French were frivolous. Sylvaine Marandon, analysing British attitudes to France in the nineteenth century, reflected on the persistence of this idea: 'the old vision, which is still there – elegance, frivolity, even vice. It is apparently indestructible.'[14] It probably was indestructible – is it not living still? It had a powerful attraction, and not only to pleasure-seekers. The historian J. R. Green, who was by no means light-minded, wrote during the Franco-Prussian War:

> France remains vain, ignorant, insufferable if you will, but still with an
> infinite attraction in her, at least to me. There is a spring, an elasticity
> about her, a 'light heart' that has its good as well as its bad side, a gaiety, a
> power of enjoyment, which Europe can't afford to miss . . . with an
> infinite respect for Berlin, I should prefer *living* in Paris.[15]

In this he spoke for many.

There were some who realised that this image was misleading. Bodley's book depicted a solid, hard-working and well-educated society, where civilisation permeated all classes, to a greater depth than in England. This society rested on 'the great mass of the people of France whose silent, sober energy makes up for the errors of its conspicuous classes'. Bodley quoted with approval a politician's remark

13. J.E.C. Bodley, *France* (second edition, in one volume, London, 1899), Preface, p. xiii.
14. Sylvaine Marandon, *L'image de la France dans l'Angleterre victorienne* (Paris, 1967), p. 669.
15. Faber, *French and English*, pp. 41–2.

that 'We present the spectacle of a tranquil people with agitated legislators.'[16] His book met the desire of a significant minority in Britain to understand France as well as enjoying the French way of life and culture. People were interested in what the French were really doing. They were neighbours, facing similar problems to those in Britain, and finding their own solutions.

This attitude found an echo in that part of the British community resident in France whose object was to promote trade. Thomas Barclay, who for many years presided over the British Chamber of Commerce in Paris (as well as founding the Franco-Scottish Society) made tremendous efforts to convince his fellow-countrymen that the French would make excellent business partners – and diplomatic partners too. During the Paris Exhibition of 1900, he actually persuaded some 500 British businessmen to visit Paris. They were splendidly entertained; but they also saw how the French *worked*.[17] Barclay doubtless failed to dent the common view of a 'business' trip to Paris, but at least he was trying to correct a fundamental error in the widespread British perception of France: a failure to grasp the serious, hard-working, down-to-earth nature of the French people. The final message of his book was to emphasise 'the steady, moral, industrious life of the French people', which continued unaffected by the more sensational aspects of French life.[18]

One Englishman understood the position better than most of his fellow-countrymen. It was not the least of Edward VII's contributions to Anglo-French relations that he enjoyed to the full the frivolous side of French life, but also grasped firmly that there was a serious side. On a visit to Paris when he was Prince of Wales he would entertain an actress one evening, but dine with Gambetta the next. When the time for the *entente* came, he was the right man in the right place.

At the turn of the century the age-old game of 'French and English' was still being played, but beneath the surface there was some earnest questioning. The old stereotypes persisted. The French deplored British empiricism and the British elite admired French culture. The British as a whole doubtless still thought that the French were frivolous. But the question was being raised: did the two countries need one another as serious partners in international affairs? If so, then the stereotypes and mental baggage of centuries would have to be accommodated in a framework of serious politics.

16. Bodley, *France*, pp. 44–5.
17. See Thomas Barclay, *Thirty Years of Anglo-French Reminiscences* (London, 1914), pp. 182–3.
18. Ibid., pp. 335–6.

CHAPTER 2

Entente Cordiale, 1902–1905

Paul Cambon disliked the telephone, and in 1904 the French Embassy in London possessed only one of these new-fangled instruments. However, on 8 April that year Cambon forced himself to use the machine. He was under strict instructions to inform the Foreign Minister, Delcassé, as soon as a certain set of documents had been signed. Not really trusting the telephone wires to convey sound from London to Paris, Cambon bellowed into the instrument: '*C'est signé*'; so that the domestic staff of the Embassy were informed of the event at the same time as the Foreign Minister.[1]

The papers whose signing was thus announced were the complicated package of Anglo-French agreements commonly referred to as the *Entente cordiale*. They had taken nearly two years to negotiate, and consisted of three elements: a Convention relating to Newfoundland, West Africa and Central Africa; a Declaration dealing with Egypt and Morocco, with five secret articles attached to it; and a Declaration concerning Siam, Madagascar and the New Hebrides. These agreements were of crucial importance in Anglo-French relations, and their name *Entente cordiale* is still in use even though their details are forgotten and the whole concept of such arrangements is alien to current thought. They form the starting-point, at once familiar and unknown, for relations between France and Britain in the twentieth century. What brought them about? What were their main characteristics? And what was their immediate significance – which was not necessarily the same as that which developed later?

What process led from the crisis of Fashoda and the ill-will generated by the Boer War to the agreements of 1904?

1. François Charles-Roux, *Souvenirs diplomatiques d'un âge révolu* (Paris, 1956), pp. 47–8.

On the French side, policy was conducted almost exclusively by Théophile Delcassé, who held the post of Foreign Minister for seven years, from June 1898 to June 1905, through five different governments. Throughout this period, he pursued three endeavours with a remarkable consistency: to infuse new life into the Franco-Russian alliance, originally signed in 1894; to detach Italy from her alliance with Germany and Austria–Hungary; and to secure an agreement with Britain. The result of these policies, if they all reached fruition, would be to strengthen the position of France, and leave Germany and Austria–Hungary isolated in Europe. The strand of his policy which led towards an agreement with Britain did not arise from any particular sympathy or friendship for that country. Delcassé was born and raised in the foothills of the Pyrenees, and for some thirty years was deputy for Foix, in the same region – far removed from the Channel coast. He does not appear to have visited England before he did so as Foreign Minister. His first ministerial posts in the 1890s were as Under-Secretary, and later Minister, for the Colonies, where he supported a policy of expansion which frequently entailed friction with Britain. He was pleased when French public opinion regarded him as a man who would stand up to John Bull. His policy was rooted in the pursuit of French interests as he saw them, and equally he believed that the English would only value friendship with countries which commanded respect and safeguarded their own interests.

At the time of Fashoda, standing up to John Bull offered no advantage to French interests. So Delcassé ordered Marchand to withdraw, and accepted the blow to French pride. He accepted also the consequence: that there was no longer the slightest chance of ending the British occupation of Egypt, or even of inducing them to accept some measure of French control there. This was now clear even to the colonial lobby, led by Eugène Etienne, which had been behind the Marchand expedition. Losing hope of Egypt, this group turned to Morocco, and began to talk of its potential wealth, its scope for settlement, and its proximity to France. If France was to take over Morocco, she would have to secure British support. The British had a strategic interest in the Moroccan coast facing Gibraltar; they had trading interests in the country; and, in one of the bizarre arrangements which flourished at that time, the Moroccan army was commanded by a Scotsman, who held the title of Caid Maclean, wore a white bernous and played the bagpipes. The French colonial party thus began to consider the idea of a deal with the British: France would give up her claims in Egypt (which were defunct anyway) in return for British support in Morocco. This would be a good bargain for France, but there was nothing in it for the British – unless there was more to it.

In the general context of Delcassé's policy, there might be much more to it. The prospect of Morocco would win over the colonial party and divert them from their complaints against the British. This would open the way, on the domestic front, for a wider colonial agreement with Britain. In 1900 this prospect began to develop a new attraction for France. By the Navy Law of 1900, the Germans set out to build a large fleet. Within a measurable period, France would either have to build against them or accept that her colonies would be at the mercy of German sea-power. The first course would be very expensive; the second would be both dangerous and humiliating. But there was a third possibility: an agreement with Britain which would gain the support of the Royal Navy.

The prospect of an arrangement with Britain thus looked increasingly attractive for France. It might secure Morocco; it offered insurance at sea; and it held out the distant prospect of the diplomatic isolation of Germany. It was to this end that Delcassé bent his efforts, in his secretive and tenacious manner; and it was to this end that Paul Cambon worked as Ambassador in London.

On the British side, Delcassé's opposite number was Lord Lansdowne, who succeeded Salisbury as Foreign Secretary in October 1900. Lansdowne was a statesman of wide experience: Governor-General of Canada, Viceroy of India, Secretary for War from 1895 to 1900, when he took much of the blame for the state of the Army at the beginning of the Boer War. He thus had first-hand knowledge of the problems of imperial defence. He also had close French connections. His mother was half-French (the daughter of Count de Flahaut, one of Talleyrand's sons, so that Lansdowne was great-grandson to Talleyrand). As a young man he visited his French relations and was at home in the language. In the 1880s he was a keen supporter of the project for a Channel Tunnel, and chairman of the Joint Committee of the two Houses of Parliament to consider the scheme. He also brought a fresh mind to bear on the problems of British foreign policy at the time when Britain was facing the question of whether the old system of a free hand would still suffice, or whether an alliance on the continental pattern was necessary. No clear-cut answer was yet apparent. In January 1902, Joseph Chamberlain (who though not Prime Minister came near to being the effective leader of the government) declared publicly that the British people must count upon themselves alone: 'I say alone, yes, in splendid isolation, surrounded by our kinsfolk' – i.e. the white populations of the colonies.[2] Yet this proud sentiment was contradicted at once. In February 1902 Britain signed an alliance with Japan. It was true that Japan was not a European country, and so the alliance counted for less than it would otherwise have done. But Chamberlain himself had recently sought an alliance with Germany; and British ministers were clearly uncertain in their minds.

The pressures which produced this uncertainty were of two kinds. One was imperial. In the Boer War it took 400,000 British troops to beat two small Republics. While this army was in South Africa, there was nothing at all to spare to meet a crisis elsewhere – in Afghanistan, perhaps, or in China. The second pressure was a growing fear of Germany. This fear developed in the late 1890s, and took root as much in the popular mind as in government policy. The Kaiser's telegram of support to President Kruger of the Transvaal in January 1896 touched off an explosion of anger in the British press. As early as 1891 Salisbury had written speculatively about the Kaiser 'It rather looks to me as if he was not "all there".' The British were puzzled by German policy because, in the words of an acute historian, 'the German challenge was at once very concrete and very abstract.'[3] It was concrete, in that the Germans on occasion threatened war over Samoa, an island in the Pacific which mattered little to either country. It was abstract in that the Germans talked in grandiose terms of *Weltpolitik* and *Weltmacht*, which no-one quite understood but which sounded menacing. In 1900 it became clear that one meaning of *Weltpolitik* was that Germany would build an ocean-going fleet, which touched the British at their most sensitive spot – sea-power. The German threat was also economic. The headlong growth of German industry after unification meant that Britain was being overtaken in the old manufacturing staples of coal, iron and steel, and was already behind in new industries like chemicals and machine-tools. The British were often conscious of their failings in management and the inadequacy of their technical education, but they also cried 'foul', and attributed their troubles to the 'dumping' of German exports at artificially low prices.

However, it was by no means certain that the answer to this double problem of overstretched resources in the British Empire and the German threat should be met by means of an agreement with France. Other courses were available. The Japanese alliance eased the British

---

2. Quoted in P.J.V. Rolo, *Entente Cordiale* (London, 1969), p. 121.
3. See Robert K. Massie, *Dreadnought* (New York, 1991), p. 211; Jonathan Steinberg, in F. H. Hinsley, ed., *British Foreign Policy under Sir Edward Grey* (London, 1977), p. 194.

position in the Far East. Proposals for the introduction of protective tariffs, combined with schemes for Imperial Federation, offered a possible solution to both economic and political problems. It was even within the bounds of possibility for Britain to meet the threat from Germany, not by opposing it, but by coming to terms with it. In 1898 Joseph Chamberlain, and in 1901 Lansdowne, made approaches to Germany about a political agreement – Chamberlain was even willing to talk about an alliance. Nothing came of these moves, which on both occasions ended in misunderstanding and recriminations; but the attempt was made.

In both France and Britain, therefore, there was some movement towards an agreement between the two countries. But between 1899 and 1902 there was little to indicate that such an outcome was probable, much less certain. In those years the two countries edged towards better relations, without getting very far. In 1899 they reached an agreement defining their zones of influence in the Sudan, along a line which left the Nile valley to Britain and Equatorial Africa to France. (Lord Salisbury described the territory allotted to France as 'very light land – that is to say it is the desert of Sahara'.[4]) Early in 1901 the French made some enquiries about the British attitude to Morocco, but Delcassé did not believe that he could get the sort of free hand there that he wanted. Cambon also raised again the centuries-old question of French fishing rights off Newfoundland. Neither approach made much progress.

If the various impulses towards a Franco-British agreement were to come to anything, there had to be a shift in opinion in the two countries. Of course diplomacy in those days was secret, but the press was vigilant and leaks were not unknown. Moreover, any far-reaching agreement would have to be ratified by the parliaments of the respective countries, where public opinion and pressure groups would make themselves felt. The state of opinion, as reflected in the press, in the aftermath of Fashoda and the Boer War was mutually hostile. In Britain, a change in the tone of the press was visible during 1902 – Bardoux, for example, traced a growth of criticism of Germany in *The Times*, accompanied by friendly comment on France. He found the same phenomenon in the periodical press, noting particularly that the *Spectator* began to advocate an *entente* with France after many years of severe comment on French policies.

French opinion too would have to change, and further than in Britain. Here lay the significance of the state visit by King Edward VII

4. Rolo, *Entente Cordiale*, p. 56.

to Paris on 1–4 May 1903, and the return visit made by President Loubet to London on 6–9 July the same year. It may well be that accounts of Edward VII's personal success in Paris have lost nothing in the telling, but there was no doubt that the King was popular in Paris. He had the great virtue of showing that he liked the city, where he was a familiar visitor. His speeches now seem full of platitudes, because they have been much copied and repeated – 'Providence has made us neighbours, let us make sure that we are friends', was a frequent theme. But at the time they sounded fresh, and they had a striking effect. The British press was delighted with the warmth of the King's reception in Paris, and so the visit affected opinion in both countries. Loubet's reception in London was equally cordial, and again the compliments in the press were reciprocal.

King Edward was a master of public relations, and also no mean diplomat. The state visits were instrumental in getting serious negotiations under way. In Paris the King went much further in political conversations than would now be thought proper for a constitutional monarch. He expressed sympathy with French aspirations in Morocco, which persuaded Delcassé that the British would be co-operative on that point. Delcassé then insisted on a rapid return fixture, and made sure that he accompanied the President to London. (King Edward had preferred to leave his Foreign Secretary at home.) During the visit, Cambon worked hard to ensure that there was serious discussion between the two Foreign Ministers. He arranged for Delcassé to have a long meeting with Lansdowne during the morning of 7 July, at which they discussed the Newfoundland fisheries, West Africa, Morocco, Egypt, Siam and the New Hebrides – nearly all the points at issue between the two countries. The conversation went well, and serious discussions between the two governments got under way.

The negotiations which followed were highly characteristic of their era, and almost completely alien – indeed repugnant – to our own. They involved the drawing of boundaries between British and French territories in West Africa without any regard for their inhabitants. They delimited spheres of influence in Siam, with little respect for that country's sovereign rights. They proposed joint Anglo-French administration of islands in the New Hebrides, far away in the Pacific. All these matters were discussed in close secrecy. It was the diplomacy of imperialism. The negotiations were also immensely slow and painstakingly detailed. Cambon wrote to his son when they were almost completed: 'We split hairs and debate about piles of pebbles in the region of Lake Chad.' And on the very eve of signing he took care to explain to Delcassé why he had agreed to replace a comma with a semi-colon in Article VIII of the Declaration on Egypt and Morocco.[5] The pace was so leisurely, indeed, that it sometimes seemed that the negotiations would never reach a conclusion. But in February 1904 war broke out between Russia and Japan. Russia was the ally of France, Japan the ally of Britain. The French and British governments realised with dismay that they might be drawn into conflict with one another over a quarrel between their respective partners, and they at last made haste to conclude an agreement.

The central core of the complicated Conventions, Declarations and secret articles which Lansdowne and Cambon signed on 8 April 1904 lay in a deal over Egypt and Morocco. France agreed not to obstruct British actions in Egypt, which she had been trying to do ever since the British occupation of that country in 1882. In return, Britain recognised that it 'appertained to France' to preserve order in Morocco and to assist reforms in that country. Britain undertook not to change the political status of Egypt, and France gave the same undertaking for Morocco. However, secret articles declared that if either power found it necessary to change its policy in Egypt or Morocco respectively, then its previous engagements (e.g. on commercial equality) would be respected. If change became necessary in Morocco, France agreed that the northern part of the country would go to Spain. Thus the published articles referred to maintaining the existing status of Morocco, but the secret articles foreshadowed its partition. For the French this was the most important part of the agreement; the more so because the two governments agreed to give one another diplomatic support in carrying out the accords on Morocco and Egypt. France had thus secured British support for her aims in Morocco.

Put crudely, without the diplomatic phraseology about it 'appertaining to France' to maintain order in Morocco, this part of the agreement meant that Britain would retain Egypt undisturbed, and France would occupy Morocco some time in the future. During the long negotiations, the French had sought territorial gains in West Africa which would make their renunciation of Egypt more acceptable at home. Cambon had tried to persuade Lansdowne to surrender the Gambia, or areas on the west bank of the River Niger, but failed. Cambon complained wryly to his son that Lansdowne objected that these were British territory – 'It is wonderful; they seem to be saying that they will only grant us territories which do not belong to

5. Paul Cambon to his son, 4 March 1904, in H. Cambon, ed., *Paul Cambon: Correspondance 1870–1924* (Paris, 1940–46), vol. II, p. 129; to Delcassé, 7 April 1904, MAE, Papiers Delcassé, 211/14, ff. 94–7.

England.' He was quite right: this was a characteristic British way of doing business. Eventually the British conceded changes to the northern frontier of Nigeria in favour of the French. Elsewhere in Africa, the British withdrew their objections to the French annexation of Madagascar, which was the merest gesture, because they had done nothing to hinder it. Further afield still, it was agreed that Britain should secure a sphere of influence in part of Siam adjacent to the Burmese frontier, while France was to have a sphere next door to Indo-China. In the South Pacific, an Anglo-French condominium was agreed on for the New Hebrides – a remarkable and implausible hybrid.

This encompassing of the world concluded with Newfoundland. Long ago, in the Treaty of Utrecht (1713), France had recognised British sovereignty over Newfoundland and its adjoining islands (with the exception of the two islands of St Pierre and Miquelon) but had retained certain fishing rights in the surrounding seas. Disputes over these rights had continued for nearly two centuries. This matter, in some ways minor yet highly sensitive, occupied an extraordinary amount of time during the talks between Cambon and Lansdowne. The British claimed that the French rights had been a declining asset for years, and that in 1903 only 258 Breton fishermen were still sailing to Newfoundland waters. The French replied that the fisheries were still of crucial importance to the economy of Brittany, and part of the local way of life. Much of the argument turned on the right of Bretons to fish for bait in order to make their main catch, and on whether they could establish fixed installations on shore in order to cure the fish. One complaint of the Newfoundlanders was that the French government offered bounties to its fishermen, giving them an unfair commercial advantage. (This part of the dispute is positively modern in its aspect.) The bargaining on these questions was hard, and as late as 30 March 1904, just over a week before the final agreement was signed, Lansdowne threatened to break off the whole negotiation if the French did not give way on a point relating to fishing for bait.[6]

Such details are not redundant. The substance of the famous *Entente cordiale*, when closely examined, was a mixed bag of bargains over territory in Africa and Asia and regulations about fishing for bait off Newfoundland. As the foundation for a lasting partnership between two countries, it looks distinctly dubious. If most of the details have now been forgotten, it is partly because they are the sort of things that people prefer to forget. Yet without the details there would have been

6. The whole passage on the making of the Anglo-French agreement rests on Rolo, *Entente Cordiale*, pp. 205–70. Cambon's remark is in a letter to his son, 9 January 1904, *Correspondance*, II, p. 107.

no agreement. The British liked facts, not principles, as Bardoux and Cambon pointed out; but when it came to the point the French too insisted on the small print being absolutely precise. The essence of the agreements of April 1904 lies in two apparently contradictory propositions. First, only the details provided the ground on which a settlement could be reached. Second, if the *entente* had been concerned *only* with the details, it would have had no more significance and no greater place in history than many another colonial agreement. What lay behind the details to give the *entente* its meaning and its longevity?

On the day when the agreements were signed, Cambon wrote to Delcassé: 'Your task is done and you may pride yourself on having carried to a successful conclusion an enterprise considered impossible, all of whose advantages will be appreciated in a few years' time. You will then be considered a great minister, and rightly so.'[7] Two phrases catch the eye. The *entente* was thought to be impossible. It went against history, and so achieved a striking dramatic effect. Moreover, it worked. The agreements did not end all colonial rivalry between France and Britain, as later events in the Middle East were to show, but they definitively closed several chapters in that rivalry. Cambon's other point was that the advantages of the agreement would be appreciated over a number of years. This was so: the consequences proved to be more important than the agreements themselves.

The immediate consequences were not remarkable. The British press, across the Conservative–Liberal divide, was almost universally favourable. Parliament approved the agreements without a division, and Liberals supported it as much as Conservatives. Among leading politicians, only Lord Rosebery (a former Prime Minister and Foreign Secretary) was critical. In the House of Lords he predicted complications rather than peace; in private he said it would lead straight to war. In Egypt, Lord Cromer, who under the titles of British Agent and Consul-General was the virtual ruler of the country, was pleasantly surprised that the French were as good as their word and abandoned their obstruction of his administration. Only the Newfoundlanders were unhappy. The Newfoundland Prime Minister claimed that the French fishermen had been given too good a deal on bounties and shore installations, and the Dominion's Parliament passed a resolution criticising the agreements. In France there was some opposition. The press, with many papers taking their lead from the Quai d'Orsay, was generally favourable, though there some criticism of what was seen as a surrender to the British in Egypt. The

7. Paul Cambon to Delcassé, 8 April 1904, MAE, Papiers Delcassé, 211/3. ff. 239–40.

31

Chamber of Deputies voted on the agreements, 436 in favour and 94 against – a sizeable opposition, including about twenty from the maritime departments who claimed that their constituencies would be damaged by the Newfoundland agreements.[8] In general, on both sides of the Channel, the whole elaborate package was accepted as a reasonable deal.

Where would it lead next? There was no doubt as to how Delcassé hoped that it would develop. He wrote to Paléologue, a senior official in the French Foreign Ministry: 'This liquidation [i.e. of colonial problems] should lead us, and I desire that it shall lead us, to a political alliance with England. . . . If we could lean both on Russia and on England, how strong we should be in relation to Germany.'[9] For Britain the answer was much less certain. Lansdowne hoped that the agreement with France would improve British relations with Russia, but it seems that in this respect his thoughts were directed more towards India and Central Asia than towards Europe and Germany. The foremost authority on British foreign policy in that period, Zara Steiner, has written that for Britain 'The Entente with France was not directed against Germany. It was the natural outcome of the need to reduce imperial tensions.'[10] Neither the Foreign Secretary, nor the government, nor the country as a whole wanted the commitment which was demanded by an alliance: that is, the requirement to go to war in certain fixed circumstances. The *entente* of 1904 looked much more attractive to British eyes: it removed causes of friction with France without involving Britain in any obligations beyond an undertaking to give diplomatic support in carrying out the agreements on Morocco and Egypt. And it appears that Lansdowne did not think that this would amount to very much. He wrote to the Ambassador in Paris at the end of 1904: 'We may in our secret hearts congratulate ourselves on having left to another Power the responsibility for dealing with so helpless and hopeless a country [i.e. Morocco].'[11] It was not the letter of a man who expected to be called upon to do anything serious about Morocco.

There was a wide gap between the French and British views on how the *entente* should develop. At bottom, Delcassé wanted an alliance, the British did not. Delcassé had his eyes fixed on Germany,

8. J.J. Mathews, *Egypt and the Formation of the Anglo-French Entente of 1904* (Philadelphia, 1939), pp. 111–12.

9. G.P. Gooch, *Before the War: Studies in Diplomacy* (London, 1936), vol. I, p. 153.

10. Zara S. Steiner, *Britain and the Origins of the First World War* (London, 1977), p. 30.

11. Christopher Andrew, *Théophile Delcassé and the Making of the Entente Cordiale* (London, 1968), p. 195.

Lansdowne did not. Such differences might have led to the rapid demise of the agreement, but events turned out otherwise. In 1905 the 'helpless and hopeless' country of Morocco became the centre of a first-class international crisis, and the British suddenly found that they could not simply leave it to the French. Germany, which had so far been in the background, suddenly and almost brutally came to the fore. The French and British governments both found that they were confronting something more than they had bargained for.

GERMANY INTERVENES

Delcassé had long intended that the *entente* with Britain should be the prelude to a French advance in Morocco. This was, after all, envisaged in the agreement, if not in so many words. In November 1904 the French made their move. Their representative in Fez, the Moroccan capital, presented the Sultan with a programme of 'reforms' which he should introduce, dealing with the banks, the police and the army. These were to be carried out with French 'assistance', and in January 1905 a strong French mission arrived to provide it. At the time, this was a standard gambit, and left no doubt that France intended to impose a protectorate on Morocco.

The Sultan opposed this pressure, and turned for support to Germany. The Germans had a diplomatic standing in the question, as one of the signatories of the Treaty of Madrid (1880), by which various powers undertook to maintain the *status quo* in Morocco. Moreover, France had taken trouble to secure in advance the acquiescence of Britain, Spain and Italy, but had ignored Germany. This meant that German prestige was involved − it was unacceptable for her to be disregarded when lesser powers had been consulted, and indeed bought off. Behind this lay the fact that the Germans had been shaken and dismayed by the conclusion of the Anglo-French *entente*, which they had believed to be impossible and which clearly weakened their position. The German government therefore agreed to intervene on behalf of the Sultan of Morocco, and chose a particularly dramatic way to do so. The Kaiser himself was on a cruise in the Mediterranean, and he was prevailed upon to land at Tangier (31 March 1905), to ride on horse-back through the city, and to put his name to a declaration issued by the German legation in Morocco the following day. This took the form of a speech (which the Kaiser did not actually deliver, but that was of no importance) drawing attention to the Sultan's status as an independent sovereign, and to Germany's determination to safeguard her interests in Morocco. This declaration, reinforced as it was by the personal presence of the Kaiser, sounded a very loud warning indeed.

Surprisingly for so experienced and astute a Foreign Minister, Delcassé was completely taken aback. When the Chamber of Deputies met later in April, members criticised him fiercely for his rashness in exposing France to such a rebuff. The French position was particularly weak because her ally Russia had suffered a disastrous defeat in the war with Japan of 1904–5, and was threatened with revolution at home. No support could be expected from that quarter. The question naturally arose of whether there would be any from Britain, which under the terms of the *entente* had promised diplomatic support over Morocco. In fact, British support proved remarkably firm. This was partly a matter of fulfilling their undertakings under the agreement of 1904, but also because Lansdowne and Fisher (the First Sea Lord) were worried that the Germans were going to claim a port in Morocco.

On 17 May 1905 Lansdowne had a crucial meeting with Cambon, at which he told the Ambassador that the British government was ready to reach an understanding with France on measures to be taken if the situation became disquieting. Cambon asked for clarification in writing, and Lansdowne replied that the two governments should treat one another with complete confidence, keep one another fully informed, and discuss in advance any contingencies with which they might be faced. Cambon reported to Paris that to take up this proposal would be to 'take the road to a general understanding which would in reality constitute an alliance'. He was not certain that the French government wished to follow such a course, and therefore proposed to offer a cautious reply, to the effect that France was already following a policy of understanding and trust towards Britain, and was ready to discuss any questions with her.[12]

This was a puzzling episode, not least because Cambon reported that Lansdowne had virtually offered an alliance. He did not. But he still did something very significant: he proposed close Anglo-French consultation and co-operation, directed against Germany. This had not been the British position when the agreements of April 1904 were signed; it was the case in May 1905. This was a striking change, brought about by the German intervention in Morocco and the naval threat which coloured all British views of German policy at that time, and which we will examine later. Cambon's response was equally

12. Lansdowne's note, 25 May 1905, and Cambon's comments, 29 May, MAE, Papiers Delcassé, 211/13, ff. 287–98.

significant, though in a very different way. When the *entente* was concluded in 1904, the French hope was that it could be developed into an alliance; yet when Cambon thought that an alliance was being offered, he advised against taking it up.

This appeared paradoxical, but in fact reflected the problems of the time in Paris. In April and May 1905 there was a deep division of opinion between Delcassé and the Premier, Rouvier. Delcassé thought the Germans were bluffing over Morocco, and would not go to war. If they did, he believed he could rely on British support. Rouvier disagreed. He thought the Germans were not bluffing, and might well launch a surprise attack which would end in a repetition of 1870. Even if the British supported France, their help could not amount to much – after all, as he remarked with obvious but painful truth, the British Navy did not run on wheels and could not defend Paris. Rather than run such a risk, Rouvier was willing to jettison his Foreign Minister, and he told the German Ambassador as much as early as 26 April. (Delcassé knew of this the very next day, from a deciphered German telegram; so in all that followed he knew that his position was undermined.) The Germans knew that they were pushing at an open door when they told Rouvier that the crisis could best be resolved by getting rid of Delcassé. That was what happened. On 6 June 1905 Rouvier brought the matter to the Cabinet, and compelled Delcassé to resign.

This was a heavy blow to the *entente*, and the Prime Minister, Balfour, wrote to the King on 8 June that Delcassé's resignation under German pressure 'displayed a weakness on the part of France which showed that she could not at present be counted on as an effective force in international politics'.[13] The consequences might well have been far-reaching. Rouvier tried to follow up his sacrifice of Delcassé by seeking a direct deal with Germany about Morocco, which in turn might have led to some wider Franco-German agreement. In that event, the *entente* with Britain would have been fatally undermined. As it turned out, the Germans declined Rouvier's approaches. They had gone too far in their public support for Moroccan independence to make an immediate private deal at that country's expense. Moreover, they wanted to press home their advantage by insisting on an international conference on the Moroccan question, which would establish Germany's standing in the matter and create the sort of public pressure which would further divide France from Britain and so finally break up the *entente*. The Germans demanded a conference, and on 1

13. Balfour to King Edward VII, 8 June 1905, Kenneth Young, *Arthur James Balfour* (London, 1963), p. 248.

July 1905 Rouvier agreed. The conference eventually convened at Algeciras in January 1906.

This final burst of German pressure proved counter-productive. Delcassé's resignation had been received, astonishingly, with almost unanimous approval in the French press. There was a general feeling that he had acted rashly, especially in excluding the Germans from discussions over Morocco; and there was little sign of resentment at the pressure which led to his resignation. Delcassé himself was understandably angry. He told a friendly journalist from *Le Matin* that it was an unusual criticism against a French Foreign Minister that he had taken insufficient care over the interests of Germany – he had thought his job was to look after the interests of France.[14] In the course of time this rather obvious point began to sink in. German insistence on pressing home their advantage after Delcassé's resignation brought a reaction in France, and during the summer of 1905 there were public demonstrations that the *entente* was still alive. In mid-July a British naval squadron visited Brest, and in August a large part of the French fleet paid a ceremonial visit to Cowes, where King Edward received the senior officers. It was an ostentatious gesture.

Where did the *entente* stand as the two fleets exchanged salutes in the Solent in August 1905, sixteen months after the signature of the agreements of April 1904? The situation was paradoxical. In making the *entente*, Delcassé hoped to secure Morocco for France and to pave the way for an alliance with Britain against Germany. In the event, he got into such difficulties over Morocco that French designs for a protectorate were put back indefinitely, and he himself had to resign. When Lansdowne offered such close consultation that Cambon thought it amounted to an alliance, the French let the proposal lie. On the British side, Lansdowne had regarded the original agreements primarily as a settlement of colonial disputes, without much thought of opposition to Germany. By May 1905 he was suggesting close co-ordination of British and French policy against Germany. In June he told the German Ambassador in London that, while there was no alliance with France, British diplomatic support over Morocco had been promised and would be given. If Germany were to start a war with France, he could not say how far British opinion might drive the government; which was a delicate way of delivering a warning that Britain might intervene in a Franco-German war.

For the French, therefore, the *entente* had failed to bring success in Morocco, and Rouvier was inclined to try for reconciliation with

14. Conversation with Lauzanne, 23 June 1905, MAE, Papiers Delcassé, 211/14.

Germany rather than seek an alliance with England. The British attitude towards Germany, on the other hand, had grown steadily sterner. For both governments it was clear that the key to their relations with one another lay in their attitudes towards Germany. The *entente* had been made, but its significance remained uncertain.

CHAPTER 3

Entente or Alliance? 1906–1914

Towards the end of 1905 the Moroccan crisis still awaited a resolution as the various powers concerned prepared for the conference which was to begin at Algeciras in January 1906. Franco-British relations remained in a state of uncertainty, which was made worse by events in British politics at the turn of the year. In December 1905 Balfour's Conservative government, which had negotiated the *entente*, resigned and was replaced by a Liberal administration headed by Campbell-Bannerman. A general election followed in January 1906, resulting in a Liberal victory by a landslide. These events were greeted with dismay in French political circles. Rouvier, the Premier, deplored the Liberal victory. He disliked the Liberals, and had less confidence in Grey than in Lansdowne. Such views found a ready echo in the mind of Paul Cambon, who was convinced that British Liberalism was strongly tinged with pacifism and pro-German sentiments.

There was some ground for this uneasiness. The idea of the balance of power was anathema to the radical Liberals who were strong in the new House of Commons. The main objectives of the new government lay in domestic reforms, whose inspiration came in part from the advanced social legislation in Germany. The instinctive Liberal stance in foreign policy was to deplore the backward tyranny of Tsarist Russia, and by extension to oppose the Franco-Russian alliance. The new Prime Minister, Campbell-Bannerman, went against this trend of thought by appointing as Foreign Secretary Sir Edward Grey, a Liberal Imperialist, a supporter of the *entente* with France, and an advocate of continuity in foreign policy. This was a crucial choice. Much of the development of British policy, and of Anglo-French relations, lay in Grey's hands for the next eight years. In some ways this was strange. As Keith Robbins has written, 'Edward Grey was totally uncontaminated by any experience of "abroad".[1] He had been to India and the West Indies, but that was all. His background was very English, of a particular kind: a family of Northumberland country gentlemen, school at Winchester, university at Oxford. His keenest pursuits were fishing and bird-watching. His integrity and the apparent simplicity of his character commanded confidence within his own party and on the Opposition benches. This was worth much. Grey was later criticised for his failure to travel, but it was more important that he should have a firm sense of the interests and sentiments of his own country, and that his judgement should be widely trusted – as it was.

Cambon met Grey on 10 and 31 January 1906, to try to find out where the new British government stood on relations with France. Grey gave his personal opinion that if Germany attacked France as a consequence of the 1904 agreement, public opinion would be strongly in favour of France, and no British government could remain neutral. He agreed to continue military and naval staff talks which had begun under the previous government. But he warned Cambon that the British people would not fight to put France in possession of Morocco, and it would be impossible for him (Grey) to give any firm undertaking of armed support without consulting the Cabinet, which contained many pacifically-minded members. Moreover, even if the Cabinet agreed to such an undertaking, it would then have to be put in writing and communicated to Parliament. Grey did not believe that the situation yet demanded such steps.

Where did this leave British policy? Grey was repeatedly willing to state his personal opinion, but warned Cambon that it would be unwise to press the question of support for France in Cabinet, and even more in Parliament. This was true.

Grey was in a serious difficulty, because there was a wide gap between his own thinking and the sentiment of the Liberal Party in general. Grey himself was prepared to use the language of the balance of power, and to consider involvement in a European war. In a memorandum of 20 January 1906, between his two meetings with Cambon, Grey wrote that if Britain remained neutral in a Franco-German war, 'the French will never forgive us . . . Russia would not think it worthwhile to make a friendly arrangement with us about Asia . . . *we should be left without a friend and without the power of making a friend . . .*' Later he added: 'An entente between Russia, France and ourselves would be absolutely secure. *If it is necessary to check Germany it could then be done.*'[2]

1. Keith Robbins, *Sir Edward Grey* (London, 1971), p. 127.
2. *British Documents on the Origins of War, 1889–1914*, vol. II (London, 1928), No. 299 – the italics are mine.

Such thinking was unacceptable to the Liberal Cabinet in January 1906, and Grey did not reveal it to his colleagues. He reported his conversations with Cambon to the Prime Minister, Campbell-Bannerman, but not to the Cabinet. There thus began an uneasy equivocation in the conduct of British policy, with Grey thinking – and telling Cambon – what he was not willing to tell the Cabinet.

In the meantime, the conference on Morocco opened at Algeciras on 16 January, and continued until 7 April. That the conference was held at all was a success for German policy, and one of its conclusions was to reaffirm the independence and integrity of Morocco, which was certainly contrary to French wishes. But in other ways the conference saw a reassertion of the Anglo-French *entente*. Britain gave France the diplomatic support promised in the agreements of 1904, and the British representative, Sir Arthur Nicolson, worked closely with his French opposite number. Among the detailed results of the conference were provisions for France and Spain to secure control over the police in Morocco, and France achieved a predominant position in the Moroccan state bank. These loopholes left the way open for French influence, and so for a possible take-over in the future. The French thus salvaged something after an unhappy start, and owed much to British assistance.

During the change of government in Britain and the long-drawn-out conference at Algeciras, it was striking that the principle of the Anglo-French agreement was not publicly challenged in Britain. This was largely because the Liberals, in the euphoria of victory, thought mostly about domestic matters; but it also showed that the *entente* had been accepted by the two major political parties. The phrase *entente cordiale* proved a public relations master-stroke. The words were vague, with none of the precision of 'alliance', and they exuded goodwill. Who could possibly be against 'cordial understanding'? That the phrase concealed ambiguities was in some ways dangerous for Anglo-French relations, but that it *could* conceal them was an immense advantage.

For the next few years, between 1906 and 1911, the main developments in Anglo-French relations were beneath the surface, and indirect in their implications. For both countries, Germany filled the horizon. Of the British, Paul Cambon wrote to his brother in February 1910: 'Hostility to Germany is implacable because it is born of fear.'[3] The British (who did not like to think that they were afraid of anyone) might not have appreciated the diagnosis, but it was

3. Paul Cambon to Jules, 26 February 1910, in H. Cambon, ed., *Paul Cambon: Correspondance 1870–1924* (Paris, 1940–46), vol. II, p. 295.

accurate. Grey and his principal officials at the Foreign Office had their minds fixed on the German menace, which was not so much that the Germans intended to attack England as that they were attaining a menacing predominance in Europe and that their methods were unpleasant. Grey in particular thought the Germans were bullies, and in his simple way he disliked bullying. As for the public, the popular mind was caught from time to time by an invasion scare, just as in the middle of the nineteenth century; but now the fictional assailants were the Germans, not the French, as in William Le Queux's novel *The Invasion of 1910*, published in 1906.

Behind everything lay the naval rivalry. In 1906 the British launched the *Dreadnought*, a new type of battleship more heavily gunned than any seen before, which rendered all pre-*Dreadnought* battleships obsolete. Britain thus seized the lead in this new type, but at the expense of virtually wiping out her vast superiority in pre-*Dreadnoughts*. The naval race with Germany was at once simplified and concentrated. New battleships laid down could easily be counted and their completion dates foreseen. In 1909 a part of British public opinion conceived an 'acceleration scare' – an alarm that the Germans were secretly speeding up their rate of building by methods of prefabrication. The scare was ill-founded, but even so it caused the British government to increase its own building programme, and lay down more battleships to increase their margin of superiority.

Grey never intended to rule out an improvement of relations with Germany, and in any case the cost of the naval race could not be justified to the Liberal Party without an attempt to reach a negotiated solution. In 1908 the British proposed an agreement to limit battleship building programmes on both sides. The Germans offered unspecified concessions on their programmes, but only in return for a declaration of benevolent neutrality from Britain in the event of Germany being at war with another power. This at once raised the issue of Anglo-French relations. So far, Grey had carefully abstained from any promise of British intervention in a Franco-German war, but he had kept the possibility open. An undertaking to remain neutral would wreck this careful balance, and remove the possibility of British support for France. Grey refused the German proposal, and the naval race continued.

The naval rivalry with Germany challenged the British both in their security and in their most cherished assumptions. If Germany controlled the sea, Britain could be threatened with starvation. (As Kipling wrote in his poem about 'big steamers', ostensibly for children: 'if anyone hinders our coming, you'll starve!') Psychologically, the

Navy lay at the heart of British pride and self-confidence. To accept German superiority was simply unthinkable, and even Liberal MPs with pacific principles knew that they could not offer such a policy to their constituents.

The general effect of the ill-defined fear of Germany, and of the only too sharply defined competition in building battleships, was to drive Britain towards maintaining the *entente* with France. Grey genuinely wanted to improve relations with Germany, but not at the cost of relations with France. The question about promising neutrality in a future war brought this issue to a sharp point. Britain could give no such undertaking without wrecking her links with France, and this was almost automatically ruled out.

The British commitment to France thus became firmer under the impulse of the German menace. Yet at the same time France was going through a period of uncertainty and reassessment. There were troubles in the vineyards of the south and on the railways, and the Army seemed to be as much occupied in breaking strikes as in preparing for war. The socialists, growing in numbers and confidence, were opposed to the whole idea of a capitalist war, and were hostile to the alliance with the Tsarist tyranny in Russia. In financial circles there were doubts about the heavy investment in Russia which accompanied that alliance. Economic co-operation with Germany looked a better prospect. French coal-producers and iron and steel manufacturers reached agreements with their German counterparts about output, prices and marketing – the first signs of that Franco-German co-operation in the field of heavy industry which was to reappear in the 1920s and take institutional form in the Coal and Steel Community of 1950.

Jules Cambon was appointed Ambassador in Berlin in 1907, and set himself to bring about an improvement in relations with Germany similar to that which his brother had achieved with England. In February 1909 he secured an agreement on Morocco, by which Germany accepted French political interest there, and the two countries were to share equally in economic development. Jules Cambon hoped that this limited agreement would lead on to bigger things, which might well have ended, not by complementing his brother's work in London but by undermining it.

In May 1910 King Edward VII, one of the architects and upholders of the *entente cordiale*, died, and there were those who wondered whether his death symbolised the demise of the relationship with which he was so closely associated.

THE AGADIR CRISIS

In 1911 another crisis blew up in Morocco. After the conference at Algeciras in 1906, the French had continued to push forward their control over aspects of the administration of Morocco. Parts of the country, notably around Casablanca, were occupied by French troops. The Franco-German agreement of 1909 to promote economic equality and co-operation in Morocco worked well within its limits, but did not check the advance of French influence in the country as a whole. The Union des Mines Marocaines, for example, had 62 per cent French capital and only 20 per cent German.[4]

In April 1911 the French government decided to send a military expedition to Fez, the capital of Morocco, ostensibly to assist the Sultan against rebels and to protect French lives, but in fact to impose a French protectorate. This decision was taken without consultation with Germany, though it was bound to affect the Franco-German agreement of 1909. The German government indicated at once that the French action reopened the whole Moroccan question, and that they considered the 1909 agreement as nullified. For some two months, that was all. Then on 1 July 1911 the German gunboat *Panther* arrived at the Moroccan port of Agadir. The *Panther* was a vessel of a mere 1,000 tons, but behind her lay the might of the German Empire. Her arrival, like that of the Kaiser at Tangier in 1905, was a dramatic signal of German concern with Morocco; indeed, it was widely interpreted as a threat of war.

The French government which faced this spectacular move had taken office only four days before, on 27 June. The new Premier was Joseph Caillaux, who had made his reputation in financial affairs and had not been involved with the Moroccan question. He had no wish to risk war with Germany, and on 9 July he approached the German government to find out what they wanted. The Germans demanded the cession of the whole of the French Congo, as what was at the time called 'compensation' for their acceptance of a French protectorate over Morocco. The French government was united in refusing such a sweeping demand, but Caillaux was willing to try for a compromise, against the wishes of the Foreign Ministry. Despite the public appearance of a war crisis, the underlying reality took the form of a Franco-German haggle about territory in Central Africa.

The British attitude to these events swung erratically between caution and bellicosity. Early in 1911 Grey had tried to dissuade the

4. Jean-Claude Allain, *Agadir 1911* (Paris, 1976), p. 84.

French from military action in Morocco, and then he urged them to withdraw their troops from Fez. But he felt bound to offer France diplomatic support, partly because it was specified in the 1904 agreement, and even more because he dare not risk weakening the *entente*. Also, while not greatly concerned about Morocco in itself, he did not want to see the Germans and French reach their own settlement there and leave the British out.

The arrival of the *Panther* at Agadir brought a new urgency to such calculations. The Cabinet, meeting on 4 July, showed little sympathy with the French, believing that they had brought on the crisis in the first place. The furthest the Cabinet would go was to authorise Grey to tell Germany that Britain must be involved in any discussions about Morocco, and to tell France that Britain would honour her obligations under the 1904 agreement, but expected the French to make some proposals for a settlement. During the next few days the Cabinet agreed that the German demand for the whole of the French Congo was excessive, but again urged the French to make some concessions. The radical wing in the Cabinet was strongly against going any further than this.

This caution makes the next British action all the more striking. The Cabinet met on 21 July, with plenty of things on its plate in addition to Agadir. There was a coal strike; the conflict over the House of Lords and the Parliament Bill was at its height; and everyone was oppressed by a heatwave. The Cabinet authorised Grey to make a strong statement to the German Ambassador, reminding him that Britain had received no reply to the declaration of 4 July about British concern over Morocco, and repeating that she would accept no settlement there in which she did not take part. Grey made this communication privately that afternoon. On the evening of the same day, 21 July, the Chancellor of the Exchequer, Lloyd George, made a speech at the Mansion House in the City. In a passage of this speech concerted in advance with Grey and Asquith, Lloyd George declared that it would be an intolerable humiliation if peace were preserved by 'allowing Britain to be treated, where her interests were vitally affected, as if she were of no account in the Cabinet of Nations'.[5] Within the conventions of the time this was an exceptionally severe statement, delivered in the most public manner possible by the leader of the radical wing in the Cabinet, generally thought to be pro-German. The tenor of the Mansion House speech was close enough to Grey's private remarks in the afternoon for the Germans to

5. David Lloyd George, *War Memoirs* (revised edition, in two volumes, London, 1938), p. 26.

be in no doubt that they were the target. Grey had a very trying meeting with the German Ambassador on 24 July, and emerged so much shaken that for a time he was afraid that war was imminent. Churchill, then Home Secretary, put guards on bridges in south-east England.

By any standards, this was an astonishing episode. Lloyd George spoke of British interests being vitally affected, but what were those interests? In Morocco, virtually none, except for the southern shore of the straits of Gibraltar, which was not at issue. Britain was certainly not vitally interested in the fate of the French Congo. The principal British concern was in practice to assert her solidarity with France, and even this took an exaggerated form. Lloyd George delivered a severe warning, and Grey was afraid of war, over a matter on which Caillaux never ceased to negotiate. In the whole inexplicable affair, the one clear point is that the British adopted at the end of July 1911 a stance which was distinctly more anti-German than that of the French.

In one way the whole episode proved to be all froth. Britain was ignored in the negotiations between France and Germany, and the final compromise was reached without her. This was what the Cabinet had declared against from the start, but in the event neither Grey nor Lloyd George nor anyone else seems to have been particularly perturbed. None the less, the froth left a solid residue. On 23 August 1911, in the face of an apparent danger of war, the Committee of Imperial Defence met to consider British strategy in the event of a conflict with Germany. The Prime Minister took the chair, and there was a large attendance at a time when in normal circumstances not a minister could be found in London. The Director of Military Operations at the War Office, General Henry Wilson, expounded a plan to send an Expeditionary Force of 160,000 men to France. With an odd flourish, he included provision for a ten-minute stop at Amiens for coffee, which raised a smile from the assembled ministers. The Navy, on the other hand, put forward only vague and impractical notions for blockading the North Sea coast of Germany. The Committee reached no conclusion, but it was plain that Wilson's proposals had made a strong impression. Thus attention was focused on military conversations between Britain and France which had been pursued in a desultory fashion since the end of 1905. The sudden possibility of war in the summer of 1911 shifted these military conversations from the periphery of British political consciousness to somewhere near the centre.

The Agadir crisis of 1911 thus had greater effects on Britain than on France. The prospect of going to war on the side of France against

Germany was contemplated and up to a point accepted. The actual means of fighting such a war were considered by the Committee of Imperial Defence. These were significant changes in Anglo-French relations, and links in the chain of events which took the BEF to France in 1914. In principle, nothing was decided. In November 1911 the Cabinet reviewed the position, and accepted a ruling by Asquith that no communications between the British and French staffs would commit Britain, directly or indirectly, to military or naval intervention. That decision lay with ministers. But Grey had told the Prime Minister that, while staff talks implied no commitment, to stop them would indicate a change in policy and so alienate the French. Not for the first or last time, there was an uneasy ambiguity in British policy towards France.

SECRET TALKS AND STATE VISITS

During the next three years, relations between Britain and France comprised three different strands. The most secret was that of talks between the military and naval staffs. The most public consisted of state visits of demonstrative cordiality. Both indicated increasing unity between the two countries. But the third strand was made up of a set of doubts and difficulties, leaving quite a different impression.

The military conversations went back to early 1905, when even before the first Moroccan crisis General Grierson, then Director of Military Operations, had told French officials in Paris that Britain would fight alongside France in a war against Germany, and had set up a war game at the Staff College based on this assumption. During the autumn of 1905 Grierson discussed the possible deployment of British forces in northern France with the French Military Attaché, Colonel Huguet. Thus far, these talks were authorised by the French Premier, but were regarded by the British as being 'unofficial'. In January 1906 they received authorisation from Haldane, the new Minister of War, with the approval of Grey, and so achieved formal status on the British side.

The military talks were pursued between Grierson and Huguet, but lapsed when Grierson left the War Office in summer 1906. His successor let the matter lie during his four years as Director of Military Operations. But in 1910 there appeared a new DMO, General Henry Wilson, who at once resumed the talks with a new impetus and enthusiasm. Wilson was convinced that war was coming, and that the decisive theatre would be in France. He spoke French fluently, and struck up a friendship with General Foch, who made a number of visits to England. Wilson himself went to France frequently and after one visit he wrote to Foch that he felt 'tout à fait un ami de la famille'.[6] This was a sentiment which did not endear Wilson to his fellow officers in the British Army, but gave a marked impulse to the Anglo-French conversations.

The substance of those conversations dealt with the size of the British force to be made available, where it was to be sent, and the details concerning its movement – ports, shipping, railway trains and timetables. As to size, Huguet has recorded a remark by Foch that he wanted no more than a corporal and four men, but they must be there at the start. You will send them, he told Wilson, and I will do my best to make sure that they get killed. That would be enough to make sure that England would be in the war.

In knowledge of the subsequent slaughter on the western front, Foch's remark appears more callous than he can have intended at the time. The actual force under discussion was four to six infantry divisions and a cavalry division. As to where the BEF should go, Antwerp was considered, on the grounds that Britain would probably be intervening in defence of Belgium, but it was soon agreed that instead it should concentrate in northern France, and operate on the left of the French army in that area. Details of movements could be worked out in principle, but in practice would depend on two dates: that of British mobilisation, and that of final concentration in France. The length of time between these two dates was obviously of great importance, especially to the French, who would have to devote some of their railway lines and rolling stock to the BEF. In the event these carefully laid plans succeeded in putting the BEF, not in a quiet area where it could complete its preparations, but right in the path of a large part of the German Army, marching through Belgium in execution of the Schlieffen Plan. It was to prove the start of a story in Anglo-French relations far more bloody and bitter than was dreamed of by staff officers working quietly on movement orders and railway timetables. As these technical arrangements went forward, the British insisted that they did not commit them to action. The government's freedom of choice as to whether to intervene in a war, or to put the plans into effect, was to remain unimpaired.

There were also naval conversations, which began at the end of 1908 but then lapsed until the Agadir crisis. They then resumed in August–September 1911, reaching a broad agreement that the French fleet should control operations in the Mediterranean in the event of

6. Jean Autin, *Foch* (Paris, 1987), p. 105.

war with Germany, with the British limiting their forces there to commerce protection by cruisers and light craft. These arrangements were developed and put in more definite form in June and July 1912. Churchill, who was by then First Lord of the Admiralty, argued in a memorandum of 22 June 1912 that the Navy could not abandon the Mediterranean, but equally could not afford to strengthen the Mediterranean Fleet either by transferring ships from the North Sea or by building new ones. The best way to remain secure in the Mediterranean without weakening the fleet at home was to reach a firm agreement with the French. This was done by the end of July. The document stated clearly that no political commitment was implied; and then went on to arrange that France should concentrate her battle fleet in the Mediterranean, while Britain concentrated on her own home waters, leaving only a limited force in the Mediterranean. A further set of agreements in January and February 1913 restated these provisions, and added arrangements for co-operation in the Straits of Dover and the Channel.

The situation created by these military and naval conversations was by no means clear. The British repeatedly insisted that in terms of policy their hands remained free. If they were to go to war with Germany at the side of France, then the technical and strategic arrangements were in place and could be activated; but the choice as to whether or not to fight was still open. Yet it was scarcely credible that all these discussions and agreements should not build up an expectation of support for the French which it would be very hard to escape. This sort of moral obligation was at its strongest in the naval agreements. Would it really be possible for the British, having at the very least encouraged France to concentrate her naval forces in the Mediterranean, to stand by and allow the Germans to bombard the French Channel ports? The British desire to avoid any formal commitment, combined with the pursuit of detailed staff talks, created a position of extraordinary uncertainty and ambiguity.

An attempt to clarify the situation was made in a formal exchange of letters between Grey and Paul Cambon on 22 and 23 November 1912. Grey set out and Cambon confirmed the following points. (1) The conversations between naval and military experts did not restrict the freedom of either government to decide whether or not to assist the other by armed force. There was no commitment to do so. (2) If either government had grave reason to expect an unprovoked attack, it might be essential to know whether it could depend on armed assistance from the other. (3) If either government had such grave reason to expect attack, 'or something that threatened the general peace, it should immediately discuss with the other, whether both Governments should act together to prevent aggression and to preserve peace, and if so what measures they would be prepared to take in common'.[7] Since this was the nearest that the two governments came to a written commitment to one another, and since the circumstances described here actually occurred in 1914, the form of words is worth close attention. The only firm undertaking was to hold immediate discussions as to whether the two governments should act together.

What did the French government and high command make of all this in their formulation of policy and strategy? The Agadir crisis in 1911 gave a new impetus and urgency to military planning. General Joffre, who became Chief of the General Staff in July 1911, began to consider a new war plan in September. One of his problems concerned Belgium. Joffre thought there would be military advantage in launching an attack into Belgium on the first news of a German attack anywhere in the west, but he wanted a political ruling as to whether this was acceptable or not. He got one at high-level meetings of ministers and officers in January and February 1912. Poincaré (then Premier) ruled that France must on no account be the first to violate Belgian neutrality, because it would alienate the British. Joffre accepted this restriction on his strategy, and planned instead for an offensive in Lorraine.

But was British support certain, and what would it amount to on the ground? When Joffre presented his new plan (Plan XVII) to the Defence Council in April 1913, he assumed that he could not count on British co-operation, because the British government did not wish to give any undertaking in writing. If they did intervene, it was not certain that all the six divisions which might make up the BEF immediately be sent to France. His conclusion was that it would be prudent not to rely on British land forces in making operational plans. (He did, however, think naval assistance would be forthcoming.)

Thus the French high command never counted on British assistance on hand. From the military point of view, the main upshot of the *entente* with Britain was a negative one: to rule out the prospect of an advance into Belgium. This in turn propelled the French high command into an attack on Lorraine, which in the event proved disastrous. For one French writer, the British influence with regard to Belgium was the cause of all France's misfortunes in 1914. 'It was to cost us, in 1914, 500,000 dead and four years of occupation of our

7. The texts of the letters, Grey's in English, Cambon's in French, may be found in E.W.R. Lumby, ed., *Policy and Operations in the Mediterranean, 1912–14* (London, 1970), pp. 106–7.

northern departments.'[8] The British have never even considered such a view of their scruples about Belgium.

The military and naval conversations were pursued in secrecy, but at the same time the two countries pursued a highly public policy of state visits to demonstrate their friendship. It became customary for each President of the Republic to go to London. The programme became settled: a welcome at Victoria station, dinners at the French Embassy and Buckingham Palace, and a banquet at the Guildhall. President Fallières went to London in 1908, President Poincaré in 1913. King George V went to Paris in April 1914, to mark the tenth anniversary of the *entente cordiale*. The King was not at home in Paris, as his father had been, and he was surprised as well as pleased by his popular welcome. In the Faubourg Saint-Antoine, where it seems that the crowds still did not like to shout 'Vive le Roi', they cried instead 'Vive la Reine', to the great delight of the normally stern and reserved Queen Mary. Paul Cambon wrote to his brother: 'She was absolutely delighted and never stopped smiling. Never had I seen her smile in London.'[9] President Poincaré declared in a speech at the Elysée Palace that friendship between the two countries had already stood the test of time: 'It is a response to the considered wishes of two powerful nations, equally attached to peace, equally passionately devoted to progress, equally accustomed to the ways of liberty. ... After a long rivalry which taught them permanent lessons in esteem and mutual respect, France and Great Britain have learned to have affection for each other, to think alike and to unite their efforts.'[10]

These now sound like platitudes, and even at the time the carefully turned sentences represented a good deal of wishful thinking. But it is important to see what the two governments were wishing for, because it is a common device in human affairs to assert that something is true in the hope that it will become so; and it sometimes works. These state visits presented Anglo-French friendship as something normal and natural, based on the common outlook shared by two democracies, both devoted to peace and progress. They proclaimed that the *entente* had a deeper foundation than power politics; and indeed it had. During the ordeal of war in 1914–18, a sense of common values was a vital cement for Anglo-French relations, as well as a first-rate theme for propaganda to the rest of the world. A few years later, the two countries became even more conscious of a common political inheritance to be defended against Nazism.

8. L. Garros, *L'armée de grandpapa, 1891–1939* (Paris, 1965), p. 186.
9. Paul Cambon to Jules, 29 April 1914. *Correspondance*, vol. III, p. 65.
10. Raymond Poincaré, *Au service de la France*, vol. IV (Paris, 1927), pp. 107–8.

THE CHANNEL TUNNEL AND THE 'SILVER STREAK'

State visits drew the two countries together, but they could not eliminate the underlying instincts and prejudices inherited from the past. In Britain, nothing brought these feelings to the surface more speedily than the old issue of the Channel Tunnel.

In 1906 this grandiose scheme was again being canvassed on both sides of the Channel. Albert Sartiaux, President of the *Société Française du Tunnel sous-marin* took the matter up with a delegation from the International Chamber of Commerce of the City of London. The French motives were a mixture of commercial enterprise and a love of great engineering projects. In England the proposal was taken up by the South-Eastern Railway Company and the Channel Tunnel Company, which together put a private Bill before Parliament. The idea had a long history, going back to 1802, when Albert Mathieu (*ingénieur des mines*) put up a suggestion to Napoleon. Between the 1830s and 1850s Thomé de Gamond pursued the concept with all the fervour of an evangelist. By the 1870s the project appeared to be reaching a practical stage, and gained support in England as well as in France. The first British Channel Tunnel Company was founded in London in 1872. In 1882 digging was actually begun. The French company drove a heading of over a mile at Sangatte, and the British about 2,000 yards at Shakespeare Cliff.

At that point British military and public opinion took fright. In April 1882 the *Nineteenth Century* gathered a large number of distinguished signatories (including Tennyson, Browning and Thomas Huxley) for a protest against the Tunnel. In June Sir Garnet Wolseley, by far the best-known and most respected soldier in the country, intervened privately with a paper on the danger of invasion. England, he claimed, was safe only when protected by her 'silver streak' – the Channel. The cumulative effect was overwhelming, and Gladstone's government brought the project to an abrupt end. It remained moribund until the renewed French interest revived it in 1906. In June 1906, Sir George Clarke, the Secretary of the Committee of Imperial Defence, argued that the controversy of the early 1880s was now out-dated. 'Our relations with France', he wrote, 'have been placed on a satisfactory footing, and the idea of French aggression no longer haunts the imagination of the public.'[11] It was not a view

11. PRO, CAB 18/25. See Keith Wilson, 'The Channel Tunnel Question at the Committee of Imperial Defence, 1906–14', *Journal of Strategic Studies*, vol. 13, No. 2, June 1990, pp. 99–125. The following passage on the Tunnel draws heavily on this

which commanded general assent. A memorandum by the Admiralty in January 1907 asserted that: 'It is true that at the present time we are happily on terms of cordial friendship with France, but the Channel Tunnel once made will be made for ever, while all history goes to prove that international friendships are not based on such secure foundations that they are able to stand the shock of a conflict of international interests or a wound to national pride.' The Director of Military Operations, General Ewart, prepared a hostile paper in April 1907. Revealingly, he wrote in his private diary in January that year: 'I have an insular prejudice against it, not on military grounds for it is easy to exaggerate the danger – but on sentimental grounds. I am prepared to admit that with France friendly or in alliance it might be a Military advantage – but its completion will Europeanise us. I hate Cosmopolitanism. I stick to my insularity.'[12]

All this, of course, was in private. In public, the military correspondent of *The Times* (Repington) pointed out that in the event of a Franco-German war the Germans might well seize the French end of the Tunnel. Lord Lansdowne, the British architect of the *entente* and previously an advocate of the Tunnel, declared in the House of Lords that he had changed his mind. On 21 March 1907 the Prime Minister, Campbell-Bannerman, announced the government's rejection of the Tunnel project in words which were often to be cited in future discussions.

> Even supposing the military dangers involved were to be amply guarded against, there would exist throughout the country a feeling of insecurity which might lead to a constant demand for increased expenditure, naval and military, and a continual risk of unrest and possibly alarm, which, however unfounded, would be most injurious in its effect, whether political or commercial. . . . These considerations lead us, while rejoicing in anything that facilitates the communication with our neighbours, to view this scheme with disfavour.[13]

Balfour, the Leader of the Opposition and Prime Minister when the *entente* was concluded in 1904, welcomed the statement. The *entente* had been welcomed across party lines; equally, the Channel Tunnel was rejected across party lines.

The issue was revived in 1913, when Sir Arthur Fell formed a House of Commons committee to promote a Channel Tunnel. Again

---

excellent article. See also the same author's book, *Channel Tunnel Visions, 1850–1945: Dreams and Nightmares* (London, 1995), which tells the whole story in fascinating detail.

12. PRO, CAB 18/25; Wilson, 'Channel Tunnel', pp. 107–8.

13. Wilson, 'Channel Tunnel', p. 110.

the project was put to the Committee of Imperial Defence, where this time it found more support. Generals Wilson and French thought it would help to get an army to France; the First Lord of the Admiralty (Churchill) claimed that it could be made safe from invasion. But neither the Foreign Office nor the Board of Trade supported the idea. Asquith, the Prime Minister, twice repeated with approval and authority Campbell-Bannerman's dictum of 1907 about the 'feeling of insecurity' which a tunnel would arouse. Nothing, he said, had yet refuted that view. The Committee rejected the project on 14 July 1914.

These discussions were very revealing. From the British point of view, expressed by the highest statesmen in the land, a permanent link with the continent would create a perpetual feeling of insecurity. The *entente* with France was welcome, but in the mutability of human affairs it was highly unlikely to last for ever; and in any case a tunnel might be used for an invasion by the Germans if the circumstances arose. Behind this reasonable view lay the sort of instincts about insularity which Ewart put down in his diary. What Wolseley had written about the 'silver streak' still touched the heart, though the head had begun to argue against it. The French, on the other hand, looked at the project with a practical eye. Their railway companies anticipated commercial and passenger traffic. Their engineers saw a great technical problem which they were sure they could solve. Their staff officers envisaged a valuable line of communication to bring British troops to France. The contrast is striking. The British might like to think of themselves as practical and pragmatic, and indeed the French too looked upon them in this way. But with regard to the Tunnel the British fell back on their insular instincts and it was the French who were pragmatic.

THE COMING OF WAR

On 2 February 1911 Eyre Crowe, a senior Foreign Office official, wrote that: 'The fundamental fact of course is that an Entente is not an alliance. For purposes of ultimate emergencies it *may* be found to have no substance at all. For an Entente is nothing more than a frame of mind, a view of general policy which is shared by the governments of the two countries, but which *may* be, or become, so vague as to lose all content.'[14] From time to time, Crowe and other officials who

14. Keith Wilson, *Policy of the Entente. Essays on the determinants of British foreign policy 1904–1914* (Cambridge, 1985), p. 37.

believed in the German menace to fundamental British security tried to turn the *entente* into an alliance, but never succeeded. British policy in the hands of Grey remained non-committal, except in the sense of refusing to promise the Germans unconditional neutrality in the event of war – which was really only another form of rejecting commitment. The same line was taken by Balfour, who ceased to be leader of the Conservative Party in 1911 but remained an influential elder statesman. Setting out his views for Grey's benefit in June 1912, Balfour wrote that the *entente* of 1904 had now developed in such a way that it would be impossible for either Britain or France to be indifferent to a serious attack upon the other, and it would be better to make a firm alliance so that the two General Staffs should know where they stood. But he went on at once to add that many British people, including himself, 'would do everything in their power to save France from destruction but have no mind to be dragged at her heels into a war for the recovery of Alsace and Lorraine'. They would need to be assured that France was truly fighting for her own independence and that of Europe, and that she was no longer 'the France of Louis XIV, of Napoleon or even of the Second Empire'.[15] Thus did history cast its long shadow.

The *entente* did not become an alliance, for a wide variety of reasons. Continuing instincts of isolation and insularity; the desire to keep the great decision of peace or war solely in British hands; divisions within the main political parties, and especially the Liberals – all played their part. So did a lurking dread that a continental alliance would bring with it that commitment common to all continental countries: military conscription. One French minister who accompanied President Fallières on his state visit in 1908 rashly urged his hosts to accept an alliance and adopt conscription. But on the whole the French did not press such questions. They would have preferred an alliance, which Delcassé had hoped for in 1904. But they thought they had secured an expectation of support, which in the last resort would be translated into action. Then in July 1914 came that ultimate emergency which Crowe had referred to in 1911, and with it the question of whether the *entente* would prove to have any substance.

The war crisis of July 1914 came with extraordinary speed and suddenness. The European powers were accustomed to crises, over Morocco in 1905–6 and 1911, and over the Balkans in 1908–9 and 1912–13; but in all of these episodes the tension had been prolonged

15. Kenneth Young, *Arthur James Balfour* (London, 1963), pp. 343–4.

54

and had ultimately been resolved by diplomatic compromise. This time the crisis lasted only about six weeks, and the final drama, when the flow of events attained enormous speed, was packed into little more than a week. On 27 July 1914 the principal states of Europe were at peace; by 5 August most of them were at war. This great European crisis contained within it a crisis in Franco-British relations.

The war of 1914 began in the Balkans. Archduke Franz Ferdinand of Austria was assassinated in Sarajevo on 28 June 1914. The Austrian government decided to use this event to crush Serbia by force, and declared war on the Serbs on 28 July. Russia supported the Serbs, as fellow-Slavs. Germany, throughout the crisis, supported Austria, deliberately seeking a limited war in the Balkans in the knowledge that this would probably produce a general war in Europe. In a war between Germany and Austria on the one hand, and Russia and Serbia on the other, France was bound to intervene, both under the Franco-Russian alliance and in terms of self-interest, because she dare not let Russia be defeated and then face Germany alone. In the event, France did not have to take any such decision. The German plan of war, devised by General Schlieffen, prescribed that in any European war the Germans must attack France first, defeat her in six weeks, and then turn on the lumbering Russians. The attack against France must be delivered through Belgium, to avoid the fortifications on the Franco-German border. That is what happened. Germany delivered an ultimatum to Belgium on 2 August, with a twelve-hour time limit. After agonised deliberation throughout the night the Belgian government rejected it. On 3 August Germany declared war on France and invaded Belgium, en route for northern France and Paris.

This developing pattern of events had its impact on relations between France and Britain. Until a very late date – 2 or perhaps even 3 August – it seemed likely that war would start in the Balkans and France would be drawn in to support Russia. In such circumstances, it was highly unlikely that Britain would have intervened to support France. The Balkans were no concern of Britain's. Russia remained deeply unpopular with Liberal opinion. A case for going to war would have rested solely on long-range calculations of power politics, and would have carried no conviction in the Liberal Party or with much of the country. Only when the crisis suddenly changed its nature, involving Belgium and France directly, did the attitude of Britain also change. In this comparatively simple fact lies the key to the conduct of the British government.

In the developing crisis it was France, not Britain, which was directly and immediately involved. The French government and people alike knew that if there were a European war they would be in it. In such a war they wanted British support. To win over British opinion, the French government took two steps. First, they claimed that Austria, not Russia, was the first to mobilise its army (in fact it was the other way round). President Poincaré went out of his way to emphasise this order of events to the British Ambassador, making it clear that Austria, not Russia, was the first to make this move towards war. Second, on the same day as the Russian mobilisation (30 July), the French Cabinet decided to order the withdrawal of all French troops to a distance of ten kilometres from the border with Germany. A telegram was at once sent to inform Grey of this decision, with the explanation that while France was resolute in self-defence she would take no aggressive measure. If there were to be any clashes between French and German forces, it could only be because the Germans were already ten kilometres inside France. In short, the French set out to demonstrate that both they themselves and their allies the Russians were on the defensive. As events turned out, they were not required to do anything else. Germany proceeded to present France with an impossible ultimatum, to declare war on France, and to invade not only France but neutral Belgium. The French could say with absolute confidence that they were at war because they were attacked.

The position of Britain was very different. No-one attacked Britain in 1914. The Cabinet was first told of the dangers of the situation on 24 July, and then only briefly, at the end of a long and difficult discussion on Ireland. Serious debate did not begin until 29 July, essentially on the question of whether to intervene in a probable European war or to stand aside. The question was left open. On 30 July the Cabinet agreed to take a decision on the next day, but it did not do so. The state of British relations with France offered only limited guidance. The British had put it in writing that the military and naval conversations left them with complete freedom of action as to whether to go to war or not. The only written obligation the government was under was that stated in the Grey–Cambon correspondence of November 1912: that if something occurred which threatened the general peace, the two governments should immediately discuss with one another as to whether they should act together to prevent aggression and preserve peace. No such discussions were held at the end of July and the beginning of August 1914, though it could have been said with the utmost truth that events were occurring which threatened the general peace.

This did not mean that there was no communication between the two governments. Grey and Cambon met daily, sometimes more than once. But as July came to an end their conversations became extremely difficult. On 31 July it was Grey's duty to tell Cambon that the Cabinet declined to make any statement about British intentions in the event of war. He explained to the Ambassador that the position was different from that in 1911, when French interests had been directly challenged. Now France was involved in the crisis only through her alliance with Russia, and in these circumstances Britain could give no undertaking to enter a war. On 1 August Grey re-emphasised this point: if France became involved in war through her alliance with Russia, at a time when Germany was willing to offer France the option of neutrality, then Britain would not join in the war or send an expeditionary force.

It was after the first of these conversations that the Foreign Editor of *The Times*, Wickham Steed, asked Cambon what he was doing, and Cambon replied: 'I am waiting to see if the word honour should be struck from the English language.' After the second conversation, on 1 August, Cambon went to see Arthur Nicolson, saying bluntly: 'They are going to ditch us, they are going to ditch us.'[16] George Lloyd, a Conservative back-bencher who kept Cambon in touch with the Opposition, told Leo Amery on 1 August that 'The French regarded themselves as completely betrayed and were in an awful state of mind.' Cambon had told Lloyd that 'if we stood out and the French won they would gladly do everything to crush us afterwards'.[17] These reactions were genuine, though the experienced Cambon was doubtless not averse to playing to the gallery in order to create an effect. They revealed how far an expectation of support had grown up in French minds, despite the fact that the British could point to their repeated statements – accepted by the French – that they retained complete freedom of action. They also show how near Britain and France came, during the war crisis of 1914, to a complete and probably fatal break. If Britain had stood out of a war, could such a breach ever have been healed?

It was not until 2 August that the British Cabinet effectively decided otherwise, by taking two decisions. On 1 August, Cambon had pointed out to Grey that, as a result of the Anglo-French naval agreements, the French Channel coast was unprotected against German bombardment, and that Britain had a duty to provide defence. Grey

16. François Charles-Roux, *Souvenirs diplomatiques d'un âge révolu* (Paris, 1956), p. 275; Harold Nicolson, *Sir Arthur Nicolson, Bart., First Lord Carnock: A Study in the Old Diplomacy* (London, 1930), p. 419.

17. John Barnes and David Nicholson, eds, *The Leo Amery Diaries*, vol. I, *1896–1929* (London, 1980), p. 103.

brought this question to Cabinet on the morning of 2 August, and the Cabinet agreed that the British fleet would defend the French coast against German naval attack. At that point, four ministers offered their resignations rather than support this decision, though two later withdrew them. The second Cabinet decision, taken during the evening of 2 August, related not to France but to Belgium. The Cabinet agreed that any substantial violation of Belgian neutrality would compel Britain to go to war. In the event, the German fleet did not try to bombard the French Channel ports, but the German Army did invade Belgium.

On 3 August the news reached London of Germany's ultimatum to Belgium and of its rejection by the Belgian government. King Albert of the Belgians appealed to Britain for help, as a guarantor of his country's neutrality and independence. There was virtually no gainsaying this appeal, though two ministers (Burns and Morley) still insisted on resigning rather than accept British entry into war. On 4 August the Cabinet agreed that if Germany did not reverse its actions in Belgium and withdraw its forces, then Britain would go to war. At midnight the ultimatum to Germany expired, and Britain declared war on Germany.

The precise role of the *entente* with France in this fateful decision has remained unclear from that day to this. It has often been said that the military and naval conversations created a moral obligation which had to be honoured, but this was not so. The British reservations, retaining their power of decision, were perfectly clear; and we know that Joffre understood that he could not count on British support. On the other hand, there was a strong case in political and strategic calculation that British security was bound up with that of France, and that German domination of Europe after defeating France would pose a fatal threat to Great Britain. Grey and Asquith held this view, which also prevailed in the Foreign Office; and they were both prepared to resign – thus bringing down the government – unless it was accepted. But as late as 2 August there was no sign that it would be accepted, either by a united Cabinet or even less by a united Liberal Party. As Grey wrote in a private letter on 9 August 1914: 'But for Belgium we should have kept out of it.'[18] In so far as we can judge a situation which did not actually arise, this is surely true. It may well be that on grounds of rational policy the British government *should* have gone to war to help France defeat the German attack, and so prevent German domination of Europe. It is very likely that such a conclusion would

18. Robbins, *Grey*, p. 297.

have been reached in the course of the next few weeks. But in actual fact it was only the German invasion of Belgium that caused a united Cabinet, Parliament and country to go to war, with a firm will and a clear conscience.

In later years, widely differing interpretations of these events grew up. In Britain, there was a widespread belief that the staff conversations had dragged Britain into war. When the war lasted for four years, with immense casualties and suffering, the lesson was drawn that there must be no more staff conversations. In France, there were unhappy memories of the period of acute uncertainty. The lesson drawn by the French was that in future the British must be tied as closely as possible by an alliance – which was the precise opposite of the lesson drawn by the British.

But that was for the future. On 5 August 1914 Britain and France were both at war, at least largely for the same purpose: to defeat Germany. The next four years were to be those of their closest co-operation and of their greatest common suffering.

CHAPTER 4
Comrades in Arms: (i) The High Command

At the beginning of August 1914 France and Britain went to war in completely different ways. The French at once mobilised almost every man of military age: in the first few days of August, some 3,800,000 men were in the Army, and by the end of September that figure rose to 4,800,000.[1] Following the plans already prepared, these armies moved rapidly onto the offensive towards Alsace and Lorraine, meeting a disastrous defeat in the Battle of the Frontiers in the second half of August. In Britain the declaration of war which took effect from midnight on 4/5 August at first had little practical effect. It was symptomatic of the national frame of mind that county cricket continued for some time, virtually uninterrupted. The Oval cricket ground was taken over for military purposes, but Surrey simply transferred their matches to Lord's. When recruitment for the Army began, it was (following tradition) on a voluntary basis, so that men could join up or not as they thought best – though there developed a considerable moral pressure to do so.

The fact was that the British government had declared war without any clear idea as to how to wage it. At 4 p.m. on 5 August 1914, the first day of British participation in the war, an unusual meeting took place at 10 Downing Street. The Prime Minister took the chair; those present included Grey, Haldane, Churchill, the CIGS and First Sea Lord, and Field Marshals Kitchener and Roberts. John Terraine, in his book on Haig (who was among those present) asks dramatically '*What were they all wanted for?*' and gives the extraordinary but accurate answer: 'to decide what to do'.[2] On 4 August, Grey had explained to

1. Jacques Desmarest, *La Grande Guerre, 1914–1919* (Paris, 1978), p. 12.
2. John Terraine, *Douglas Haig: The Educated Soldier* (London, 2nd edn, 1990), p. 72.

Cambon that Britain would not at once send an expeditionary force to the continent, because the Army was needed for home defence and public opinion would not support the despatch of troops to France.

Thus, despite all the military conversations, the British government had not decided to send an army to France. At the Council of War at Downing Street, the naval representatives declared that the fleet could protect the country against invasion, so that it was safe to send five or six divisions overseas. Discussion then turned on where they should go – perhaps to Antwerp, to help the Belgians directly, or to Amiens, which would be a safe concentration area. But here the military talks did come into play. The only transport arrangements which had been worked out were those designed to get a British Expeditionary Force (BEF) to Maubeuge, a town in France near the Belgian border. The Council of War agreed to send troops, and as provided by the staff talks and the railway timetables, they were to assemble round Maubeuge; which put them directly in the path of a large part of the German force advancing through Belgium into France.

The episode is a further reminder of the British uncertainty. Until 4 August the government had hesitated about declaring war, then they hesitated about sending the BEF to France. As late as 6 August the French Minister of War, Messimy, still did not know whether the British had made up their minds, and sent Huguet, the former Military Attaché, to London to find out what was happening. The French dismay if the British Army had stayed at home can only be imagined, but we can guess at it by the relief and enthusiasm which later greeted the British arrival. It is salutary to remember that the *entente* almost foundered on the sandbanks of British hesitation.

FIRST CONTACTS: A HESITANT START

In the event the BEF went to France, starting a British military commitment on an unprecedented scale. But at the beginning its strength was only five divisions. Its commander, Field Marshal Sir John French, was to exercise his command independently of the French, though he was instructed to co-operate with them. Because his force was so small, and had few reserves, he was also ordered to incur as few casualties as possible.

In practice, co-operation with the French proved difficult to achieve. The first meeting between Sir John French and General Lanrezac, commanding the neighbouring French Fifth Army, on 17

August 1914 was by common consent a disaster, from which their personal relations never recovered. After the battle of Mons on 23 August, both the British and French were driven back by powerful German forces. Almost inevitably, they blamed one another for their retreat. Lanrezac claimed that his troops had to fall back because the British failed to hold their ground; the British made similar complaints about the French. At one stage at the end of August the two armies came near to a complete breach. Sir John French, in a mood of deep discouragement, considered retreating with his whole force towards its main base at Le Havre, and he even talked of shifting his base to Nantes or St Nazaire, far away on the Atlantic coast. Barely a week after the British had fought their first action there was a danger of them pulling out to head for the ports. The situation was saved by ministerial intervention, both British and French. British ministers despatched Kitchener (now Minister of War) to Paris, where he arrived on 1 September wearing his Field Marshal's uniform, and ordered Sir John French to stay in the line and co-ordinate his movements with those of his allies. At the same time the French Minister, now Millerand, and the C-in-C, Joffre, also used their influence to persuade the British commander to give up his talk of retreat. The danger of a breach was averted, but it was to recur in 1918, and again (in even more dramatic circumstances) in May 1940.

The orders to the British commander to minimise casualties also caused some difficulty. On 30 August Sir John French wrote to Joffre about this problem. Since the French Army had already incurred about 21,000 casualties, amounting to a fifth of the total strength of the BEF, this concern seemed to Joffre almost absurd; and yet for the British the BEF comprised most of their trained troops, with not much in reserve except territorials.[3] The French and British points of view on this painful matter were deeply opposed, and each was in its own way well founded.

At the beginning of September 1914 the German advance through northern France came to a halt, almost within sight of Paris; and Joffre made preparations for the counter-offensive on the Marne which was to turn the tide. As late as 5 September, a day before Joffre's attack was due to begin, there was still some doubt as to whether the BEF would take part in the battle. Joffre himself went to see Sir John French to explain his plan, and according to Spears's graphic eyewitness account made an intense appeal for British co-operation. 'Monsieur le Maréchal, c'est la France qui vous supplie.' ('Marshal, it is

3. Edward Spears, *Liaison 1914. A Narrative of the Great Retreat* (London, 1930, 2nd edn, 1968), pp. 240, 287–8. All references are to the second edition.

France who implores you.') One of Joffre's biographers writes that what he really said was "Il y va de l'honneur de l'Angleterre, Monsieur le Maréchal' ('England's honour is at stake, Marshal'). Sir John, after struggling with his French vocabulary for a moment, said to one of his officers: 'Damn it, I can't explain. Tell him that all that men can do our fellows will do.'[4] The scene was dramatic, and the roles were emblematic, almost stereotypes, with Joffre's appeal to honour and Sir John's tongue-tied bluffness. It was as though some tableau of French and English had come to life.

The BEF duly played its part in the battle of the Marne, which marked the end of the great German offensive designed to knock France out of the war in six weeks. During this opening phase of the war, the French and British armies had made a bad beginning in their co-operation, with much recrimination and loss of confidence. For two or three days they had come dangerously near to a fatal break. But they survived. By the end of November 1914 the western front had settled down in the shape which it was to maintain until the final battles of 1918. Two lines of trenches confronted one another from the Swiss border to the coast. On the Allied side, the French held the greater part of this long front, with the BEF on the left, towards the sea. The line itself lay, for the most part, deep in French territory, with the Germans occupying a large part of north-west France and all Belgium except one small corner.

At that stage, no-one knew that the war was going to last another four years; but at any rate it was clear that it would not be short. Relations between France and Britain had to assume wholly new and sterner aspects. Armies had to fight side by side and their commanders had to work together. Politicians had to get used to crossing the Channel frequently and doing business face to face in a manner which was quite unprecedented. In all this, language presented a serious difficulty, and neither soldiers nor statesmen were blessed with the gift of tongues. When the war began, the compulsory foreign language at St Cyr (the French equivalent of Sandhurst) was German, on the principle of knowing your enemy. Joffre, the French C-in-C, could manage almost no English. Foch, despite visits to England, could scarcely conduct a conversation in the language. Sir John French spoke French only with great difficulty; and his successor, Haig, was notoriously inarticulate in English and worse in French. Of the generals who later reached high posts, only Nivelle on the French side and Henry Wilson on the British spoke the other language fluently;

---

4. Spears, *Liaison 1914*, pp. 414–18; Pierre Varillon, *Joffre* (Paris, 1956), p. 322.

and as it happened Nivelle was C-in-C for only a short and disastrous period, and Wilson's influence was limited. Among the politicians, nobody on either side could manage much of the other language, until Clemenceau (who had married an American and spoke good English) became Premier near the end of 1917. In these circumstances, the interpreters faced hard work.

An alliance had to be forged, and made to work at a number of different levels. Methods had to be found of directing the war at the highest strategic and political level. The economic demands of war had to be met. Long-term war aims had to be devised and held in some sort of balance between the two countries. The two peoples had to settle down to a conflict of unprecedented severity and hardship, in strikingly different conditions. The French had the immediate and powerful incentive of fighting to liberate their own territory from German occupation. British troops, on the other hand (millions of them before the war was over), had to fight in foreign lands, for territory not their own; and, even more remarkable, so did hundreds of thousands from Canada, Australia, New Zealand and South Africa. It is a notorious fact in the history of warfare that alliances are subject to many strains; and it is remarkable that in 1914–18 France and Britain held so well together at all these different levels.

STRATEGIC CHOICES AND MEANS OF CO-OPERATION

In fundamental strategic terms, the French had no choice as to where to fight the war or what their prime objective must be. They had to fight in France, and they must drive the Germans out of the occupied departments. In order to do so, they became increasingly dependent upon British help. French losses in 1914 (killed, wounded and missing) amounted to 995,000, and in 1915 a further 1,430,000.[5] Such casualties could not be sustained much longer, and therefore France had to rely on British assistance on a scale unexpected when the war began. The British for their part believed that they had a strategic choice. There were politicians and soldiers who believed that the war could only be won in the west, by defeating the German armies in France; and others who as early as December 1914 regarded the western front as offering no more than a blood-stained stalemate, and

5. Casualty figures from Douglas Porch, *The March to the Marne. The French Army 1871–1914* (Cambridge, 1981), p. 213. Terraine, *Haig*, p. 126.

who therefore looked for other areas in which to fight. These areas varied over time – the Dardanelles in 1915, Italy and the Balkans in later years; but their advocates were usually called 'easterners', if only to differentiate them from the 'westerners' who were committed to the campaign in France.

In 1915 the British tried to follow both courses at once. In April they effected a landing at the Dardanelles, in an attempt to knock Turkey (then allied to Germany) out of the war and bring assistance to Russia by way of the Straits and the Black Sea. But in August the same year Kitchener visited France, and returned convinced that Britain must do all in its power to help the French, even at the cost of very heavy casualties indeed on the western front – otherwise, France would not be able to sustain the war in the west. It may be that this was the point at which the British effectively committed themselves beyond recall to the western front; but for a long time that was by no means obvious. Troops were not withdrawn from the Dardanelles until January 1916, and by that time another landing had been made at Salonika in northern Greece, to try to create a Balkan front against the Central Powers. For the second part of 1915 and all of 1916, Allied meetings were often taken up with questions of whether to reinforce either the Dardanelles or Salonika with comparatively small forces, even when whole armies were being swallowed up at Verdun and on the Somme. Other campaigns in Mesopotamia and Palestine continued to engage large numbers of British and Imperial troops throughout the war. Even if the British had made their fateful choice by August 1915, its consequences were not fully acknowledged.

The French obviously had a vital interest in this internal British dispute between westerners and easterners. Even though France joined in the Dardanelles expedition, and provided the commander for the Salonika force, they remained fundamentally opposed to any substantial diversion of forces from the western front.

In these circumstances, it was natural for each government to play its own hand; but they were also compelled to consider their problems together. Under the pressure of war, something quite new in Franco-British consultation and co-operation began to emerge. This process began sporadically. As we have seen, Kitchener made a hasty visit to Paris on 1 September 1914 to fend off an immediate military crisis. In January 1915 Millerand, the French Minister of War, went to London to try to persuade the British to send more troops to France. Between 31 May and 4 June 1915 Asquith went to France to visit the British armies, and met the British and French commanders and Millerand. Later in June Lloyd George, the Minister of Munitions, went to Boulogne to confer with his French opposite number. At much the same time, in June and July 1915, there were formal conferences at Chantilly and St Omer (the headquarters respectively of the French armies and the BEF) between the military commanders.

The first formal inter-governmental conference took place at Calais on 6 July 1915, eleven months after the start of the war. It began amid some confusion. The French Premier, Viviani, with the two service ministers, arrived by train from Paris at an early hour, intending to start the conference at 9 a.m. Hankey, acting as secretary to the British delegation, had to tell them that his team 'wouldn't be out of bed by then', on the rather weak grounds that they had arrived in Calais only at midnight. When the conference got under way, the opening speeches were translated, but after that the French required that proceedings should be in their own language, leaving the British to muddle along as best they could. Not surprisingly no formal minutes were kept or conclusions recorded.[6]

On 17 November 1915 there was a more formal and better-prepared conference at Paris. Asquith, Grey, Balfour (Admiralty) and Lloyd George (Munitions) were welcomed by Briand (the new French Premier) and the opposite numbers of the British ministers. Briand opened with a statement that victory could only be achieved by closer Allied co-operation, and that this conference was to be the first in a series which would continue until the war was won. The two delegations agreed to set up a Joint Standing Committee to co-ordinate policy. The British further proposed that this Committee should have a permanent secretariat; the French demurred, but Hankey and a French officer, Captain Doumayrou, were appointed as Secretary–Liaison Officers. It was only a limited step, but future Allied conferences at least had minutes taken and conclusions recorded. The year 1915 ended with another conference between Briand and Asquith at Calais on 5 December, and a formal meeting of military commanders at Chantilly on 6–8 December. This military conference made a serious attempt to grapple with the whole strategy of the war. Joffre proposed that the early part of 1916 should be devoted to wearing-down attacks against the enemy, to be followed by simultaneous offensives by all the Allied powers, now four in number – France, Britain, Russia and Italy. This broad pattern was accepted in principle; though it was shortly to be disrupted by the Germans launching their own wearing-down assault at Verdun in February 1916. In March 1916 a vast Allied conference was held in Paris, with

6. Maurice Hankey (Lord Hankey), *The Supreme Command, 1914–1918* (London, 2 vols, 1961), vol. I, pp. 348–9.

representatives from France, Britain, Russia, Italy, Belgium, Serbia, Portugal and Japan. Again, Joffre expounded his general strategic concept, to the effect that at present France could do no more than stand on the defensive, and it was for the British, Russians and Italians to take the offensive, in their different theatres of operations.

There thus developed, somewhat haphazardly, a system of Franco-British conferences, with an improving administrative organisation. They sometimes got bogged down in comparatively minor matters (for example, the Calais conference of December 1915 was almost entirely taken up with questions concerning Salonika rather than with the major front in the west), or were lost in high generalisations which could not be made good. Even so, France and Britain were developing a form of consultation which had not been conceived of when the war began.

During these first two years of the war there also took place a profound shift in the balance of forces between France and Britain. At the outbreak of war, even though the independence of the BEF's command was insisted upon, there was no doubt whatever that the French Army was in charge of operations. The French forces were far stronger than the British, and their generals were more accustomed to commanding large numbers. The French government had desperately wanted Britain to enter the war, but more on moral and political than on military grounds. By early 1916, however, the French had suffered heavy casualties which could no longer be replaced. They had to look to the British to take an ever greater role in the fighting. Joffre was painfully aware of this late in 1915, when he said at the Chantilly conference that the wearing-down attacks in 1916 must be made by those states which still had large reserves of men – which did not include France. The BEF, on the other hand, had grown from its original five divisions in August 1914 to 43 divisions in January 1916 and 52 in June 1916.[7] This force was as yet inexperienced, despite its battles in 1915; but it still had reserves of manpower to draw on, in Britain and the Dominions.

As time went on, therefore, the French became steadily more dependent on British help, and the balance of force shifted within the alliance. This process reached a new stage during the terrible battle of Verdun, which began in February 1916 and continued for months, with almost every division in the French Army at home being drawn through the carnage at one time or another. French losses rose to some 200,000 in the early stages, and on 26 May Joffre went to see

---

7. Correlli Barnett, *Britain and Her Army, 1509–1970* (London, Pelican edn, 1974), p. 389.

Haig, who had taken command of the BEF in December 1915, and told him that if this continued the French Army would be ruined. Joffre asked formally that the British should take the weight off the French. Haig had already made his mind up. He knew that his troops, the men of the Kitchener Army, were not fully ready; but equally he knew that they must take the offensive some time in 1916 and he believed that they could do so successfully. But for some obscure reason he almost teased Joffre, reviewing in his dour Scots manner the possible dates for an attack, and concluding that 15 August would be the best. At that Joffre exploded, shouting that if the British did nothing until then the French Army would cease to exist. Haig then agreed to attack on 1 July.[8] It was to be a sombre date in British history: the first day of the battle of the Somme.

Military relations between the French and British had thus reached a stage completely unforeseen in 1914. Joffre told Haig, without the slightest ambiguity, that without British help by 1 July the French Army would be finished. The French depended on the British to survive. At that time, events worked out as Joffre hoped, for the benefit of the French Army and of the alliance. The offensive on the Somme relieved the pressure on Verdun, and by the end of August all German attacks there ceased. But for years afterwards these events proved deeply divisive. In a history of the Great War published in 1991 and aimed at a wide readership, Guy Pedroncini wrote that 1916, which might have been the year of the Somme, was in fact the year of Verdun. 'Who remembers Thiepval?' he asked rhetorically. It is Douaumont, Vaux and *la voie sacrée* (by which Verdun was supplied) which have remained in French memories. But in Britain the opposite is the case. It may well be that only the very well-informed now remember Thiepval, but the British people long remembered the Somme. As John Bourne wrote, at about the same time as Pedroncini, 'The Battle of the Somme was to be a unique experience for the British people. Never before had they attempted to wage war on this scale. Not since have they wished to do so.'[9] Some 20–25 years later, the desire to have no more battles like the Somme was to have serious effects on British policy, and the marks of the historical and folk memories lasted longer still.

In order to sustain this new role as a great military power, Britain

8. Robert Blake, ed., *The Private Papers of Douglas Haig, 1914–19*, (London, 1952), pp. 144–5.

9. Guy Pedroncini in Paul-Marie de la Gorce, ed., *La Première Guerre Mondiale* (Paris, 2 vols, 1991), pp. 91–2; John Bourne, *Britain and the Great War, 1914–1918* (London, 1989), p. 51.

was compelled to introduce compulsory military service, for the first time in history (if we except the very different use of the press-gang for the Navy). An Act imposing conscription for unmarried men was passed through Parliament in January 1916, and another extending the obligation to married men in May 1916. At the time, what seemed the British slowness in reaching this decision (which was highly controversial in the Liberal Party, where it was seen as an unwarranted intrusion on personal liberty) exasperated many Frenchmen. In France, since the time of the Revolution, the idea of the 'nation in arms' had been widely accepted, and conscription was simply a fact of life. British reluctance to impose it was regarded as a sign that the British were not pulling their weight in the war. As with the battle of the Somme, this question of conscription was to cast a long shadow. In the late 1930s, French politicians and generals were to regard the re-introduction of conscription in Britain as a touchstone by which to measure British determination to assume a military commitment to France. The British, for similar but opposite reasons, were reluctant to accept a return to conscription. It was a matter which went much deeper than strategic calculation, involving as it did strongly held national assumptions and emotions.

The shock of the casualties on the Somme – about 400,000 over the four and a half months of the battle's duration – had a profound effect in Britain. Such a toll for the gain of perhaps ten miles of territory strengthened the hand of the easterners, who sought some alternative to such dreadful methods. Among these, Lloyd George was the most dynamic and influential. He had lost all confidence in Haig, against whom his hostility became personal as well as strategic. During the autumn of 1916, Lloyd George used all his political skill and devices to undermine Haig's position and to change the direction of the war. He visited France and asked Foch how he had managed to keep French casualties proportionately lower than British, even during the battle of the Somme. He prepared a long paper for Asquith to take to a Franco-British conference in Paris, arguing the case for switching the main Allied effort away from the western front.

Lloyd George was thus using the means provided by the Franco-British alliance to control, or even subvert, Haig. While Joffre, who was a determined westerner and got on well with Haig, remained Commander-in-Chief, this device had little success. Equally, Lloyd George's influence was limited by his subordinate position within the British government. But in December 1916 Joffre was dismissed from his post, and replaced by General Nivelle; and in Britain, Asquith was deposed as Prime Minister and replaced by Lloyd George. The way was opened for a new phase in relations between generals and politicians, and between Britain and France.

SUPREME WAR COUNCIL AND A SINGLE COMMAND

At the beginning of 1917 the war had lasted for two and a half years. The Germans still held nearly all the territory they had captured in 1914. The French had suffered terrible losses, and their Army was almost exhausted. The British had fought their first great battle on the Somme, to depressingly little visible effect. Within the Franco-British alliance, the period of unquestioned French military leadership was drawing to a close, without much to show by way of results, and the balance of strength was moving towards the British. The two governments had instituted a system of regular conferences, but so far with little effect on strategic issues. The year ahead was to prove even more difficult for the Allies. In February the Germans began unlimited submarine warfare, with devastating effect on shipping across the Atlantic. In March the Tsar was deposed, and it looked increasingly as though Russia was effectively out of the war. In May there began a series of mutinies in the French Army. The only heartening event was the entry into the war of the United States in April; and even that was unlikely to produce American troops on the ground in any significant number before 1918. It is against this grim background that the working of the Franco-British alliance must be seen.

The year opened with apparently hopeful developments. As Prime Minister, Lloyd George introduced sweeping changes in British methods of government, creating a small War Cabinet and several new ministries, with better means of deciding on priorities. He also promised new energy and resolution in the conduct of the war, advocating a 'knock-out blow'. In France, the new C-in-C, Nivelle, was comparatively young (a mere 60), brisk and confident in manner, and with a good command of English. He claimed to have the secret of success on the western front without heavy casualties, and was willing to promise that if he undertook an offensive which did not produce rapid results he would break it off at once, instead of persisting for months as Haig had done on the Somme. Lloyd George found Nivelle very persuasive, and for a time dropped his objections to an offensive on the western front. He agreed that the British should take over an extra section of line in France to release French troops for Nivelle's attack.

Haig proved reluctant to take part in these new plans, and delayed taking over the French line. Lloyd George decided that the way to deal with this problem, to control Haig and perhaps get rid of him, was to change the system of command. On 15 February 1917 he told the French liaison officer at the War Office that he wished to place the British Army in France under Nivelle's command – a complete change from the independence which had been insisted on since the start of the war. Lloyd George then set out to achieve the change by means of what might charitably be called stage management, or more brutally, trickery. He arranged a Franco-British conference at Calais (26–27 February 1917), at which he prompted Nivelle to propose that the French C-in-C should be given full authority over the BEF in all operational matters. This was fiercely opposed by Haig, and by Robertson (the CIGS), who were both present at the conference. Haig declared that British troops would not fight under French command. At this Lloyd George partially climbed down, and accepted a compromise to the effect that British subordination to French command should only last for the duration of the impending offensive, and that the British C-in-C should retain the right to appeal to his government if he thought the safety of his Army was being endangered by French orders. At a further conference in London on 12 March, it was agreed that Nivelle would not communicate with the British government over Haig's head.

After these compromises, no-one was satisfied. Lloyd George had achieved neither a permanent unified command nor the neutralising of Haig. Robertson and Haig were furious with Lloyd George, with whom their relations were so bad that it was astonishing that they could work together at all. Haig also felt betrayed by Nivelle, because he thought that soldiers should stick together against the politicians. The French too felt deceived. Lloyd George, on his own initiative, had proposed a unified command under a French general, and then pulled back when it came to the point. Indeed the very concept of unity of command, which was in principle a valuable one, was undermined by the air of conspiracy and deception which pervaded the Calais conference. Not until another year had passed, and under the stress of dire necessity, did the Allies come round to a unified command.

In the event, Nivelle's offensive on the Chemin des Dames in April 1917 was a failure, made all the worse by the expectations which he had built up. Lloyd George and the British War Cabinet then went back on everything they had decided in February. On 1 May they agreed to urge the French to keep up the offensive, instead of breaking it off. If this still did not work, they wanted the restoration of complete freedom of action for the BEF in France, and the French to take back the section of line recently handed over to the British. These British proposals raised two issues which were to plague the Allies for the rest of the year: the independence of the BEF's actions, and the length of line being held by the two partners.

In mid-1917 the long process of the weakening of France within the alliance reached a new stage. French resources of manpower were now completely exhausted, and the morale of the Army gave way under the appalling strain. In May and June 1917 there were widespread mutinies, affecting about one-third of the 109 divisions in the French Army to a greater or lesser degree. The Army was out of action as an offensive force for the rest of the year. Haig did not know the full extent of these mutinies, but he knew enough to understand that his own Army, though still smaller than the French, was now the stronger of the two. This confirmed him in his determination that the offensive which he was planning in Flanders later in the year should be totally under British control. This caused considerable anxiety among the French high command and politicians, who were afraid that the British were trying to take control of the war for their own political purposes – Nivelle, for example, thought that a British victory in Flanders would result in British control of Belgium after the war. In July, General Herbillon, a senior French liaison officer, noted with annoyance that the British kept talking about 'our battle' in the north-east. Unhappily, this battle when it came was that which the British now remember as Passchendaele, a terrible and fruitless struggle in the mud which did much to restore the balance between the British and French armies – though alas it was a balance of despair.

The length of line held by the two armies was a bone of contention throughout the war, reaching a stage of particular difficulty in 1917. At the beginning of that year, the French held about 360 miles of front with 109 divisions, the British about 85 miles with 62 divisions. The French claimed that they used only five men per metre of front, while the British had thirteen. The British replied that the French line included long stretches (notably in Alsace and Lorraine) where there was little or no fighting. The British section, on the other hand, was all active, and early in 1917 they were facing nearly half the German forces in the west. At the end of the year, after much bickering, the French held about ten fewer miles of front than at the beginning, the British ten miles more. The French public still saw in their newspapers maps showing that their armies held a disproportionate length of line, and concluded that the British were not pulling their weight. The

British were convinced that they were doing more than their share of the fighting. Each side had, by its own lights, a strong case; and on each side the resentment against the other ran deep.

The situation of France and Britain was made worse by the progressive collapse of Russia, where the Bolsheviks seized power in November 1917 and concluded an armistice in December, leaving Germany free to concentrate on the west.

But at much the same time the alliance was strengthened by two developments. One was that Clemenceau became Premier in France, on 19 November 1917. His sole purpose, as he told the Chamber, was to wage war, and he at once instilled a new vigour and urgency into the French war effort. He commanded admiration and respect among the British leaders. Haig wrote to his wife (31 January 1918) that Clemenceau, 'though 76 is the soundest and pluckiest of the lot. He is a grand old man, full of go and determination.'[10] Clemenceau turned to Lloyd George during a conference (1 February 1918) and said: 'You know you like me. You can't help yourself. You like me!' Hankey, who noted these words, added: 'The old fellow is just like a schoolboy, a great character.'[11] In fact, Clemenceau brought a rock-like certainty of purpose to counteract Lloyd George's mercurial changes of mood. Lloyd George had come to power as the advocate of victory and a 'knock-out blow', but he wavered during 1917, and it was Clemenceau who brought him back to his previous determination. In the last year of the war the two formed a close partnership.

Clemenceau's advent to power came in the midst of a change in the method of Allied co-operation. On October 1917 the then French Premier, Painlevé, arrived in London with a couple of ministers and General Foch, apparently without anyone having the slightest idea what they had come for. Lloyd George took them off to Chequers, which had just been given to the nation as a country house for the Prime Minister of the day, for a sort of housewarming weekend. There, on Sunday 14 October, he put forward a proposal to set up an Allied Supreme War Council and a Permanent Allied General Staff. Both would be located in Paris, and together they would impart a central direction to Allied strategy. The French were taken aback. After the disastrous attempt at a unified military command earlier in the year, they would not have dared to raise the question; but since the British did so, they were willing to look at it favourably.

There was much scepticism as to Lloyd George's motives. He was

10. Blake, *Haig Papers*, p. 281.
11. Stephen Roskill, *Hankey: Man of Secrets*, vol. I *1877–1918* (London, 1970), p. 491.

still trying to subvert Haig, and a new Allied General Staff would be a new means of getting round Haig's blocking power. Hankey wrote in his diary that the Prime Minister was 'pleased at the prospect of "dishing" the soldiers by establishing the allied council'.[12] Lloyd George also proposed to bring the Italians into the Council and the Staff, which would help him to shift the centre of operations away from France. But Lloyd George himself stressed the obvious truth that the enemy had a single strategic direction, which the Allies must match. His private fight with Haig and Robertson did not invalidate that proposition.

But would the Supreme War Council provide such direction? The formal British proposal, as approved by the War Cabinet on 2 November 1917, was that the Council would be advisory, i.e. that it would agree on recommendations to the individual governments, which would each retain its own power of decision. It might prove therefore to be no more than a talking shop; or, as President Poincaré put it more elegantly, an Aulic Council – an ancient Greek court which was reputed never to decide anything. Clemenceau, when he came to office, was at first sceptical, on these very grounds – he wanted to get things done, not to talk.

Despite these doubts, the Supreme War Council came into being with remarkable speed. Lloyd George made his first proposal on 24 October; the War Cabinet formalised it on 2 November; and Lloyd George bore it to Paris on the 3rd. With the French Premier (still Painlevé at that time) he went to Rapallo to meet the Italians. There, on 7 November, the three Prime Ministers settled the main lines. The Council was to consist of the three Premiers and one other minister from each country, and each government was to nominate a permanent military representative to give technical advice. With masterly tact, Lloyd George proposed that the normal meeting-place for the Council, and the permanent headquarters for the Allied Staff, should be at Versailles. Prussian domination, he declared, would be broken at the very place where the German Empire had been proclaimed in 1871.

For some time the Supreme Council seemed to achieve little. Lloyd George tried to use it for his own schemes, urging an offensive against the Turks; but Clemenceau opposed any diversion of forces from the western front. The Council agreed to set up a General Reserve for the whole of the French and Italian fronts, to be controlled by the permanent Allied Staff at Versailles, with Foch in the chair. However,

12. Ibid., p. 449.

in practice, in February 1918 neither Haig nor Pétain (now French C-in-C) would hand over any forces for this General Reserve, preferring to make their own arrangements to support one another in case of need. The Supreme War Council saved face by claiming that the British and French forces serving in Italy should be regarded as a reserve, but this was the merest pretence. The opening phase of the Council's existence was thus unpromising.

FOCH IN COMMAND

On 21 March 1918, the Germans launched a tremendous offensive in the west, seeking a decisive victory before the arrival of the Americans. They struck at the junction between the French and British fronts, and especially at the British Fifth Army, and they won spectacular successes, provoking a crisis between the French and British commanders similar to that at the beginning of September 1914, when it had seemed likely that the BEF might retreat to the ports.

Three days after the German assault began, on 24 March, Pétain went to see Haig. There is no absolute certainty as to what passed between them, but the consequences of their meeting were far-reaching. Pétain was already moving large forces to help the British – he had ordered twenty-one French divisions to reinforce Haig's front, and he was to add another thirteen divisions in the next two days. But also, on the evening of the 24th, Pétain told his commanders that his intentions were to maintain the cohesion of the French armies, and if possible to maintain liaison with the British. Guy Pedroncini has argued that the words 'if possible' merely indicated that Pétain was preparing to cope with different situations if they arose, and were not a sign that a break with the British was imminent. But Haig's impression at the time was very different. He described Pétain as 'very much upset, almost unbalanced and most anxious'; and recorded that Pétain had said that he had given orders for his troops to fall back to cover Paris if the German advance was maintained. Haig asked if he meant to abandon the British right flank, and wrote that 'He nodded assent'.[13]

Haig concluded that there was an immediate danger of a gap being opened between the French and British armies; and, more important, he was convinced that Pétain had already accepted defeat. On 25

---

13. Compare the accounts of this crucial meeting in Terraine, *Haig*, pp. 420–1, and Guy Pedroncini, *Pétain. Le soldat et la gloire, 1856–1918* (Paris, 1989), pp. 330–7.

March he telegraphed to the British government asking that 'General Foch or some other determined general who would fight should be given supreme control in France'. This was a complete departure from Haig's previous objections to a French C-in-C, and testifies to the gravity of the situation as he saw it. The key lies in his reference to a general *who would fight*. Haig believed that Pétain would not fight, but Foch would.

In response to this acute crisis in Allied affairs, Milner (representing the British War Cabinet) and General Henry Wilson (now CIGS) went to France on 26 March and met Clemenceau, Poincaré, Foch and Pétain at Doullens. Before the meeting, Clemenceau spoke to Pétain, and formed the same impression as Haig of Pétain's frame of mind – he told Poincaré that Pétain had said that the Germans would beat the British first and the French afterwards.[14] At the Allied meeting it was agreed that Foch should be appointed to co-ordinate the action of the Allied armies on the western front. In a first draft, Clemenceau had referred only to the armies in front of Amiens, and it was Haig who argued that this was too restricted and the whole front should be included. Just over a week later, at a conference at Beauvais, attended by Clemenceau, Lloyd George and the American commander, General Pershing, Foch's remit was changed to 'the strategic direction of military operations'; and on 14 April he was formally accorded the title of 'Commander in Chief of the Allied Armies'.

Foch's precise position in the light of these successive decisions remained unclear. It was nothing like that of General Eisenhower as Supreme Commander of the Allied Armies in Western Europe during the Second World War, with a large and integrated staff. Foch never had a staff of more than twenty, with no attempt at integration between French and British. His primary role lay in the realm of morale and attitudes, not planning and administration. On the very day of his appointment as 'co-ordinator' (26 March), Foch descended on General Gough, commanding the British Fifth Army, and ordered him to hold the present line, with no more retreats. It was an order which simply could not be carried out, and in fact the Fifth Army continued to retreat until 1 April; but Foch was striving for a moral rather than a material effect. In the same way, he instructed Pétain that the French must hold on and on no account lose contact with the British. In fact on 27 March a gap of some ten miles opened up between the two armies, to the south of the river Somme, but the French managed to close it before the Germans could exploit it.

14. David R. Watson, *Georges Clemenceau. A Political Biography* (London, 1974), p. 303.

Foch's appointment did not end the Allied defeats. The first German offensive came to a halt, but two more followed, virtually without pause. At the beginning of May it again appeared that there might be a breach between the British and French armies. On 2 May Clemenceau, Lloyd George and several generals debated anxiously as to whether, if the German advance continued, the BEF should defend the Channel ports and part company with the French, or maintain contact with the French and abandon the ports. Foch declared that the loss of the ports would be grave but not fatal, and that if he were forced to choose he would keep the armies together. But, he insisted, events would never come to that – 'jamais, jamais!' He carried Clemenceau and Lloyd George with him. The meeting accepted this, insisting that the choice would not arise; but (somewhat paradoxically) if it did the armies must fall back together. Thus Foch's moral authority prevailed, and he proved to be right. The choice did not have to be made. The armies held together, and the ports were held. It was a close-run thing, and it was the vindication of Foch's new position.

From the point of view of relations between France and Britain, it was not the specific achievements of either the Supreme War Council or the Allied Commander-in-Chief which mattered, but their very existence. Neither had been dreamed of in 1914. If anyone had told Haig even six months before March 1918 that he would actually *ask* to be put under the command of a French general, he would have got a dusty answer. But so it was. The two governments grasped the problems of how to wage a coalition war slowly and painfully. The solutions which they produced were improvised and imperfect. But finally they worked, and in the desperate crisis of March–May 1918 the Supreme War Council and the Allied C-in-C produced crucial decisions. This was partly a matter of personality. Lloyd George's flexibility and agility were complemented by Clemenceau's stability and fortitude. Foch proved the right man for an unusual job. But the institutions were also important. The very existence of the Supreme War Council, even if its members did not always know what it was to do, and an Allied Commander-in-Chief, even with ill-defined authority and no proper staff, changed the character of the alliance.

At the end of July 1914 no alliance had existed at all. There was no certainty that France and Britain would be engaged in war together, or whether, if they were, a British army would go to France. By 1918 the two countries had built up from nothing the institutions and working habits of an alliance. In four years of suffering, death and destruction, it was no small achievement.

CHAPTER 5

Comrades in Arms: (ii)
Economics and War Aims

When war broke out in 1914 almost everyone expected it to be over by Christmas. Only Kitchener, rising above the conventional wisdom of the European General Staffs, predicted at once a war of three years or even longer. Kitchener was right. A war of attrition developed at the front. Behind it lay a war of resources: manpower, industrial production, raw materials, food, shipping. In order to make their alliance work, France and Britain were compelled to co-operate on these practical matters. In so doing they produced a form of partnership previously unknown to either of them, and new in the whole history of war.

ECONOMIC CO-OPERATION

France faced economic problems from the very start of the war. Total mobilisation for the Army brought an immediate drop in industrial production. The harvest had to be brought in by women, children, and men too old to be called up. In the first two months of fighting, the Germans occupied a large area of north-eastern France, a zone of coal-mining, industry and arable farming. French coal production, which stood at 40.8 million tons in 1913, fell to 19.5 million tons in 1915. The figures for steel were 4.7 million tons in 1913, 1.1 million in 1915.[1] In autumn 1914 France began to put a prodigious effort into armaments production, as it became clear that the war would not in fact be over by Christmas, with the inexorable consequence of a rise in

---

1. G. Hardach, *The First World War* (London, 1977), p. 91.

imports. France became a large-scale importer of coal, raw materials, finished industrial goods, and food for both man and beast. These imports had to be transported by sea, and within two years of the outbreak of war Britain leased to France about 600 cargo ships. They also had to be paid for, in gold or foreign currency or by loans, because there were few goods available for export. So there emerged the linked problems of imports, shipping and payments.

For Britain, the problems came later. Voluntary recruitment played almost as much havoc with the British economy as conscription did with the French, though more slowly. The British were accustomed to vast imports, and in 1914 possessed some 4,000 merchant vessels to transport them and huge overseas investments to help to pay for them. Even so, by mid-1915 the pound sterling (which had been taken off the gold standard at the outbreak of war) was in disquieting decline against the dollar, and in August the British government accepted that it would have to raise a large loan in the United Sates to finance imports. In May 1915 another cloud appeared on the horizon: the German declaration of unrestricted submarine warfare. At that time there were not enough U-boats to make this effective, but the second attempt, starting in February 1917, was a different matter. Sinkings were very high in the early months of 1917 (850,000 tons in April). British food supplies neared exhaustion, and ship-building came nowhere near replacing losses. It was a desperate situation.

By 1917, therefore, Britain and France faced an acute economic crisis. They had to buy imports, especially from the United States; and they had to ship those imports across the Atlantic in the face of the U-boats. It was a remarkable fact that they tackled these problems together.

In making purchases from neutral countries, and especially the United States, Great Britain held the key position. As early as February 1915 the British and French agreed to create what they called a 'gold pool' to secure the common use of their gold reserves. With the City of London being at that time the centre of the world's money markets, this meant in effect that Britain became for a time the banker to the alliance. The British began to arrange loans from the USA and transfer some of them to France. The French too played their part. They sold some of their large gold reserves to Britain to finance purchases from abroad, and also lent gold to the Bank of England for use as a guarantee for loans. In August 1915, at a conference at Boulogne between the British Chancellor of the Exchequer (McKenna) and the French Finance Minister (Ribot), it was agreed to raise a joint Franco-British loan in the United States rather than a British loan from which advances would be made to France, and the two governments agreed to transfer gold to the value of $200 million each to New York to promote this loan. There thus developed a large degree of financial interdependence between the two countries. This system worked reasonably well until the end of 1916, when gold stocks were running down and Allied credit was nearing exhaustion. The situation was then saved only by the American entry into the war in April 1917, and the beginning of direct loans by the United States government. These were extended only on a month-to-month basis, and were subject to tough bargaining, but they were always there, and resolved the problem of payments – at the cost of the later problem of war debts.

One simple necessity for Britain and France was to import food. For the two countries to compete against one another to buy foodstuffs was wasteful when they could combine to purchase jointly. This took some time to sink in, and it was not until February 1916 that McKenna and Clémentel, the French Minister of Commerce, agreed that the Royal Sugar Commission (set up to control British purchases of sugar in August 1914) should buy sugar for both countries, and then supply France with 29,000 tons of sugar per month. Such use of British machinery, though convenient, was unwelcome to French pride and in the long run dangerous for French interests, and during 1916 Clémentel's representative in London, Jean Monnet, pressed the case for joint purchasing agencies. This was particularly important with regard to wheat, for which, during 1915, different French and British organisations had continued to compete with one another, to the benefit of cereal producers in Canada, the USA and the Argentine. In November 1916, on the initiative of Monnet and Arthur Salter, a British civil servant in the Department of Transport, a Wheat Executive was set up. It consisted of representatives from the British, French and Italian governments, and was authorised to purchase, apportion and transport wheat on behalf of all three countries. This was a remarkable departure. Jean Monnet, then a civil servant only 28 years old, wrote in his memoirs that 29 November 1916, the date of the signature of this agreement, had remained for him a vital date – 'the first step on the long road that led me gradually to discover the immense possibilities of collective action'.[2] Monnet's views on collective action were to affect Franco-British relations again, during the next forty years and more.

Even the best arrangements for purchasing wheat (or anything else) were of no avail unless the commodities could then be shipped across

2. Jean Monnet, *Memoirs* (English translation by Richard Mayne, London, 1978), p. 58.

the Atlantic. From 1 February 1917 this was increasingly difficult, as the German U-boats came to dominate the sea-lanes. The British took what seemed to them common-sense action by prohibiting the importation of all 'luxury goods', so as to save shipping space for necessities. The trouble was that this struck at once at what were still the major French exports to Britain, which were all classified as luxuries – wines, spirits, hats, ribbons, jewellery. Thus what seemed a sensible British measure threatened serious damage to French interests. Then in April 1917 the British government asked the French to return, by the end of June, some half-million tons of shipping previously leased to France. It was natural for the British to want the use of their own vessels in a crisis, but the potential disruption to French transport was enormous. The French government inspired protests in the press (which needed little urging when the facts became known), and a drastic dispute was in prospect.

Yet at this point the alliance showed its strength. In a series of negotiations in August 1917 the British went back on both their earlier decisions. They agreed to resume imports of French luxury goods, and they allowed the French to retain most of the British shipping whose return had been requested. The British also introduced the convoy system for the protection of shipping, and slowly brought down the rates of losses. September was the first month in which Allied ship-building exceeded sinking. Moreover, new methods of coping with the shipping problem by common action were introduced. The inspiration again came from Jean Monnet, who persuaded his Minister of Commerce, Clémentel, to propose the establishment of a 'shipping pool', a means of allocating all shipping to various tasks, not by individual governments but by an inter-Allied agency. On 3 November 1917 the British accepted this arrangement, though at that stage only for the limited task of transporting food supplies. At the Allied Conference on 29 November which set up the Supreme War Council, it was agreed to create an Inter-Allied Maritime Transport Council, with a permanent Executive to carry out its decisions. This Council met for the first time in London in March 1918. It speedily proved impossible to confine its activities to the shipping required for food. Ships allocated to the transport of foodstuffs had to be diverted from some other purpose, and decisions on priorities had to be made. Food, raw materials, manufactured goods, the troops of the American Expeditionary Force (two millions of them in 1918): all crossed the Atlantic under arrangements made by the Maritime Transport Executive.

Once this system had begun to work, inter-Allied Executives,

Councils and Committees began to multiply, to deal with munitions, nitrates, chemicals, explosives, and aircraft. The time came, indeed, when they were treading on one another's toes and beginning to compete with one another. But the system worked when it was needed, and its successes were far greater than its difficulties.

These were extraordinary developments. Just as in 1914 it was inconceivable that there should be a Supreme War Council to co-ordinate French and British policy, or a joint Commander-in-Chief to direct their armies, so no-one would have dreamed that French and British civil servants would be meeting every day to decide on the purchase of wheat or the allocation of shipping. Meeting the demands of total war had transformed Anglo-French relations.

In the course of this transformation the balance of influence tilted against France. Britain provided most of the shipping, and so exercised a predominant, if informal, influence in the Maritime Transport Council. Britain was the principal financial partner in the Franco-British alliance. By the end of the war, France owed Britain something like the equivalent of $3,000 million.[3] France became dependent on Britain in the spheres of finance and economics. At the same time, both became dependent on the United States. Here was an element which was to transform relations between France and Britain in the years to come.

WAR AIMS

The French and British achieved remarkable feats of co-operation to fight the war and to survive its economic problems. But throughout the war they faced also a quite different set of problems, which might well have disrupted their alliance. What were they fighting the war for? What were their war aims? How could the alliance cope with the politics of war? To look at these questions, it is necessary to go back to 1914.

The French and British never operated alone. They were allied to Russia from 1914 to 1917, and to Italy from 1915 onwards. In April 1917 the United States entered the war. There was a host of smaller allies. None the less, France and Britain represented the core of the alliance against Germany. They were in closer contact with one another than either was with Russia; they were stronger than Italy;

3. A. Sauvy, *Histoire économique de la France, 1919–1939*, vol. I (Paris, 1965), p. 169.

they were old and experienced European powers, whereas the USA was young and Utopian. They were the only great powers to sustain the war against Germany from start to finish.

Franco-British relations were therefore of particular importance. At the beginning of the war, no-one knew how they would develop. Only the issue of Belgium had truly united the British government, Parliament and people at the beginning of August 1914, and that might have been translated into a very narrow war aim indeed: simply the restoration of Belgian independence and integrity. In practice, events worked out differently. Once in the war, the British government quickly saw it as a means of crushing the German Navy, annexing German colonies, and eliminating the German economic menace – which were very wide aims indeed. Perhaps strangely, yet also quite naturally, the British also maintained a strong element of idealism in their approach to the war, genuinely seeking a new international order at its conclusion. The French for their part concentrated from the first on the recovery of Alsace and Lorraine, and then on a European settlement which would give them security. To achieve this they thought mainly in terms of power, but they too could use the language of idealism.

From these rather different elements, the two countries rapidly constructed a fundamental unity of purpose which sustained them throughout the war and proved strong enough to absorb the various disputes which inevitably arose. This unity of purpose was first affirmed in the agreement signed on 5 September 1914 between Britain, France and Russia not to conclude a separate peace. The three powers also agreed that, when the time came to discuss peace terms, none of them would individually propose terms without the previous consent of the other two. The initiative for this agreement came from the Russian government, but its conclusion was of great significance in Anglo-French relations. It was their first commitment to one another, and the first formalisation of their alliance.

The three-power agreement left open the question of what sort of peace terms would be acceptable. The British and French governments considered this matter very quickly, in response to enquiries about mediation from two widely different sources: the United States and Luxembourg. Early in September 1914 President Wilson raised the possibility of American mediation. The French reply was that they could not end the war without securing legitimate reparations from Germany for the invasion of their territory. The British laid down the more far-reaching condition that a peace settlement must include guarantees of its permanence, so that there could be no repetition of such an event as the violation of Belgian neutrality. When the Prime Minister of Luxembourg offered to mediate, Delcassé (now back in his old post as French Foreign Minister) wrote on 6 November that the Allies would continue the war until Germany was reduced to impotence.[4] This was indeed a formidable objective, considering the scale of German power and the position of the German armies at the beginning of November.

But, however startling it may appear, it was true. The British and French governments set themselves far-reaching aims, which could only be achieved by the destruction of German power. On 9 November 1914 the British Prime Minister, Asquith, speaking at the Guildhall, summed up the British position thus:

> We shall never sheathe the sword which we have not lightly drawn until Belgium recovers in full measure all and more than she has sacrificed, until France is adequately secured against the menace of aggression, until the rights of the smaller nationalities of Europe are placed upon an unassailable foundation, and until the military domination of Prussia is wholly and finally destroyed.[5]

To this programme could be added two points which Asquith did not make in his speech, though they would have commanded wide support: the destruction of the German fleet, and the dissolution of the German Empire. Shortly afterwards, on 22 December, the French Premier, Viviani, set out French objectives to the Chamber of Deputies. The first was the recovery of Alsace and Lorraine – which Asquith had not mentioned. Belgium was to be restored in its independence and prosperity. France was to secure indemnities to restore the areas devastated by German invasion. The Allies must crush Prussian militarism.

These were not mere words. They were real objectives, arising out of what had become a common Franco-British view of the German menace. For France, Germany had been the enemy since 1871. For Britain, she had emerged as such since the turn of the century, mainly as a result of naval rivalry – though it is striking to see Asquith shifting the emphasis to Prussian 'military domination' in general, which gave common ground with France. The stated war aims of the Allies – the restoration of Belgium, reparations, security against aggression, crushing Prussian militarism – could certainly not be achieved short of total

4. Georges-Henri Soutou, *L'or et le sang. Les buts de guerre économiques de la Première Guerre mondiale* (Paris, 1989), p. 113.
5. *Speeches by the Earl of Oxford and Asquith*, selected by Basil Herbert (London, 1927), p. 224.

victory. They would mean beating the German Army, and trying to break the traditions and way of life which gave that Army its strength. The two governments were united in these far-reaching aims, and among their peoples, in so far as popular sentiment can be discerned, there was a similar resolution. The French were conscious that their country had been invaded and that the Germans must be driven out. The British were not affected in the same way – there were no German soldiers in Kent; but they still had a powerful impression that the Germans were a menace, and would have to be stopped.

There was here a striking unity of sentiment and purpose which in the event saw the two countries through the long and terrible war. There were of course points of difficulty which imperilled that unity. The worst of these was Alsace and Lorraine, which was the signal point of difference between Asquith's and Viviani's speeches on war aims. As far as the French were concerned, there was almost complete agreement that the return of the provinces was vital. (A few socialists argued that the population should be consulted by a plebiscite, but that was an eccentric view.) This was primarily a matter of emotion, though it had its strategic and economic aspects – the Rhine frontier and the iron ore of Lorraine. The French government wanted British support for this fundamental demand, from the government and from public opinion. In 1915 a prominent French socialist, Marcel Sembat, went to London to explain to the British Labour Party that the claim to Alsace and Lorraine was not an annexation but a restitution, like the return of a stolen watch. But British ministers refused to commit themselves publicly. They said nothing at all in public on the subject until 1917. Then in October 1917 Lloyd George declared that Britain would stand by France 'until she redeems her oppressed children from the degradation of a foreign yoke', which was singularly vague. In a speech on 5 January 1918, designed as a general statement of British war aims, Lloyd George referred to the 'reconsideration of the great wrong' done to France in 1871. Neither of these speeches referred specifically to Alsace and Lorraine, and it is clear that the Prime Minister did not want to commit Britain to fighting on until Germany agreed to give up the provinces.[6]

This was a dangerous point of difference. The return of Alsace and Lorraine was the principal French war aim, and yet it was one on which the British studiously avoided public commitment. If Germany

---

6. Speech of 11 October 1917, David Stevenson, *The First World War and International Politics* (Oxford, paperback edn, 1991), p. 168; that of 5 January 1918, M.L. Dockrill and J.D. Gould, *Peace without Promise. Britain and the Peace Conferences, 1919–23* (London, 1981), p. 19.

had chosen to play the diplomatic card of offering to withdraw from Belgium and north-east France, while keeping Alsace and Lorraine, they could have put the British government in a grave dilemma and the Anglo-French alliance under severe strain. Would British public opinion have been prepared to continue the war in such circumstances? Perhaps not. But the Germans did not think in such terms. They wanted to retain both Belgium and Alsace-Lorraine, and parts of France as well; and so the question was never put.

Economic war aims formed another area of potential conflict between France and Britain. In 1915 and early 1916 the French developed economic aims which went beyond the simple demand for reparations. As Clemenceau pointed out in 1915, the German danger was in many ways greater in times of peace than in war. Before 1914, the Germans had outstripped the British in commerce and industry, were economically far stronger than the French, and even succeeded in exporting to the United States across the tariff barrier. With another half-century on such lines, the world would have been theirs through economic domination. Clemenceau argued that the Kaiser and the German generals had actually *saved* Europe by going to war, and so calling into being the coalition which would defeat them.[7] How could France prevent the recurrence of this danger after the war? The answer lay in continued Allied economic co-operation, and in a post-war policy of active discrimination against Germany. Tariffs should prevent the 'dumping' of German exports. Germany should be refused 'most favoured nation' status in commercial affairs. By the beginning of 1916 these ideas formed the basis of French economic war aims.

They seemed likely to meet British opposition, from two widely different quarters. The Liberal Party was still in principle the upholder of the long-standing orthodoxy of Free Trade – the McKenna tariff introduced in October 1915 breached that principle, but could be regarded simply as a wartime measure. On the other hand, the advocates of protection, mainly in the Conservative Party, favoured a system of tariffs based on Imperial preference, turning the British Empire into a trading bloc. In such circumstances, British tariffs would discriminate against France as well as against other countries.

It was a tribute to the power of anti-German sentiment in Britain, and to the reaction against German economic competition before the war, that for a period in 1916 these objections were largely overcome. At a secret meeting between Runciman, the President of the Board of Trade, and Clémentel, the French Minister of Commerce, in February

7. Clemenceau's preface to F. Bernhardi, *Notre Avenir* (Paris 1915), quoted in Soutou, *L'or et le sang*, p. 150.

1916, the two ministers agreed that, both during and after the war, their countries would seek to restrict German access to raw materials, and to develop their own resources and purchasing policy so as to avoid dependence upon Germany. They thought it prudent not to raise the question of tariffs directly, because of its likely divisive effects in Britain. Then, at a full-dress Allied Economic Conference in Paris, 14–17 June 1916, the Allied Powers, led by France and Britain, agreed on a series of measures to be taken against Germany, both during the war and after the peace. These were to include the withholding of 'most favoured nation' status from enemy countries for a period to be agreed upon, and protection against dumping and other forms of unfair competition by means of special rules and quotas. It is true that the Economic Conference tended to avoid thorny questions by agreeing on principles, while postponing the means of applying them. Moreover, the entry into the war of the United States, with its strong objection to any economic blocs other than its own, eventually nullified much of the effect of the Conference. Even so, the Economic Conference of 1916 marked a large degree of Anglo-French agreement on a subject which seemed likely to generate friction, and some of its resolutions were to find their way into the Treaty of Versailles in 1919 – for example, the Treaty deprived Germany of 'most favoured nation' status for five years.

The fate of the Ottoman Empire in the Middle East also raised problems between Britain and France. The Ottoman Empire entered the war on the side of Germany in November 1914. During the conflict, the Allies produced an extraordinary series of plans for the partition of the Empire after its defeat – a classic case of wanting to cut up the skin of the bear before ensuring that the animal was dead. In 1915 the British raised an Arab rebellion against the Turks by promising Sherif Hussein of Mecca recognition for a large Arab state in the Middle East, though only subject to British and French claims to spheres of influence in Mesopotamia (modern Iraq) and Syria respectively. This arrangement was set out in an exchange of letters between the British High Commissioner in Egypt, McMahon, and Hussein. Then in 1916 the British and French, in the Sykes–Picot agreement (named after the two countries' respective negotiators), simply decided to partition a large area of the Middle East between themselves. The French were to control Syria and the Lebanon; the British would secure Mesopotamia, though excluding the northern zone of Mosul, which was to be under French influence. Arab states in the area were to fall under either French or British influence. This agreement reconciled French and British ambitions in the area, but at the expense of earlier British undertakings to Sherif Hussein. In April 1917 the Treaty of St Jean de Maurienne allowed Italy into the plans of partition, with a sphere of influence in southern Anatolia. Then in November 1917 the British added a further complication with the Balfour Declaration, offering to the Zionists the hope of a national home for the Jewish people in Palestine. From the British point of view, this device was at least in part anti-French, with the intention of counter-balancing French influence in Syria.

This bewildering series of devices, which were sometimes in contradiction with one another, comprised certain consistent elements. The British sought to control a large part of Mesopotamia, with its sources of oil; and to this they sought to add influence in Palestine. The French, for long-standing historical reasons, claimed a zone of influence or control in Syria and the Lebanon. In 1915 and 1916 they each acknowledged the other's sphere and came to agreements about them; but in 1917 and 1918 they came to regard one another as rivals. By the end of 1918, the British government concluded that, since British and Imperial forces had done practically all the fighting against the Turks, with only token contributions from the French, they had every right to change the earlier agreements in their own favour. They put forward a claim to Mosul, which the Sykes–Picot agreement had allotted to the French; and they supported the aspirations of Feisal, the son of Sherif Hussein, to become King of Syria. These issues threatened to produce serious disputes between Britain and France, and indeed were to do so at the peace conference and for long afterwards. While the war with Germany continued, however, they were largely suppressed and not allowed to disrupt the broad Franco-British agreement on war aims.

PEACE MOVES, 1917

The greatest dangers arising from questions of war aims and peace terms appeared during 1917, when moves for a compromise peace proliferated. The French and British had agreed to fight the war to a finish, until Germany accepted defeat. In 1917 a German defeat seemed far distant, and it seemed that there might have to be a compromise peace. The end of 1916 and 1917 produced a flurry of peace moves. In December 1916 President Wilson invited the belligerents to state their objectives, in the hope that a basis for compromise would emerge – a 'peace without victory'. In spring 1917 the new Emperor Charles of Austria–Hungary began an elaborate attempt to get his country out of the war before the war broke up his country. The remains of the Second Socialist International, along with the Petrograd Soviet, tried to summon a socialist peace congress at Stockholm. In August the Pope issued an appeal for peace. In November Lenin, after seizing power in Russia, appealed to the peoples of the belligerent states to impose on their rulers a peace without annexations or indemnities. Even in Germany the Reichstag passed what was euphemistically called a 'peace resolution'. It was a year of war weariness, of revolutions, and of doubt, when Europe looked with dismay at what it was doing to itself.

In this crisis France was deeply involved. The army mutinies were the gravest sign, revealing the deep weariness and agony of the French soldier, normally remarkable for his steadfastness. Among the politicians, autumn 1917 saw the final collapse of the *union sacrée* formed at the outbreak of war. The Socialist Party left the ranks of government. A strong current of opinion, headed by Caillaux, a former Premier and a leading figure among the Radicals, favoured a compromise peace. At first sight, Britain seemed less affected. Lloyd George became Prime Minister in December 1916 as the advocate of the knock-out blow. He was pledged to the efficient conduct of the war, and brought about a far-reaching transformation of the British system of government to achieve that end. Yet in November 1916 Lord Lansdowne, the former Foreign Secretary and architect of the *entente*, had put to the Cabinet a suggestion that the time had come to seek the best terms available from Germany. A year later, no longer in government office, he put the substance of his case in a letter published in the *Daily Telegraph* (*The Times* had refused to print it). In May 1917 the Labour Party Conference voted to send a delegation to the socialist peace congress at Stockholm. The German submarine offensive, however tight the censorship on its detailed effects, was manifestly successful. Queues outside bread shops testified to that. It was plain that the war was not being won, and it might even be lost. Lloyd George might talk of the knock-out blow, but he had no idea of how to deliver it, and he began to doubt its possibility. Britain too felt the profound crisis of 1917.

Any serious attempt at a compromise peace in 1917 might well have broken the unity between France and Britain. What might be the terms of a compromise? The British had not yet committed themselves in public on the return of Alsace and Lorraine to France. The French were less adamant than the British about Belgium. But in fact there was no serious chance of peace at all. In France, even Caillaux, the most significant advocate of negotiation, insisted on the return of Alsace-Lorraine, and there is no sign that the German government ever contemplated such a move. What the Germans were set on doing was to keep Alsace and Lorraine, and to retain control of Belgium as well. Neither Clemenceau nor Lloyd George prevented the negotiation of a compromise peace in 1917, because no compromise was on offer. Clemenceau told the Senate Foreign Affairs Commission on 19 April 1918: 'Although many people have had the illusion of a half-peace over the last three or four years, events have shown very clearly that we are not going to have a half-peace: we must either conquer or be conquered.'[8] It was bleak doctrine, but it was true. For Franco-British relations it was, at any rate in the short run, the doctrine of salvation. Negotiations for a compromise peace would almost certainly have divided them. They could remain united, as they had been since 1914, on war to a finish.

This did not mean that the two countries were agreed on everything. When Lloyd George made his speech on war aims on 5 January 1918, he put great emphasis on stripping Turkey of all territory outside its basic Turkish heartland, about which the French were not greatly concerned, and yet he still referred only to the 'reconsideration' of Alsace and Lorraine, about which the French cared very much indeed. He also showed plainly that he was prepared to abandon eastern Europe to its fate – if the Russians did not want to fight to save themselves, that was their own affair. This was not Clemenceau's view: he knew very well that French security was bound up with the fate of eastern Europe. There were other points of dispute, for example over the partition of former Turkish territories in the Middle East, to which we shall have to return. There was an emerging conflict of interest in French and British relations with the United States. Both France and Britain wanted the Americans to regard them as their favoured associate: the French invoked the name of Lafayette, while the British appealed to a common language and heritage. It took some time for them both to grasp that the Americans intended to run their own war, and were very likely to impose their own peace.

Such differences were unavoidable. There is no such thing as complete identity of view and interest between two countries, even when they are close allies. But during the war the differences were much less important than the basic unity of purpose between France and Britain. In 1914 they had determined to fight until they had

8. David R. Watson, *Georges Clemenceau. A Political Biography* (London, 1974), p. 292.

beaten Germany, secured firm guarantees against the repetition of German aggression, and crushed Prussian militarism, whatever that might mean. In the pursuit of the war, they developed organs for the conduct of policy, strategy and economic affairs which were inconceivable before 1914. By the end of 1918 they had, to a great extent, achieved their aims. The German Army was beaten in the field. The German government asked for terms. The Kaiser abdicated and the old Imperial system collapsed. The question of whether this achievement was worth the price which had been paid for it was another matter. France and Britain fought the war with a remarkable display of unity, not matched before or since. But in the deeper impact of the war lay the causes of division.

CHAPTER 6
The Shock of War

The war of 1914–18 rapidly became known, by common consent and on both sides of the Channel, as the Great War. It was a catastrophe without precedent, all the more terrible for coming after a century of comparative peace in Europe. It struck both France and Britain like a bolt from the blue, though in different ways and for different reasons. In one sense, the French had been expecting a war with Germany ever since 1871, and many had looked forward to it as the opportunity to revenge the defeat of the Franco-Prussian war. The prospect of war had constantly been in French minds. Yet the war when it came was utterly different from all expectation. No-one was prepared for the system of mechanised devastation and desolation which was established on the western front. The British, for their part, had not seriously expected war at all, despite some voices raised in fictional prophecy. They were utterly unprepared for the event itself as well as for the form it took. As the war pursued its frightful course, both countries came under the harrow, and their reactions to the ordeal marked the relations between them as well as their own separate national lives.

Of the two countries, France suffered much the more severely. The country was invaded, nine departments were occupied, and a great scar of destruction was cut across the whole of north-eastern France. French military deaths totalled approximately 1,327,000. This amounted to 34 in every thousand of the pre-war population, and 168 per thousand of those mobilised. The comparative figures for the then United Kingdom were 723,000 dead, amounting to 16 per thousand of the pre-war population and 63 per thousand of those mobilised. The British war dead thus amounted to rather more than half the French in total numbers, rather under half per thousand of population, and only one-third per thousand of those mobilised.[1] The long-term effects of the war on the French population were heightened by the very sharp fall in the number of births during the war, amounting to an estimated deficit against 'normal' totals of about 1,770,000. This compared with an estimated wartime deficit of births in Britain of about 670,000.[2] The consequences were all the more severe in France because they fell upon a population which was already static and ageing, while Britain was still showing a natural increase.

In statistical terms, the British experience was therefore markedly less harsh than the French. This fact was probably never fully appreciated by the British, whose minds were concentrated on their own sufferings. The Great War was the first occasion when Britain put into the field an army on a continental scale. The total strength of the British Army (including Territorials and Reserves) in August 1914 was approximately 733,000. The total serving in the Army, 1914–18, was 5,704,000. The maximum British strength on the western front at any one time was just over 2,000,000; with Dominion forces, this reached 2.7 million. It was a prodigious effort.[3] The British Army, though recruited from the whole nation (by voluntary enlistment in 1914–15, and by conscription from 1916 to the end of the war), was not a complete cross-section of British society. During the period of voluntary enlistment (August 1914–January 1916) about 2,400,000 men joined the army. Among these there was a marked social bias. The higher up the social scale a man was, the greater were the chances that he would volunteer, and – of crucial importance – that he would be fit for combatant duty. This reflected the social and medical conditions among the poorer sections of the population. Therefore, while in terms of numbers the army was predominantly working-class, reflecting the structure of the population, there was still a disproportionately high intake from the professions, finance, commerce and even from the world of entertainment. Among the working class there was a very high proportion of volunteers among coalminers: by mid-1915, 230,000 miners (about a quarter of the mining workforce) had enlisted. So, even among manual workers, it was an elite that suffered disproportionately.

1.   Table in Jay Winter, *The Great War and the British People* (London, 1986), p. 75. This splendid book underlies much that follows.
2.   French figure, Colin Dyer, *Population and Society in Twentieth Century France* (London, 1978), p. 56; British figure (excluding Ireland), Winter, p. 253.
3.   Brian Bond, *British Military Policy between the Two World Wars* (Oxford, 1980), p. 3; I.F.W. Beckett and Keith Simpson, eds, *A Nation in Arms. A social study of the British Army in the First World War* (Manchester, 1985), p. 8.

The result was what Jay Winter has called 'a slaughter of social elites'. Officers (especially junior officers in the infantry) suffered a higher death rate than other ranks. During the first year of the war, 14 per cent of the officer corps as against 6 per cent of other ranks were killed. This disproportion continued, though at a lower level, throughout the war. (The same was true for the French Army, where during the whole war 29 per cent of infantry officers were killed compared to 23 per cent of infantrymen.) British officers were largely recruited from the public and grammar schools and from the universities. This was the factual basis for the belief that grew up so rapidly when the war was over that there was a 'lost generation' of talent, courage and devotion. There was a strong sense among those who survived that the best had gone.[4]

The British people therefore believed, with good reason and with painful memories, that they had contributed heavily to the war in men and in blood. This was only partially and patchily recognised by the French, who had their own sacrifices to bear. Neither nation fully comprehended the sufferings of the other.

THE BRITISH IN FRANCE: TOO FEW OR TOO MANY?

In August 1914 many French eyes were on Britain. At first no-one knew what the English were going to do. In Calais on 1 August there was anxious speculation: if the port was protected by the British fleet, they would be safe; but if not they would be open to German bombardment. Far to the west, at Paimpol in Brittany, people were afraid of invasion unless they were defended by British warships. When the British declaration of war was announced, prefects' reports from all parts of France recorded relief, satisfaction and even enthusiasm. At Angoulême a primary school teacher wrote that 'Everyone is breathing a sigh of relief. . . . Everyone believes that with the help of the British fleet fortune could smile on us this time.' When British troops began to pass through the station at Arras later in August, the prefect reported that they were greeted all day by enthusiastic crowds.[5]

An important key to these early reactions is to be found in the words 'this time'. People felt the contrast with 1870, when France had

4. Figures from Winter, pp. 25–37, 83–99; the phrase quoted is on p. 92.
5. Jean-Jacques Becker, *1914. Comment les Français sont entrés dans la guerre* (Paris, 1977), pp. 516–17; Albert Chatelle et G. Tison, *Calais pendant la guerre* (Paris, 1927), p. 6.

faced Prussia alone. This time she was not alone, and it is interesting that the sense of being supported arose less from the alliance with Russia (presumably because the Russians were so far away) than from the presence of the British. There were not many British troops but they were welcome; though there were some odd ideas about them. Jacques Bainville noted reports that the British officers were encumbered with tea-tables and ice for their whisky. A writer in *La Revue* was puzzled and yet impressed by British troops singing 'Tipperary'.

> This appears puerile, with a sentimentality bearing no relation to the grave events we are facing. It has nothing to do with outpourings of bravado, with curses called down on the enemy . . . it is in strange contrast to the *Marseillaise* of the French, but Tommy Atkins has given life to what was at first sight something purely commonplace and has given it the stamp of imperishable greatness.[6]

This last phrase proved absolutely true, and 'Tipperary' still bears the stamp of greatness which belongs not to the song but to the singers. It was a remarkable tribute to the British by a certain French mentality.

This early sense of welcome and relief at the British presence was something quite new in France. Two liaison officers with the armies in the north-east in August 1914 (Spears and Huguet) were both struck by the fact that when the challenges rang out – 'Who goes there?' or 'Qui vive?' – it was the first time in that much-fought-over territory that they could receive a friendly answer. But such acute awareness of a new comradeship could not last. At the end of August the French were suddenly confronted by their own danger. The military communiqué to the press on 29 August was a shock: 'Situation unchanged, from the Somme to the Vosges.' The *Somme*? How could the Germans have reached the Somme? In the Var, the prefect thought this must be an error in transcription: he struck out Somme, and put in Sambre. But it was indeed the Somme, which remained a battlefield for the next four years. France was in terrible danger, and the French had to get themselves out of it. They were still glad the British were there, but wished there were more of them.

6. Charles Simond, 'Chants nationaux et chansons de guerre des Anglais', *La Revue*, vol. 111 (15 March–1 April 1915), pp. 77–82. The author provided a translation:

Il y a loin à marcher jusqu'à Tipperary. Il y a beaucoup de chemin à faire.
Il y a loin à marcher jusqu'à Tipperary, jusqu'à la douce amie que je connais.
Au revoir Piccadilly. Adieu Leicester Square.
Il y a loin à marcher jusqu'à Tipperary, mais mon coeur est là tout entier.

From that time onwards, despite the increasing co-operation between governments and military commanders, the French and British armies fought separate wars. Spears records that in August 1914 the soldiers of the French Fifth Army were given postcards illustrating British uniforms, so that they should know who their allies were. Afterwards, in 1915 and 1916, it was not unusual for French troops not to know that there were British forces fighting only a mile away. The demarcation line was strict, and even at the point of junction the units involved rarely mixed, separated as they were by language, customs and the inward-looking nature of men at war.

This picture is confirmed by the records of ordinary French soldiers. The trench newspapers presented a picture of men living from day to day, enclosed in their own units and their own surroundings. There was some communication with the enemy trenches, and much respect for the German soldier, but very little reference to allied troops – and what there was indicated the unpopularity, first of the British and (much later) of the Americans. The French soldiers were so convinced that the weight of the war rested on their own shoulders that they resented the attention paid by the press, and sometimes by the civilians, to the Allied armies.[7] A few examples from the letters and diaries of the men in the trenches illustrate the same point. One notebook kept by *un poilu moyen* makes a reference to the French artillery firing a salute for a Russian victory in April 1916, but mentions no other outside events at all. A soldier who served in Lorraine, then near Nancy, then at Verdun, where he was killed, came nowhere near the British and never mentions them in his letters. Another set of letters exchanged by a Savoyard family testifies to official recognition of France's allies, in the form of field postcards bearing the flags of Britain, Russia, Belgium and Italy; but that was all. Even the historian Marc Bloch, who served in 1914 at the Belgian frontier and later at the Marne, and was presumably sensitive to the wider bearings of the war, made no mention of the British in his *Souvenirs de guerre*, written while the war was going on.

There is a rare exception to this pattern in a man who was himself exceptional – a Jewish lawyer and infantryman, who kept a journal in the form of letters to his fiancée. He was sent to Ypres in November 1914, and met British troops, with whom the French were at that time much mixed up. He noticed the dull British uniforms among the colourful garb of the French cavalry, and saw 'an elegant lady of the English Red Cross', wearing boots and khaki uniform, looking for

---

7. Stéphane Audouin-Rouzeau, *14–18: Les combattants des tranchées* (Paris, 1986).

somewhere to set up her ambulance station. He welcomed this apparition, as offering hope that the British might be taking over his section of line. Other remarks were less friendly to the British. He heard that German warships had bombarded British coastal towns (December 1914). 'Bravo! That will make Messieurs les Alliés think.' Perhaps they would now get round to sending over the million men they had promised for so long, but who had never arrived. By spring 1915 he was meeting a lot of English – 'fine lads, freshly shaved, dressed in new uniforms'. He encountered them again on the Somme in July 1916, when some Tommies visited his unit talking of a mysterious weapon which would amaze the world – presumably the tanks.[8]

But this is the exception which proves the rule, which was that in the normal course of events the vast majority of French soldiers fought their own war, within the closed circle of their own units. At the end those who survived knew without a shadow of a doubt that they had borne the heat and burden of the day and won the victory. After the war, the voluminous war literature said almost nothing about the British Tommy. The same was true in reverse for the British troops. Recent books drawing on the letters, diaries and memories of 'ordinary' soldiers contain almost no mention of the French Army. Denis Winter's *Death's Men*, for example, making careful use of the massive material in the archives of the Imperial War Museum, makes no reference to French soldiers; though the author devotes a chapter to attitudes to the Germans, and a few pages to French civilians.[9]

As the war went on, indeed, there were civilians in France who saw rather too many British soldiers. Any army stationed in a foreign country, however necessary its presence and friendly its intentions, is bound to create friction with the local population. There were vast numbers of British and Dominion troops in north-east France for some three years of the war. In the normal routine of trench warfare, about half of each division in the line would be resting or in reserve, and from time to time whole divisions would be moved to the rear to recuperate. There were rarely enough army huts to go round, so most men had to be billeted on the local population. Careful and elaborate

---

8.   André Kahn, *Journal de guerre d'un juif patriote, 1914–18*, (Paris, 1978; preface by Jean-François Kahn, the writer's grandson). The writer survived the war, and married the girl to whom he wrote the letters in this book.

9.   Denis Winter, *Death's Men: Soldiers of the Great War* (London, 1978); cf. Malcolm Brown, *Tommy Goes to War* (London, 1978). Peter Simkins reviews a host of publications in 'Everyman at War: recent interpretations of front-line experience', in B.J. Bond, ed., *The First World War and British Military History* (London, 1991), without once mentioning the French Army.

arrangements were made by the two governments for payment and compensation for damage, but it goes without saying that they were not universally observed. In 1916 there was an increasing stream of protests to the French Ministry of War from the deputies and senators of what were sometimes called the British-occupied departments. The deputies themselves were careful to say that their constituents were basically sympathetic to the British forces, but there were still real causes of grievance and resentment. This is borne out by British accounts, which reveal a whole variety of relations, good and bad. Some British troops found French houses and farms intolerably squalid. Some stole or got drunk. Some quarrelled with the family, others got on only too well, notably with the women. Some were simply and generously grateful for being given a meal, or full of admiration for French civilians carrying on their lives in the war zone. The Tommies cared little about the French language, and the sort of French phrases which appeared in the trench newspapers, and at one time found their way into the language ('napoo' is a harmless example meaning 'no more') indicate the basic level of communication with the civilian population.

Thus some Frenchmen thought there were not enough British troops in France, but others were conscious that there were altogether too many on their own doorstep. A particular case in point was that of Calais. At the beginning of 1915 the BEF needed a new base nearer to the front than Le Havre, and Calais was the obvious choice. By agreement with the French government, the British requisitioned buildings, set up tented camps, built barracks for the troops and vast warehouses for their supplies. The *Place d'Armes* displayed directional signs in English, and the traffic was directed by British military police in uniform. There was a big Church Army club, and a camp for First Aid Nursing Yeomanry, with a balcony where the nurses could sit in basket chairs. In August 1917 there were over 56,000 British officers and men in Calais, plus another 1,725 in military hospitals; and at different times there were some 2,000 nurses, FANYs and members of the Women's Auxiliary Army Corps. (There were also, at various periods, about 50,000 Belgians, plus Portuguese in 1917 and Americans in 1918.)[10]

The original population of the town was swamped by this foreign presence, and a very natural resentment and anxiety arose. As early as August 1914, Spears noted that it was a joke in the French officers' mess to which he was attached that if the English got into Calais they would never leave it. (Those with a historical turn of mind amended

10. Chatelle et Tison, *Calais*, pp. 40–3.

this by saying 'got back into Calais'.) German propaganda quickly tried to exploit such feelings. In December 1914, even before the British base was established, the German press published a report that a British *maire-coadjuteur* had been appointed in Calais, and had attended a meeting of the *Conseil Municipal.* Later, in 1916 and 1917, the Germans often returned to this theme, and invented the story that the French government had leased Calais to England for 99 years. The French military governor of the town was keenly aware of the problem. He told his superiors in 1917 that the local population hardly ever saw a French uniform, and that there was a strong impression that the town and its hinterland had become a foreign country. He recommended that some troops should be sent to show the flag, and in August 1917 two battalions of *chasseurs* marched through the town, held a review, and gave military band concerts in the public gardens. The governor reported great relief among the population, and suggested that two or three regiments should always be posted near Calais during their rest periods.

After the armistice, the rumours that the British intended to stay in Calais took on a new life, because for a long time that was what happened. Calais became the main base for demobilisation and the removal of equipment from France. The British actually occupied new areas, put up new buildings, and took an indefinite lease on a piece of communal land for a concert-hall. In 1919 there were 50 marriages between British soldiers and local girls (there had only been 51 in all the war years).[11] It really seemed as though the British were settling down. For the historically minded, there was an ominous sign in that the British commander was a descendant of one of Edward III's barons, and was entitled to bear the insignia 'Caen–Crécy–Calais' on his coat of arms. The last troops did not leave the town until the end of 1920, more than two years after the armistice.

Calais was a particularly prominent example of a common phenom-enon in north-eastern France, where a number of towns assumed a very British appearance. The British Army, unlike the French, brought with it a train of voluntary organisations for the welfare of the troops, and the whole strange assembly made itself at home. Sometimes this impinged upon protocol at the highest level. In December 1914 King George V disturbed President Poincaré, a punctilious man, by inviting him to dinner at Field Marshal French's headquarters at St Omer. Poincaré thought that the King, in the midst of his own troops, was behaving as though he was at home; whereas he was of course in

11. Figures for marriages, ibid., p. 246.

France, and it was for the President of the Republic to issue the invitation. It was a tiny matter, but it was symptomatic. The British were setting up house in north-eastern France.

The impression left by this British presence was more fleeting than seemed likely at the time. In 1928 Spears went back to Montreuil (where Haig had established his headquarters from 1916 to 1918) and found that the woman at his habitual pastry-cook's, who had only been a child during the war, could scarcely remember the British being there at all. The British soldiers had kept to themselves, 'uninquisitive and detached, insular even when overseas, preserving their own habits and secure in their own routines'.[12] Yet there was more to Montreuil than the lady at the pastry-cook's. In 1931 a monument was put up in front of Haig's former headquarters, and when during the Second World War the Germans removed the statue (apparently not out of vindictiveness, but simply to melt it down for metal) a group of citizens gathered at the plinth on Armistice Day – a significant gesture of Franco-British solidarity against the Germans. In 1950 the statue was replaced, in the presence of the British Ambassador.

The British presence in north-eastern France left good memories as well as bad. At Arras, well after the Second World War, there was still a perceptible liking for the British and respect for the British Army – which was still very much present in the solemn form of the massive British military cemetery. Moreover, the north-east was not only the area of British presence, too easily called an occupation; but of the real German occupation. Richard Cobb, in an evocative description, has written that the *Feldgendarmerie* was remembered with fear and hatred, and the ordinary German soldier with a lingering respect. In either case, 'people were glad to see them go, and even gladder to see the British arrive' at the end of 1918.[13] That sense of welcome lasted a long time.

LIAISON AND CROSS-PURPOSES: SPEARS AND HUGUET

The Great War made a tremendous impact on both countries, and its effects continued to be felt for generations to come through its

---

12. E.L. Spears, *Prelude to Victory* (London, 1939), pp. 76–7.
13. Richard Cobb, *French and Germans, Germans and French. A personal interpretation of France under two occupations, 1914–1918, 1940–1944* (Hanover, Australia and London, 1983), p. 32.

impression on the memories of the two peoples. Never was war remembered with such solemnity and agony. It was recalled in the memoirs of participants, and in a stream of war novels and poetry. It was commemorated in stone, by the war memorials erected in every town and village in Britain and France. Before those war memorials gathered, every 11 November, the members of the ex-servicemen's organisations, which themselves existed in part to preserve the memory of those killed in the war. This memory was shared by the French and British people, and formed a bond between them; yet with a sad inevitability it also divided them.

During the war, as we have seen, it was a natural tendency for each country to grumble that the other was not pulling its weight. Both governments complained that the press of the other country was one-sided in its reporting. French newspapers were only interested in the French Army, and British newspapers in the British. This was like complaining that the sea is wet – for newspapers to be interested in their own troops is simply a fact of nature, and since few people read the press of the other country it probably did little harm. It was more serious that this wartime grumbling continued and intensified when the war was over. Striking examples may be found in books written by two of the officers most closely concerned with liaison between the British and French armies, Spears and Huguet.

Spears was a young man at the start of the war. Born in Paris in 1886, he was barely 28 when he took up his post as liaison officer between the BEF and the French Fifth Army in August 1914. As a boy he had been brought up in France, and he had an excellent command of the language. He had the reputation of being an ardent Francophile. In 1930 he published *Liaison 1914*, with a highly complimentary foreword by Winston Churchill, praising Spears's achievement in maintaining confidence and contact between the two armies. In his own Preface, Spears emphasised his 'profound admiration . . . for the French nation' and respect for the French soldier.[14]

In the book there are indeed admiring passages. He portrays Joffre as a hero, a man of impenetrable calm, rare but formidable anger, immense self-confidence and great clarity of vision. He describes the galvanic shock administered by Franchet d'Esperey when he took command of the French Fifth Army, and conveys an indelible impression of his force of personality. He pays tribute to the courage

14. Edward Spears, *Liaison 1914. A Narrative of the Great Retreat* (London 1930, 2nd edn, 1968), p. xxxi.

and adaptability of the ordinary French soldier. Of the battle of the Marne he writes: 'It seems to me that the real miracle was the feat of the French private soldier. . . . No people but the French – the most adaptable and intelligent race in the world – having started so badly could in so short a time have learnt so much.'[15] He offers sharp vignettes of French life, deep-rooted in its customs and virtues, embodied in the postmistress at Châtillon-sur-Marne, who refused to leave her post as the Germans advanced. 'It was her duty to stay. So she went on quietly with her work. I felt for her an admiration and respect that is undimmed to this day.'[16]

But the general impression left by the book is different. In the preface, Spears recounts a visit to the French Senate, after the war. Senators were saying that British military participation in the war had been negligible until 1916, and that Sir John French had let General Lanrezac down during the campaign of August 1914. He knew these statements to be 'fantastically untrue', and decided to correct them. Throughout the book he insists that Lanrezac blamed the British for his own failures in August 1914. More important, the British contribution to the campaign was not negligible but vital: 'the verdict of history will be that but for the small British force, final and irremediable defeat would have overtaken France'.[17] The BEF first imposed a fatal delay on the German advance, and then played a decisive role in the miracle of the Marne. 'That the victory of the Marne would have been impossible without the BEF will be the inevitable conclusion of posterity.'[18] Spears certainly did his best to make sure that it would be.

In his general impressions of France and the French, Spears's method was to damn with faint praise. How sad it was that the British troops met 'the hard-bitten and often grasping peasants of Northern France', or 'old and shabby Territorials guarding bridges and railways', and did not see the French as Spears knew them. 'Even those who met good French troops found their mentality and methods of fighting entirely different, [and] were apt to conclude they were unreliable.' Spears knew they were not unreliable; but as with the grasping peasants, he left the negative impression to sink in. In a passage on the problems of liaison he writes:

> Sometimes the French would sense an assumption of superiority on the part of their Allies which they found intolerable. On the other hand, they

15. Ibid., p. 432.
16. Ibid., p. 339.
17. Ibid., p. 328.
18. Ibid., p. 329, and cf. pp. xxxii, 433.

had to concede that the British were always where they said they would be, and that if they undertook to do anything they honestly endeavoured to carry it out. To the British the French often seemed unreliable. To be there one minute and gone the next suited their mentality but bewildered the British.[19]

This superficially even-handed description leaves in practice a picture of the dependable, honest British and the unreliable French. Even Spears's praise of French courage was sometimes double-edged; at the battle of Guise 'the men, as always, were brave but ignorant, the officers uninstructed'.[20]

The book was brilliantly written, highly praised and much read. Spears followed it in 1939 with *Prelude to Victory*, dealing with the early months of 1917, again with an enthusiastic introduction by Winston Churchill. In this book, Spears's theme was not liaison in the field but the working of governments and high commands. His villain was Lloyd George, the political intriguer, and his heroes were Haig and Robertson, the honest soldiers. So the book was mostly about the British, but the state of France and the French Army runs as a sub-plot throughout the narrative. This time Spears was genuinely sympathetic but deeply gloomy. He gave a moving account of French sufferings during the first three years of war. Their recovery of morale early in 1917 was like a sail filled by a great but short-lived wind – 'something not unlike despair galvanised into action'. He ended the book with an extraordinarily vivid account of the Nivelle offensive, which opened with immense *élan* and ended in disaster. His description of the French wounded is unforgettable:

> They were discouraged as French wounded had never been discouraged before. 'It's all up', they said, 'we can't do it, we shall never do it'. '*C'est impossible*', and the words whispered from ashen lips swept over the rows of stretchers like a cold gust rustling dead leaves and dead hopes in a cemetery.[21]

It was a sombre picture of a nation and an army tried to breaking-point. Spears's title was *Prelude to Victory*; but not long after his book was published in 1939 his description began to read uncannily like the prelude to defeat – the defeat of 1940.

In 1928 General Huguet published a volume of memoirs entitled

19.   Ibid., pp. xxxi–ii, 331–2.
20.   Ibid., p. 270.
21.   Spears, *Prelude to Victory*, pp. 329, 507.

L'Intervention militaire britannique en 1914.[22] Huguet had been French Military Attaché in London from 1904 to early 1914, when he returned to his old regiment. He had been the principal French representative in the Anglo-French military conversations before the war. Immediately after the outbreak of war he was appointed as Joffre's liaison officer with Sir John French, at the headquarters of the BEF. Though the book was published in 1928, the preface is dated November 1922 and explains that the writing was completed in 1921–22, and publication postponed out of a sense of tact, until the major actors on the British side were dead. Huguet writes in the preface that it is useful to describe the real value of the British effort at the start of the war, but that his main purpose is to explain the English character, the essential nature of English policy, and the principles which must govern French policy towards England. There is thus a signal at the start that this is more than simply a volume of memoirs. Huguet was a man with a message.

On the events of 1914, Huguet presents broadly the opposite picture to that of Spears. In his view, it was the British who precipitated French retreats by their own hasty withdrawals. Sir John French, though personally brave, was at bottom irresolute, and needed to be solidly wedged in between French forces. He constantly refused to take the offensive, and put off taking over extra line when British reinforcements arrived, so that French territorial divisions had to hold dangerous sectors of the front which the British could have occupied. In short, Huguet – despite some favourable comments – was unenthusiastic about the British contribution to the battles of 1914.

Much of this was a matter of detail, where there could well be different interpretations. In any case, no-one could dispute that the numbers of British troops involved in the battles fell far below those of the French. The real essence of Huguet's message lay elsewhere. He did not believe that the British had ever truly acknowledged what was at stake *for them* in the war. Early in his book, he explained the arguments which he had used while he was Military Attaché in London to convince his British contacts that their fate was bound up with the continent of Europe. If Germany won a European war, he reasoned, Britain would face an empire of a hundred million people, and would eventually succumb to the same domination. To prevent this, neither a naval effort nor keeping forces at home would suffice. Britain must concentrate on the decisive theatre, which was the soil of France, where a war would be won or lost. But he sensed that this

22. General Huguet, *L'intervention militaire britannique en 1914* (Paris, 1928).

logic never got through, except to a few individuals. After the war, he felt that this situation was unchanged. He quoted Lord French, wondering in his memoirs what Napoleon would have thought to see a friendly invasion of British soldiers landing at Boulogne to save France. Huguet comments that this was the view of most British people, who still did not understand that they had been fighting in France for their own security. This led all too often to the belief that the British had sacrificed themselves for the sake of France, and the French were not sufficiently grateful.

This was only a part of Huguet's message. He was profoundly convinced of the persistent insularity of the 'English race', which he believed was distinct, not only from the French but from all continental peoples. 'When one crosses the Channel, one finds one's self suddenly and without any transition in contact with habits, customs and a cast of mind which are not only different in essence from ours, but are sometimes directly opposite.'[23]

In a whole section devoted to the post-war scene, Huguet brings his interpretation of the English character to bear in order to explain the fact, as he saw it, that when the war was over France faced a Britain determined to cheat her of the fruits of victory and emerging as her enemy, even to the extent of defending Germany. Why had this come about? Huguet's answer was that British policy was primarily governed by their national character, and above all their 'splendide et tranquille égoïsme'. What counted for them was strength, material goods, and the power of money; and behind money lay the Jews, whose influence was growing steadily in England. They were everywhere: the financial world was full of them, there was an increasing number in the House of Lords, they were to be found in all governments, and some had even become Prime Minister.[24] The Englishman might be honest and loyal in private life, but was bitter, pitiless and treacherous in public policy, which was dominated by the great industrialists and financiers. Summing up, Huguet pronounced England to be 'grim, implacable, somewhat unscrupulous, sometimes treacherous'. As for her people, they were an unlikeable race, whose humiliation 'would be generally welcomed in the world with a sigh of relief and release'.[25] The British were regarded with hatred abroad, faced unrest at home, and had been forced into the partition of their own territory in Ireland; so the time might be coming when the

23. Ibid., p. 21.
24. Ibid., pp. 240–2. There was Disraeli, of course, but one wonders who else Huguet had in mind.
25. Ibid., pp. 244–6.

whole edifice of British power would crumble. But meanwhile France would have to deal with England as she was, with her policy decided by egotism and material interest. The only answer was for France to be strong and on her guard, following her own policy and dealing firmly with the British.

The portrait is harsh, and in some respects – for example, the comments on the Jews – tells us more about Huguet himself than about the British or about more general French opinion. But some traits in it have a long pedigree. 'Perfide' is a description we have met before, and will meet again. The assertion that British policy was dominated by financial and economic interests made much sense in the period of the 1920s. Above all, Huguet was right to stress that the British had not really understood, or even wanted to understand, that their security was bound up with that of France, and therefore claimed that all they had been doing was *helping* France. This sentiment was very much alive between the two World Wars, and by no means dead after the Second – it is probably living still. Huguet's message was strident in tone, and the burden of it was not welcome across the Channel – there was, perhaps fortunately, no English translation. But it contained substantial elements of truth.

MEMORIES OF WAR: 'NEVER AGAIN'

There were other, and much more sympathetic, representations of the two peoples to one another produced by the Great War. In France, André Maurois's *Les silences du Colonel Bramble* enjoyed a remarkable popularity, which persisted well into the post-war years. Maurois was himself a liaison officer with the BEF, and his novel is a humorous introduction to the atmosphere and customs of a British officers' mess. His companions and friends are unobtrusively brave and immensely reliable. They are every bit as insular as Huguet accuses the British of being, but in a far more amiable fashion. They transplant as much of their domestic habits as possible to the alien soil of France and the grim surroundings of trench warfare. 'Amid the horrible wickedness of the species, the English have established an oasis of courtesy and phlegm', writes the narrator – who is told more than once that no Frenchman really understands how to make tea![26]

26. André Maurois, *Les silences du colonel Bramble* (Paris, 1918). Cf. the translation, *The Silence of Colonel Bramble* (London, 1919) – the quotation is on p. 33; for tea-making, see pp. 73, 75.

Colonel Bramble and his officers are gentle caricatures rather than portraits. The war is usually off-stage, though the young subalterns and the padre are all killed. Nonetheless, *Bramble* presented a picture which many British readers of that time were happy to accept – it was how at least some of them wanted to appear. It also relaunched in France the old stereotype of the English gentleman – even though Maurois was writing about a Scottish regiment. The book was translated into English, and enjoyed a high reputation and strong sales in both countries. Maurois himself went on to become a generally accepted interpreter of England and the English to the French – his biographies of Edward VII, Disraeli and Queen Victoria were very successful, and he produced a widely read one-volume *History of England.*

In Britain, John Buchan had a similar reputation to that of Maurois, as a popular novelist, biographer and historian. Unfit for active service, Buchan held a commission in the Army, on the Intelligence staff, and later worked in the propaganda service. In February 1917 he became head of the newly created Department of Information. From 1915 onwards, he wrote *Nelson's History of the War*, a multi-volume serial story of the conflict. It was vivid, well written, and reasonably priced, and it won a wide readership. Buchan's emphasis was naturally on the British role in the war, but his portrait of the French was notably sympathetic. In a long account of Verdun, he wrote that: 'The glib commentators who before the war praised French *élan* and denied French fortitude were utterly put to shame. It was the fortitude and stoicism of the French that were their most shining endowments.' He was full of praise for Pétain ('simple, modest, patient, gentle and brave'), and for Clemenceau ('his courage, his ardour, even his narrowness were the qualities most needed. . . .'). Buchan described the French as an armed nation working under self-imposed discipline, and it was to the French that he paid for him the greatest compliment of applying to them the words of Cromwell: 'the plain russet-coated captain who knows what he fights for and loves what he knows'.[27]

Maurois and Buchan were later condemned for failing to describe the conflict in its true horror. But they wrote from knowledge and sympathy for the other country, and the widespread popular appeal of these two authors did something to help the French and British think well of one another. This proved to be a passing phase. The literary memory of the war which later emerged, with such power as to swamp other versions and distort the truth, had quite a different impact.

27. John Buchan, *A History of the Great War* (4 vols, London, 1921–22), vol. II, pp. 576–7; vol. IV, p. 161; vol. I, p. 465 for the russet-coated captain.

The actual content of war literature was mixed. In France, Henri Barbusse's *Le Feu*, which appeared in weekly parts before being published as a book in 1916, was itself a mixture. It was both a realistic description of life in the trenches, and a protest against war – an anti-war novel while the war was still going on. It was awarded the Prix Goncourt, and sold some 230,000 copies in the two years after publication. It was accompanied by other, and quite different war novels. René Benjamin's *Gaspard*, published in 1915 and also awarded the Prix Goncourt, had as its hero one of the natural survivors of army life, and displayed some of the humour which helped men to endure in the trenches. Gabriel-Tristan Franconi's *Un-Tel de l'armée française*, published in 1918, depicted a prosaic acceptance of the routine of war which must have come somewhere near the reaction of most soldiers. Of these, it was *Le Feu* which had the greatest impact in both France and (through its translation) Britain.

In Britain, it was not so much the war novel as war poetry which took root in the national consciousness. The sifting of time has produced a remarkable effect. John Bourne has established that over 2,200 poets published verse during the war, and were in some sense 'war poets'.[28] Literary selection, and the intricate two-way traffic between the poems and the public, have left a handful of names – Owen, Sassoon, Blunden, Rosenberg. The words 'war poetry' have become synonymous with 'anti-war poetry', and war literature is represented by men who were unrepresentative of the millions who fought the war, and even of the hundreds who wrote verse about it.

Yet paradoxically even these very few novelists and poets were not untypical. They represented their fellow-soldiers because they shared their suffering and fought the war through. Wilfred Owen was killed in action. Barbusse the anti-militarist volunteered for the Army in 1914 even though he was 41 and had been exempted from further service. Roland Dorgelès, whose novel *Les croix de bois* was as successful as *Le Feu*, was another anti-militarist who volunteered although medically exempt, and won the Croix de Guerre. Such men could write with authority and command attention.

The principal result of the evocation of the war in literature, in both countries, was to give weight and focus to the revulsion against war itself which followed the terrible events of 1914–18. Previous wars had seemed worth the cost, or perhaps the cost had not been counted too carefully. But this time the price was too high. The effects were felt in the next generation, which differed profoundly from that which

28. J.M. Bourne, *Britain and the Great War, 1914–1918* (London, 1989), pp. 225–6.

fought the war. John Bourne rightly wrote of Britain that: 'The war lit a slow fuse under the values which had done most to sustain it. When the explosion came they suffered near mortal damage.'[29] This was equally true of France. The consequences were inevitably felt in the relations between the two countries. The alliance which had fought the war, and drawn new strength from its conduct, was bound to suffer from the revulsion against the war, and against war itself.

The memory of the war was also engraved in stone. Other wars have had their memorials, but none to match those of the Great War, in number, in significance, or in the solemnity with which they were inaugurated. The determination to commemorate those killed in the war was common to both France and Britain. War memorials from the Pyrenees to the north of Scotland have a similar character, despite differences in symbolism and insignia. The names carved on innumerable columns tell the same story. Sometimes the memorials themselves were shared by the two countries. There are British and Dominion memorials and war cemeteries, great and small, all along the old battle zone in north-eastern France, on the Somme and Vimy Ridge, in Arras and Bapaume. Here the British war dead and their monuments have become a part of the French landscape. Their meaning in the popular mind is now much diminished, but for many years after 1918 it was sharply etched.

At these monuments there gathered every year on Armistice Day the representatives of the ex-servicemen's organisations – the Royal British Legion in Britain, the various associations of *anciens combattants* and *victimes de la guerre* in France. These movements were particularly strong in France. As early as July 1919, when the government proposed to make the parade on Bastille Day a celebration of victory, it was former soldiers (as yet scarcely organised) who asserted that it would be wrong to mark the victory without also paying respect to the dead. Clemenceau, who knew the *poilu*, accepted this sentiment. During the night of 13–14 July a cenotaph was set up at the Arc de Triomphe, and a silent crowd kept vigil before the next day's parade. This tide of emotion ebbed with time, but even so the *anciens combattants* were always more than a pressure group. They were of course concerned with pensions and all kinds of practical questions; but in the words of their historian they were 'conscious of having accomplished something that no generation had even imagined before, or would ever again experience – they want to believe that'.[30]

29. Ibid., p. 231.

30. Antoine Prost, *Les anciens combattants en la société française, 1914–1939* (Paris, 1977), vol I, p. 131.

The *anciens combattants* wished to believe that later generations would not have to repeat their sacrifice. In October 1931 the French National Confederation of ex-servicemen's organisations passed unanimously a resolution that: 'French ex-servicemen are at one in their devotion to the idea of peace and in their determination to contribute to its establishment.'[31] This was formally phrased, but represented a deeply held sentiment. The ex-servicemen's organisations were much involved in attempts at Franco–German reconciliation, and often met their German opposite numbers. The same current of feeling was strong in the British Legion. The old soldiers were on the side of peace.

How did all these memories of war – in literature, in stone, and among the ex-servicemen – affect relations between France and Britain? They evoked two very different responses. One was simple, and in a sense exclusive. Men remembered their old companions, their units and their regiments. Their symbols were patriotic, and their acts of remembrance found a natural framework in the nation. The other response was that of pacifism, sometimes in the sense of an absolute rejection of the use of force, more often in a general desire for peace. This tendency led towards internationalism and the League of Nations. Both these responses worked against any close relationship between France and Britain. The patriotic reaction was essentially closed in upon itself, while the international reaction rejected all alliances.

The conduct of the war had drawn France and Britain together, at the level of government and high command. The memory of the war separated the two peoples. Each had suffered grievously, and each felt that it had borne the main burden. The French knew – it was the simple truth – that they had fought in great numbers from start to finish. The British knew that at the end, in the summer and autumn of 1918, they had won the decisive victories. The calamitous casualties of the French Army had begun in August 1914, in battles on the German frontier and at Charleroi, which the British to this day know nothing about. The agony of the British Army began later, but left the lasting scars of the Somme and Passchendaele. When all was over, people in each country withdrew into their own grief to mourn their own losses.

In other and less dignified ways, the end of the fighting saw a continuation of the carping between the former allies, each complaining that the other had not borne enough of the burden. These unhappy disputes fed a much deeper resentment which arose

31. Ibid., pp. 140–3.

out of radically different views of what had happened within the alliance. The British believed that they had sent a great army to help the French, and perhaps even to save them. For this the French were not sufficiently grateful, or in some eyes not grateful at all. Worse still, there grew up the suspicion that Britain had been inveigled into the war by the French, especially through the military conversations before 1914, whose secrecy assumed a sinister aspect. This view still found expression as late as 1972, in Paul Johnson's *The Offshore Islanders*: 'The English entered the great Continental war as a French political puppet...'[32] This stands in stark contrast to the view, expressed forcibly by Huguet and widely shared in France, that the British did not enter the war to help or save France, but to protect themselves from the German menace. To this the French could add that while they had *tried* to draw Britain into the war, they had signally failed to do so. The British declared war for their own reasons and in their own time. Between these opposing convictions no bridge of understanding could be built.

Behind everything lay the feeling common to all hearts, on both sides of the Channel: 'Never again'. But what did this mean? For a comparative few, it meant absolutely 'No more war' – the flight into complete pacifism. For very many, it meant 'No more 1914s'. War was to be prevented by a new diplomacy and the machinery of the League of Nations. Both these interpretations put an Anglo-French alliance beyond the pale. For the pacifist, alliances were evil, and for the League supporter they were unnecessary. For the British in general 'never again' meant above all 'no more continental wars' – no more Sommes, no more Passchendaeles. For the first time in their history the British had sustained the full burden of a great war on land. They had won, but they did not want to do it again. For the French there was no clear-cut meaning to 'never again', but simply an immense weariness. France could afford no more victories like that of 1914–18. Geography did not allow the French to say 'no more continental wars'. They could only say, 'no more wars with Germany', as long as that was humanly possible.

All this told against the Anglo-French alliance. If the British were to keep out of continental wars, there must be no more *ententes* or military conversations. The French were not so sure. They wanted a British alliance to insure against another war with Germany, but a better insurance policy might be to improve their relations with Germany, and make a deal with Berlin. In the event they failed to

32. Paul Johnson, *The Offshore Islanders. A History of the English People* (Revised edn, London, 1992), p. 374.

secure an alliance with Britain at the right time, nor did they – or could they – make a deal with Nazi Germany.

Whatever meaning was attached to the phrase 'never again' – and there were several – it had an ominous ring for relations between France and Britain. They had fought a great war together with remarkable success and increasing closeness, but the memories of that war later stood between them and held them apart.

CHAPTER 7
Peace-making, 1919–1920

During the last stages of the Great War, the emergence of the United States as a combatant nation introduced a new element into relations between France and Britain. The old triangular relationship between France, Britain and Germany was complicated by the addition of another centre of power and influence, with consequences which continue to the present day.

The early reaction of the two countries to this newcomer on the wartime stage was, rather like children with a new friend, to compete for attention and favours. The British, claiming a common language and shared traditions, tended to see the Americans as their own special partners. American battleships were welcomed to the Grand Fleet at Scapa Flow, where they served under British command. Lloyd George went out of his way to emphasise that his ideas about self-determination and a just peace were close to those of President Wilson. The French for their part invoked the name of Lafayette, not wholly in vain, and hoped to become the favoured ally of the Americans. It took them both some time to realise that the United States intended to pursue its own interests.

American attitudes were in many ways ominous. President Wilson, in a speech on 8 January 1918, had expounded a set of principles supposedly embodying right and justice, the Fourteen Points. These were followed by Four Principles and Five Particulars, adding up to a formidable collection. Among these ideas was an insistence on 'the freedom of the seas' which would undermine the traditional British weapon of blockade. Another watchword was self-determination; and if this were to be applied to the peoples of the Hapsburg Empire, it would be logical to extend it to Ireland. The French for their part had lost an ally in Russia which had supported French territorial claims in

Europe, and gained an 'associated power' in the USA which regarded nearly all territorial claims with suspicion. President Wilson stated at the end of November 1917 that the American people would not fight for the selfish aims of any belligerent, with the possible exception of the French demand for Alsace-Lorraine. From the French and British point of view, what aim was there which might not be classified as 'selfish'? Indeed, what was the point of fighting the war unless they achieved quite a number of objectives which Wilson would call 'selfish'? France and Britain were in a cleft stick. They desperately needed American help to win the war; but they wanted to avoid the political consequences which were likely to be attached to that help. If the war had continued until the autumn of 1919, when the Americans would have had perhaps 80 divisions on the western front and thus been the predominant military power, the British and French position would have been very difficult indeed. For that reason, among many others, the armistice of 11 November 1918 came none too soon.

In the event, the split between Britain and France which threatened to develop when the United States entered the war did not become serious. Indeed, during the negotiations for an armistice in October and November 1918 the two drew closely together, affronted and dismayed by the conduct of Woodrow Wilson. On 5 October the German government addressed a note to the President requesting an armistice. Wilson then opened an exchange with the Germans which he continued for over a fortnight without even consulting the French and British. For a full three weeks the Germans communicated only with the United States, disregarding the two great powers with which they had been at war since August 1914. It was an extraordinary state of affairs, deeply resented by Lloyd George and Clemenceau, partly out of a proper pride in what their countries had achieved and partly out of fear that their interests would be disregarded. Clemenceau said to Lloyd George, 'Have you ever been asked by President Wilson whether you accept the Fourteen Points? . . . I have not been asked.' Neither had Lloyd George.[1]

At this stage the Supreme War Council stepped in to wrest some of the initiative back from the Americans. On 7 October 1918 Clemenceau, Lloyd George and Orlando (the Italian Prime Minister) set out their own terms for an armistice, including demands for the evacuation of all occupied territory in France, Belgium, Luxembourg and Italy, the evacuation of Alsace and Lorraine, and the retreat of German forces to the east of the Rhine. On 9 October the Council

---

1. Alan Sharp, *The Versailles Settlement: Peacemaking in Paris, 1919* (London, 1991), p. 13.

told Wilson that an armistice was a military matter, and terms could not be arrived at without consulting the Allied military commanders. Eventually the soldiers took over the main role in drafting the armistice. There remained much confusion as to the meaning and status of the Fourteen Points, but at least Foch made sure that militarily the Germans would be placed at the mercy of the Allied armies.

The British and French were also determined that, if the terms were right, an armistice should be made at once. Politicians and generals alike were agreed that no further sacrifices should be imposed on the men at the front. The stern old Clemenceau, who could be accused by no-one of being soft on the Germans, wanted no more Frenchmen killed. The American General Pershing, on the other hand, whose troops had scarcely begun to suffer, urged that the Allies should press on with the war and impose unconditional surrender upon the Germans. He did not prevail, though later there were those who claimed that he had been right, and in the next war 'unconditional surrender' became the policy of the Allies.

THE PARIS PEACE CONFERENCE: THE GERMAN QUESTION

In making the armistice, the British and French stood together against the Americans as well as the Germans. Could they do the same at the peace conference, which opened in Paris on 18 January 1919? It later became a commonplace in France to say that the British and French had been allies at 11 a.m. on 11 November 1918, but thereafter they were enemies. That went too far, but there were bound to be problems. Clemenceau told the Chamber on 29 December 1918 that in the peace negotiations he intended to remain in close accord with the wartime allies, but he was also determined to defend the interests of France to the full. Lloyd George would have said exactly the same. The question was how far their separate interests would impede the maintenance of a close accord.

Some differences were fundamental. The French were convinced that they had played the major part in the war, fighting with their whole forces from start to finish. They had been the principal sufferers, in death and devastation. They therefore felt entitled, almost in a moral sense, to reward for their efforts and redress for their sufferings. Moreover, the facts of geography were remorseless. France would remain next to Germany, and had to seek security on that basis. France thus needed reparation for past losses and safety for the future. Clemenceau was determined to pursue these objectives by the methods of power politics and old-fashioned diplomacy, secret and ruthless if need be, and not through Wilsonian idealism or the 'new diplomacy' of the Fourteen Points. As a French journal put it in January 1919, in a choice between Wilson and Metternich, Clemenceau would follow Metternich.

The British for their part felt that they were the true victors in the war. Also, though their country had not been invaded, they had suffered grievously and they wanted compensation. They too demanded security, by getting rid of the German fleet and the German colonies. In these ways, their attitudes resembled those of France. But at bottom the British believed that they had a choice which was not open to the French. They could turn their backs on Europe and seek safety and prosperity in their Empire, which the war had made a reality in ways undreamed of before. Dominion troops had fought in France in large numbers and with great success. An Imperial War Cabinet had met for long periods in 1917 and 1918. A Dominion minister (Smuts, the South African) had actually been a member of the British War Cabinet. The Dominions were all to be represented at the peace conference. An old dream, fading before 1914, had come back to life.

There was something more that came between the British and the French. Britain, like France, was an old European country, whose rulers thought primarily in terms of interests and power, and practised secret diplomacy of the old-fashioned kind. But Wilsonian idealism, which was itself the offspring of the British liberal tradition, touched a strong responsive chord in Britain. Lloyd George, a chameleon among men, was both an underhand conspirator, who could have lasted a round or two with Machiavelli, and an old radical idealist. British policy tended to veer between power politics and idealism, to the dismay and bewilderment of the French. Moreover, the affinity between American and British idealism reinforced the French tendency, which became prominent in 1919, to lump the two together as 'Anglo-Saxons'. There were indeed 'Anglo-Saxon attitudes'. Looking back after many years, a French diplomat wrote of 'the varnish of humanitarianism which the Anglo-Saxon governments meant to spread over the peace'.[2] This was an accurate remark, and it

2. MAE, Papiers 1940, Chauvel 94, MS. 'Origines de la défaite', not dated but probably 1944, f. 7.

must be doubted whether the varnish really did much good. To Anglo-French relations it certainly did harm.

The two countries thus came to the Peace Conference with some widely different assumptions; but the key to their relations lay in the detailed working out of a number of different issues. The British and French had to consider what to do about Germany: how to attain security against future German aggression; how great a demand for reparations to impose; how to settle Germany's eastern frontiers; how to crush German militarism. The peace-makers faced a formidable series of problems.

At the Peace Conference, Clemenceau was on his home ground in Paris. The French Premier was elected as the President of the formal plenary sessions, which gave him certain advantages. He was remarkably strong and resilient for his 78 years; and even when shot by a would-be assassin on 19 February 1919 he was back in action inside ten days, with the bullet still lodged in his ribs. After that, understandably, he showed signs of weariness and an occasional failure of concentration. Lloyd George remained vigorous, wily and fertile in devices throughout the conference. On two occasions, with his Fontainebleau memorandum (25 March) and his list of objections to the proposed treaty with Germany (2 June), he tried to exert a large-scale influence on the conference's conclusions, and he also kept up a constant pressure on individual issues. The two Premiers were well matched, and retained some of their wary wartime respect for one another.

One aspect of the conference's proceedings had a particularly jarring effect on French sensibilities. For a long period before 1919 French had been the official language of diplomacy and of great international congresses. In 1919 Clemenceau, as President of the Conference, agreed that French and English together should be the official languages. With the United States and the British Empire looming so large among the victors, and their delegations playing key roles in the conference, it is hard to see that he had much choice in the matter. Even so, he was accused of having sold the pass and betrayed the standing of the French language to the advantage of the Anglo-Saxons. It was a sign of the sensitivity of the French to the status of their language *vis-à-vis* English, which we shall meet again. Meanwhile, and on a practical level, it was fortunate for Clemenceau that he spoke good English, which was the working language of the Council of Four (Wilson, Lloyd George, Clemenceau and Orlando).

The central issue of the conference was the German peace treaty, and the basic question for the French and British was what to do about Germany. French public opinion early in 1919 was overwhelmingly convinced that Germany, though now defeated, would again become a danger in the future. 'The Hun will always be the Hun' was the general sentiment. *Le Temps* put it more elegantly: 'If the world's thinking has changed, Germany's has remained unchangeable.' It meant the same thing. The great majority of the French press, both Parisian and provincial, therefore demanded 'a victorious peace', which would render Germany harmless and ensure the future safety of France.[3]

This straightforward view met with little sympathy from the British. This was partly a matter of national temperament – sympathy for 'the underdog' rapidly displaced the anti-German feelings of November 1918. The British were also afraid that harsh peace terms would push Germany into Bolshevik revolution, which would then overwhelm the whole of Europe. Above all it was a matter of geography, as Clemenceau knew well: 'there is a difference of psychology between your people and ours: you are on your island, behind the rampart of the sea; we are on the Continent, with a bad frontier'.[4]

For these diverse reasons, the British were completely out of sympathy with the French view of Germany. Balfour, the Foreign Secretary, wrote that the French took a 'lurid view' of the German danger. German militarism could only be cured by a change in the international system, which the French were doing nothing to promote. Even if they were right about the German character (which he did not accept), then 'no manipulation of the Rhine frontier is going to make France anything more than a second-rate Power, trembling at the nod of its great neighbour on the East'. Lloyd George told President Wilson that 'For France, the great danger is the German danger; I believe it is averted for a century. I fear the Slavs much more.'[5]

This general conflict of view came to a head in an exchange between Lloyd George and Clemenceau at the end of March 1919. Lloyd George and some of his closest advisers withdrew from Paris to Fontainebleau for a weekend, and there produced the 'Fontainebleau Memorandum' (25 March), in which the Prime Minister argued the

---

3. Pierre Miquel, *La Paix de Versailles et l'opinion publique française* (Paris, 1972), pp. 236–7, 245–6.

4. Arthur S. Link, ed., *The Deliberations of the Council of Four (March 24–June 28, 1919.) Notes of the official interpreter, Paul Mantoux* (Princeton, 1992), vol. II, p. 440. Clemenceau was talking to Lloyd George, Bonar Law and Barnes, 13 June 1919.

5. M.L. Dockrill and J.D. Goold, eds, *Peace without Promise* (London, 1981), pp. 35–7; Link, *Council of Four*, vol. II, p. 325.

case for a peace settlement which might be stern, but would also be so clearly just that the Germans themselves would accept it of their own free will and it would not need to be enforced. Reparations should be imposed only on the generations which were responsible for the war, and not on their successors. Germany must be allowed equal commercial opportunities with other countries. No more Germans should be transferred to other states than was absolutely necessary. Germany must not be driven into Bolshevism. Lloyd George pleaded for a peace of reconciliation, magnanimity and 'appeasement' – a word which was not yet devalued.

Clemenceau replied severely and shrewdly. Britain had already eliminated the main threats to herself: the German fleet lay under British guns at Scapa Flow; the German colonies were all occupied. With their own position secure, the British could afford to be magnanimous; or rather, to urge magnanimity upon others. But France had not eliminated her main danger, which remained the presence of a powerful Germany just across the Rhine. Besides, if a policy of reconciliation was to be pursued, it should not be limited to Europe. If Germany was to be 'appeased', this should include naval and colonial concessions as well.

This exchange was sharp and revealing. Clemenceau pounced on the hypocrisy of the British, who urged magnanimity upon others after securing key advantages for themselves. On the other hand Lloyd George grasped what was to become the central problem of later years: how to enforce a treaty which the Germans were determined to oppose or evade.

The treaty itself began with a flourish: the Covenant of the League of Nations, which formed the first Chapter in all the treaties which brought hostilities formally to an end. The League was mainly an Anglo-American affair. President Wilson was the driving force, and the detailed drafting was largely the work of Lord Robert Cecil and General Smuts. The French played little part, though one of their delegates, Léon Bourgeois, had been planning a 'Société des Nations' for some time. The League, with its mixture of Wilsonian idealism and British liberal internationalism had the broad appearance of an Anglo-Saxon combination against the French. For their part, the French did not believe that the League would be an adequate guarantee of their security. In this they were quite right. The USA insisted on the League, but then Congress refused to ratify the Treaty and so the Americans took no part in their own creation, undermining the League from the start.

A more solid guarantee might be found in the Rhineland. Marshal

Foch took the lead in demanding that Germany's western frontier should be moved back to the Rhine. In a memorandum of 10 January 1919 he argued that it would be a mistake for France to abandon the natural barrier of the Rhine for the sort of security offered by the League. He proposed permanent military occupation of the left bank of the river, and of three important bridgeheads on the right bank. The area on the left bank should be detached from Germany, though he left open the question of its exact political status. (Possible solutions were outright annexation by France, or the formation of one or more Rhineland republics under French influence.) Foch's proposal was firmly opposed by Lloyd George, who said it would create an Alsace-Lorraine in reverse. 'On my last visit to Paris my strongest impression was the statue of Strasbourg in its veil of mourning. Do not allow Germany to erect such a statue.'[6] Though a man of many devices, he never wavered from this stance. President Wilson took the same view, which meant that the Anglo-Saxons were lined up again.

For Clemenceau the issue presented a severe test of his policy of working closely with his allies and pursuing French interests. He believed that French interests required the Rhineland to be detached from Germany, and he gave general support to Foch's proposals. But to press them to a conclusion would mean a breach with the British and Americans, which he knew would be extremely dangerous. The question threatened the worst crisis of the peace conference.

In the event, a breach was avoided. On 14 March, on Lloyd George's initiative, the Prime Minister and President Wilson reaffirmed their opposition to the detachment of the Rhineland from Germany, and to anything other than a temporary military occupation of the area; but they proposed to meet the French need for security by offering an Anglo-American military guarantee against any future unprovoked aggression by Germany against France. Clemenceau welcomed the proposed guarantee, and knew that he would have to accept it rather than lose British and American goodwill. However, he and Foch both pointed out that in the event of a German attack France would have to stand alone until British and American forces arrived – which might be a long time. He therefore requested, to supplement the guarantee, the permanent demilitarisation of the Rhineland, i.e. that Germany should not fortify the area or maintain forces there. Demilitarisation should be verified by a permanent system of inspection. Any breach should be countered by immediate French

6. J.C. King, *Foch versus Clemenceau. France and German Dismemberment, 1918–1919* (Cambridge, Mass., 1960), p. 24.

occupation of the line of the Rhine, and at once bring the Anglo-American guarantee into action. Clemenceau also demanded a thirty-year Allied military occupation of the left bank, plus bridgeheads at Mainz, Coblenz and Cologne. Finally, he accepted a number of compromises. There was to be a permanent demilitarised zone, on the right bank of the Rhine as well as the left. There was to be a temporary allied military occupation of the Rhineland, lasting for five, ten and fifteen years in different areas. A breach of demilitarisation would be deemed a 'hostile act', but would not automatically bring the Anglo-American guarantee into effect. There was no provision for permanent inspection, but instead a system of notifying the League of Nations of suspected breaches.

These agreements were embodied in the Treaty of Versailles with Germany. Two treaties of guarantee, one between Britain and France, the other between the USA and France, were signed on the same day as the Treaty of Versailles, 28 June 1919, providing for immediate assistance by Britain and the United States respectively in the event of unprovoked German aggression against France. The treaties of guarantee were bound together, so that if one were not ratified the other would not take effect. In fact, Lloyd George inserted the word 'only' into the drafts as late as 27 June, so that *only* when the American treaty was ratified would the British treaty come into force. In the event, the United States Senate failed to ratify the Treaty of Versailles, and Wilson did not even put the American treaty of guarantee before it. The British treaty thus also became null, though it could be argued that the British still had a moral obligation to uphold the arrangement in which they had taken the initiative. The guarantees to France therefore came to nothing.

The results of this complicated failure were disastrous for Anglo-French relations. There was an air of deception about the whole affair. Even in June 1919 it was unlikely that the American Senate would accept the treaty of guarantee. Foch said so openly. Lloyd George knew it, and it seems plain that the French knew that he knew it. The proposed guarantee thus appeared a mere trick, by which Lloyd George got round the problem of the Rhineland without committing Britain to anything. Worse, the whole idea was probably baseless from start to finish. Even if both Britain and the United States had ratified the treaties, was not Foch right to think that actual British and American military help would be too little or too late? If so, the guarantee which was supposed to underpin the Rhineland settlement was simply meaningless. The French felt they had been deceived. The British for their part, government and public opinion alike, were relieved to have escaped from a commitment which they had not really wanted in the first place. It was a disastrous episode.

One purpose of the military occupation of the Rhineland was to ensure that the Germans paid reparations. When the war ended, everyone was agreed that Germany should pay a substantial sum towards the cost of repairing its damage. Even the Germans expected this, because it was an established tradition that the loser paid; though naturally they would try to keep the payment as low as possible. On this question, the French and British positions were not at this stage far apart, and were certainly closer to one another than they were to the views of the Americans. It was only later, over the questions of the justice of reparations imposed and the problems of enforcing payment, that fatal differences between the two countries developed.

When the peace conference opened, neither France nor Britain had a clear-cut conception about reparations. In Britain, when the issue is remembered at all, there survives the idea of France as the villain of the piece, firmly decided from the start upon revenge and the ruination of the German economy. The reality was not so simple. At the end of the war, French government policy remained one of trying to keep in being the wartime system of Allied economic co-operation, including the organisations to co-ordinate purchasing from the USA. This would reduce France's balance of payments problem, assist her economic reconstruction, and at the same time control Germany by maintaining the economic front against her. This policy, which was in effect a continuation of wartime co-operation, broke down on American opposition. President Wilson was in principle a free-trader; or rather he was a free-trader for others, with no intention of dismantling American tariffs. He denounced the idea of any selfish economic combinations within the bosom of the new League of Nations. He would not accept any continuation of Allied co-operation which impinged on the American economy when the exigencies of war had come to an end. By the end of February 1919 it was clear that the Americans were immoveable on this issue. The French therefore turned to the alternative policy of dealing with their own economic problems and controlling Germany by imposing substantial reparations payments. Even then, they were by no means intransigent in their approach to the question. Clemenceau instigated secret conversations with members of the German delegation, offering a modest reparations settlement in return for German co-operation in carrying it out.

The British position was uncertain, and in some ways inconsistent. On the one hand, Lloyd George said from time to time, notably in the Fontainebleau memorandum, that he wanted a figure for reparations which the Germans would accept and co-operate in paying. He also claimed that he did not want to crush the German economy and so impede general European recovery. On the other hand, during the general election campaign of November and December 1918 he pledged that Britain would demand the whole cost of the war from Germany, and allowed his ministers to make dramatic speeches about squeezing the German lemon until the pips squeaked. More important, at the same time as he was preparing the Fontainebleau memorandum, he accepted a proposal by Smuts (supposedly a 'moderate') that reparations should include pensions and allowances to servicemen or their widows or dependants. By common consent, this approximately doubled the amount to be demanded from Germany, as so far envisaged. The point was that Britain had suffered little material loss to compare with the devastation of north-eastern France, and without the claim for pensions would have had little basis for a large reparations payment. The Dominions had suffered heavy casualties but no damage, and so would have had no claim to reparations at all. This would not have been acceptable to public opinion in any of the countries involved, and it was natural that the demand on pensions should be pressed. But it meant that the British reparations claim was greater than the original French demand – though the French rapidly gave their support to the British proposal when it was made.

At that stage, the British and French made broadly common cause on the question of reparations. They postponed the issue for as long as possible, and then successfully opposed the fixing either of a total sum for Germany to pay, or a time-limit in which to complete payment. Almost at the last moment, on 9 June 1919, President Wilson made a final attempt to set a maximum figure of £6,000 million, but Lloyd George and Clemenceau both resisted, and got their way. The whole issue was referred to the Reparations Commission, which was to prepare an assessment of damage suffered, to include pensions and allowances, and to report by 1921. At the time, this suited both the British and the French, who knew that they could not arrive at a figure which would be acceptable to the Americans, the Germans and their own public opinions. Later, however, the delay was to sow discord between them, because opinion in the two countries developed on divergent courses.

One crucial reason for this divergence was that, by a process which was almost accidental, an assertion of German responsibility for causing the war was placed at the head of the reparations chapter of the Treaty of Versailles. This became almost universally known as the 'war guilt' clause, though the word 'guilt' did not appear in it. As 'revisionist' thinking about the origins of the war gathered pace in Britain during the 1920s, casting doubt on the thesis of sole German responsibility, the moral basis for reparations was eroded in British minds because reparations were linked to war guilt. The French too had their revisionists, who argued that the war had been caused, not by the Germans, but by a conspiracy between President Poincaré and the Russian Ambassador in Paris, Iswolsky; but they had much less influence than in England. French opinion as a whole remained convinced that Germany had attacked France in 1914, and it was perfectly right that the Germans should pay reparations.

Among the discussions about reparations at the peace conference, one item passed almost unnoticed at the time but assumed greater significance in the light of later events. This was coke, a fuel vital for the French steel industry and which France could import only from Germany. Almost at the last minute, the delivery of coke as well as coal under the heading of reparations was written into the treaty. Coke represented an aspect of the economic interdependence of France and Germany, which was actually increased by the Treaty of Versailles. Before the war, Lorraine (now part of France) had received about four million tons of coke each year from the Ruhr, and if its iron and steel industries were to continue to work, Lorraine would still need that coke. Thus through all the horrors of war and the wrangling of peace-making, there persisted an underlying bond of common economic interest between France and Germany. It was in one way astonishing, and yet in another only rational, for Louis Loucheur, the French Minister for Industrial Reconstruction and an ardent advocate of reparations, to propose to the German government on 1 August 1919 the creation of a cartel between the French, German and Belgian steel industries. In the event, this was not followed up. The German government showed interest, but German industrialists felt they were not yet ready. But, not for the first time, the outlines of the later Coal and Steel Community can be discerned on the horizon. It was not proposed that the British steel industry should form part of the cartel.[7]

In eastern Europe, the restored state of Poland brought out political differences between France and Britain. France, having lost her former ally in Russia, sought to make Poland as large as possible, by pushing her frontier with Germany westward. Lloyd George, on the other

---

7. Georges-Henri Soutou, 'Le coke dans les relations internationales en Europe de 1914 au plan Dawes (1924)', *Relations Internationales*, 43, 1985, pp. 249–67.

hand, while supporting the concept of an independent Poland, wished to keep to a minimum the number of Germans within the new state, on the ground that a large German minority would store up difficulties for the future. The French were interested primarily in security against Germany, and a continuing Polish-German antagonism was by no means unwelcome to them. The British had no idea that their own security might be involved in the Polish-German border, and were more concerned with the principle of self-determination and the hope of stability in eastern Europe. In this they sided with President Wilson, causing the French to resent the Anglo-American propensity for high-sounding principles.

Throughout the war the French and British had asserted that their objective was to destroy German (or sometimes Prussian) militarism – and they had meant what they said. To achieve their aim, they had virtually to destroy the German Army, and if possible the mentality which had shaped it. Everyone agreed that the German Army must in future be small, and a French proposal of a total of 100,000 was accepted. The French suggested that this force should be raised by conscription for a period of one year, but Lloyd George argued that this would allow the Germans to build up a reserve of trained men, and instead the principle of a long-service professional army was accepted. This difference of view reflected the great gulf between the British and French attitudes to military conscription: for the British, conscription and militarism went hand in hand, but for the French conscription was linked to democracy. Behind this lay another and more dangerous element of discord. The preamble to the disarmament Chapter of the Treaty declared that the limitation of German armaments was to be the prelude to the general disarmament of all nations. The British actually meant this to come about, though only for armies – navies were another matter. Sooner or later they would turn their attention to the reduction of the French Army.

On the whole, France and Britain came through the making of the treaty with Germany with their relations intact in the short run. On the most contentious issue between them, the Rhineland, they reached a compromise. On reparations they were more closely aligned with one another than with the Americans. The British and Americans sometimes worked together against France, but equally there were sharp differences between them, notably on the freedom of the seas and on naval armaments. But there were also difficulties between France and Britain. Clemenceau rightly pointed out from time to time that the British always urged moderation and concessions to Germany at the expense of others, usually France. French public opinion was firmly convinced that France had not secured peace terms to match her efforts in the war, and tended to blame this on the Anglo-Saxons, whose impractical idealism emphasised the League of Nations and self-determination at the expense of stern realism. The British for their part emerged with an impression that French intransigence had somehow obstructed Lloyd George's hopes of a moderate peace. They came to feel, obscurely at first but more and more strongly as time went by, that the Germans had not been fairly treated, and that this was the fault of the French. In reality, the treaty itself – a long and complicated document – allowed much scope for interpretation, and much depended on how it was to be construed and imposed in the years to come.

THE MIDDLE EAST AND LAWRENCE OF ARABIA

It was one of the peculiarities of the whole 1919 peace settlement, which included several different treaties arrived at over a period of some eighteen months, that the principal defeated power, Germany, survived very largely intact. Germany lost in fact only about 13.5 per cent of its 1914 territory, mostly to Poland. It was Germany's two main allies, Austria–Hungary and the Ottoman Empire, which ceased to exist. The disintegration of Austria–Hungary affected Anglo-French relations only slightly. France played an active role in the successor states, especially Czechoslovakia, but Britain did not. The fall of the Ottoman Empire proved a different matter. Anglo-French rivalries over the Middle East which had been suppressed during the war emerged with astonishing bitterness, which was to persist for some thirty years.

During the early stages of the peace conference, in March 1919, the British put forward proposals about Syria which would abrogate French control there in favour of an Arab kingdom to be headed by the Emir Feisal, the son of Sherif Hussein of Mecca and a friend of Lawrence of Arabia. France was to retain only the Lebanon and Alexandretta. At this Clemenceau exploded, and said outright 'Lloyd George is a cheat'. He yielded so far as to agree that an allied commission should visit the Middle East to ascertain local opinion, but he continued to accuse Lloyd George of going back on his word, and on 21 May the two quarrelled very sharply in the Council of Four. Lloyd George denied that he had broken any undertakings, and said that Clemenceau should apologise. Clemenceau replied at once 'Don't wait for apologies on my part', which has been interpreted as an offer to fight a duel – which would certainly have added spice to the peace conference and to Franco-British relations. The next day went little better. Clemenceau continued to insist on French occupation of the whole of Syria. Lloyd George said that France had refused to take part in the conquest of these areas, to which Clemenceau replied that France had sent only small forces, 'but they carried our flag'. He also told Lloyd George that the large British forces in the Middle East might have been better employed on the western front. It was an unedifying quarrel between two great statesmen over a matter which was essentially of only minor importance to their countries, but which came to assume disproportionate significance.[8] The poison of the Syrian affair, once at work, ran deep. Just over twenty years later, two other great statesmen, Churchill and de Gaulle, were again at loggerheads over Syria. A sort of fatality dogged the two countries over this strange affair.

In 1919 the quarrel was pushed aside for a time by more pressing questions. By September the British had changed their minds radically. It made no sense to keep large numbers of troops in Syria, or in the Middle East as a whole, when they could not maintain order in Ireland and were scraping together an army of occupation in Germany from fresh conscripts. In September 1919 the British government agreed that its forces would leave Syria and be replaced by the French. In October they told Feisal that he must accept his fate and make what terms he could with France. Feisal found that the French were not interested in anything less than complete control. In March 1920 the Syrian National Congress, meeting in Damascus, tried to defy both France and Britain by electing Feisal King of a 'Greater Syria', to include both Syria and Palestine. But by July the French occupied Damascus and Feisal was driven out of the country – only for the British to make him King of Iraq.

It was an episode in which nothing went right, and neither country acted rationally. It is doubtful whether Clemenceau cared much about Syria, but he could not abide being tricked by Lloyd George. The British, when it came to the point, decided that Syria was not vital, and left it to the French. Moreover, when it came to a choice between Feisal and the French they dropped Feisal, and yet continued to exasperate the French by finding him a new kingdom next door to Syria.

---

8. Link, *Council of Four*, vol. II, pp. 132–8, 160–4. Sharp, *Versailles Settlement*, p. 181, thinks that Clemenceau was offering to fight a duel with Lloyd George.

France finally secured the League of Nations mandates for Syria and the Lebanon, which they proceeded to run as French colonies for the next twenty years. But the French knew that this had only been achieved in the first instance against British opposition, and they continued to believe that they maintained their control of Syria in the face of a British conspiracy with the Arabs to get them out.

It was through the Syrian affair that there entered a new figure in the French demonology of England – Lawrence of Arabia. There developed in France during the 1920s and 1930s a picture of Lawrence as an agent of the British Secret Service, devoted to the Arab cause and a persistent and insidious enemy of France. In part this picture arose from specific alleged incidents. It was said that Lawrence's hatred of France was so strong that in 1919 he took his Croix de Guerre, put it on the collar of a dog belonging to one of his friends and walked round Oxford with it. (This bizarre story was actually put into circulation by one of Lawrence's brothers. It was still being repeated in a serious French biography of Lawrence published in 1955, but has been demolished by another, more scholarly, French historian.)[9] Other allegations were more general. Pierre Benoît, in a novel published in 1924, *La châtelaine du Liban*, which achieved wide circulation in the *Livre de Poche* series, depicted Lawrence as a member of the English Secret Service, vying with Gertrude Bell in their attempts to undermine the French in the Middle East. Lawrence was often seen as the instigator of the Druse rebellions against the French in Syria in the early 1920s. Henri Béraud, in his pamphlet *Faut-il réduire l'Angleterre en esclavage?* (1935) made the intrigues of Lawrence one of his many charges against the English. A writer in the *Mercure de France* in 1931 depicted Lawrence as working against France in Syria, Afghanistan, Kurdistan and Palestine – mostly in 1929, when Lawrence was in the RAF at Plymouth.

The events of the Second World War and the continuing rivalry between France and Britain over Syria perpetuated these views of Lawrence. A recent biographer of General Catroux, Henri Lerner, speculated as to whether Spears regarded himself as the successor of Lawrence, dedicated to the completion of his work by removing the French presence from the Middle East. He was certain that the spirit of Lawrence was still alive in the British headquarters in Cairo. For Alfred Fabre-Luce, writing in 1950, it was Churchill who had finally realised the dreams of his former friend and adviser. The belief in Lawrence's hatred of France, and his undermining of French influence in Syria both in his lifetime and even from beyond the grave, was thus

9. Maurice Larès, *T.E. Lawrence, la France et les Français* (Paris, 1980), pp. 243–5.

entwined round the story of Anglo-French rivalry in the Middle East. Maurice Larès has demonstrated that for the most part the story is a legend – there is little sign that Lawrence cherished a hatred of France, and much evidence that his pro-Arab feelings led him to oppose British policy even more than French. But this was of no importance for those who found in Lawrence another focus for their Anglophobia.

The French were convinced that the British betrayed them over Syria. In the Turkish settlement they turned the tables. The question of what was to happen to the central core of the old Ottoman Empire, in Anatolia and Turkey-in-Europe (including Constantinople) was repeatedly put off by the peace-makers in Paris, who had more urgent business on their hands – or so they believed. It was only in February–April 1920, at a conference in London, that terms for a peace treaty with Turkey were drawn up. They were largely the work of the British representatives, and were very severe. Much of Anatolia was to be divided into French and Italian spheres of influence, in Cilicia and Adalia respectively. The Greeks were to gain territory in Thrace, and were to hold Smyrna and its hinterland until a plebiscite was held there in five years' time – which would give them every opportunity to fix the results in advance. Turkey was allowed to retain Constantinople, but the Straits were to be controlled by an international commission. These terms were embodied in the Treaty of Sèvres, which was signed on 10 August 1920 but never came into force.

While the Allies had been postponing a Turkish settlement, in the belief that Turkey was in effect dead and would simply wait to be carved up, the supposed corpse was in fact returning vigorously to life. Mustapha Kemal (Kemal Ataturk) formed a new government in Ankara, supported by strong nationalist feeling and commanding a reorganised army. In 1921 the Greeks tried to crush Kemal, but were defeated outside Ankara in August and driven back to the coast. Italy and France took the measure of the Turkish revival, and concluded that they had no chance of making good their claims under the Treaty of Sèvres at any bearable cost. The Italians withdrew from their zone in Turkey as early as June 1921. Then the French government despatched an emissary, Henri Franklin-Bouillon, to negotiate with Mustapha Kemal, independently of Britain or any other of the Allied Powers. On 20 October 1921 Franklin-Bouillon signed an agreement with the Turks, recognising Mustapha Kemal's administration as the *de facto* government of Turkey, giving up French claims in Cilicia, but saving some economic advantages. The French also agreed, though less publicly, to sell arms to the new regime. This was undoubtedly a realistic course of action. But it destroyed the Treaty of Sèvres, signed with all formality only fourteen months earlier. The French acted without any consultation with the British, and left their former allies out on a limb. The British were understandably furious. The press was fierce in its condemnation of French treachery. Lord Curzon, the Foreign Secretary, denounced the French government as unscrupulous and the press as full of lies. There were protests by the Ambassador in Paris, but to no avail. The French had set their course, and they stuck to it.

This Turkish quarrel reached its nadir in the Chanak crisis of September 1922. Chanak was a town on the Asiatic shore of the Dardanelles, occupied by a small British and French force still supposedly supervising the now defunct Treaty of Sèvres. Mustapha Kemal's victorious armies, having driven most of the Greeks out of Smyrna and massacred those who remained, moved north to Chanak and confronted the British and French garrison there. At that very moment, with the air charged with danger and with a battle apparently imminent, Poincaré, the French Premier, decided to order the withdrawal of the French contingent from Chanak, leaving the British to face the Turks alone. Curzon hastened to Paris on 20 September to protest and to try to find some way out of the crisis. Harold Nicolson's description of his meeting with Poincaré is justly famous.

At the first session of the Conference Lord Curzon, in precise but cutting phrases, summarised the disloyalty of the French during the last two years, of which the betrayal of their British comrades behind the wire entanglement of Chanak was but the final culmination. In the afternoon M. Poincaré responded to this attack. His voice was dry, his words were clipped, his insults were lancets of steel. Curzon's wide white hands upon the green baize cloth trembled violently. He could stand it no further. Rising from his seat he muttered something about an adjournment and limped hurriedly into the adjoining room . . . He collapsed upon a scarlet settee. He grasped Lord Hardinge by the arm. 'Charley', he panted, 'I can't bear that horrid little man. I can't bear him. I can't bear him.' He wept.[10]

This tragi-comic scene was the dénouement of a double débâcle for Anglo-French relations, in Syria and Turkey. Accusations of treachery and double-dealing abounded, and were mostly justified. Lloyd George went back on the Sykes–Picot agreement, and then on his deal with

10. Harold Nicolson, *Curzon: The Last Phase, 1919–1925* (London, 1937), pp. 273–4.

Clemenceau in London over Mosul. The French, in the Franklin–Bouillon agreement, deserted the British and abandoned the Treaty of Sèvres. Behind these betrayals lay calculations of self-interest. In the Middle East, the British were mainly concerned with the security of the Suez Canal and their oil supplies, and in a vague way they saw France as a danger to both, simply by being a rival power in the area. In Turkey the French judgement of the situation was cold and correct. Mustapha Kemal was going to win, and there was no point in sticking to a policy, or a treaty, which was bound to end in failure.

These calculations explain much, but not everything. Behind them there lay that most sensitive of all issues, prestige. The French people as a whole were not much interested in Syria. But for those who were, the country evoked long memories of the crusades, Napoleon at Acre in 1799, and the idea of a French cultural mission in the Levant. Similarly, the Turkish question left most of the British public bewildered or indifferent. Very few can have known where Chanak was, and the country was shocked to find itself on the brink of war over such an outlandish spot. But Lloyd George staked his own reputation and that of his government on the Turkish settlement, which he had done much to shape; and he lost. Chanak was the last straw for Lloyd George. His coalition government broke up, and he had to resign. He never held office again.

Looking back, these Turkish scenes now seem to have been enacted upon another planet. Even at the time they bore an air of unreality. But the wounds inflicted on French and British pride and sensitivities were real. The French and British, who had got through the serious part of their peace-making business (the settlement with Germany) with their relations intact, fell into a disastrous muddle and squabble over the marginal issues of Turkey and the Middle East. The consequences were to persist for over twenty years.

CHAPTER 8
The German Question, 1920–1926

Anglo-French co-operation survived the making of the Treaty of Versailles in 1919. It was not to survive the problems of applying that treaty in the 1920s. Looking back from the vantage-point of 1944, the French diplomat Jean Chauvel reflected that the ruin of the Versailles Treaty arose, not so much from its inherent defects, as from the fact that the powers which had combined to devise and impose the settlement did not remain united to maintain it. That is surely true. If France and Britain had acted together during the 1920s, and through into the 1930s, they could either have imposed the main elements of the treaty even upon a recalcitrant Germany, or if they had agreed upon change, they could have supervised an orderly revision of the treaty. In the event they could agree on neither course, and their divisions led to the collapse of Versailles. How did these divisions come about?

There is a general impression in Britain and France alike that France was the only great power determined to impose the treaty. This was not so at the beginning. French policy at first bore the marks of indecision, not of single-minded severity. French politicians thought sometimes of seeking a reconciliation with Germany, and at other times of crushing her. This was not simply a split between doves and hawks. The same man could be at different times hawk and dove. Briand, who usually appears as the quintessential dove, had a plan ready in 1921 for the occupation of the Ruhr in order to enforce the treaty. Poincaré, the strong man, was quite willing in 1921 to attempt a policy of economic co-operation with the Germans. There was thus scope for flexibility in French policy, and room for interpretation in the treaty of Versailles.

On one point, however, there could be no flexibility. The facts of geography were unchangeable. After 1919 the United States withdrew into isolation, with the broad Atlantic lying between it and the troubles of Europe. The British dearly wished to do the same, and escape from the calamities which a continental commitment had brought upon them; and they tended to believe that the narrow strip of the Channel would allow them to do so. The French could harbour no such thoughts. France was next door to Germany and would inevitably take the brunt of any renewed German attempt to dominate Europe. France needed security: but how could it be attained? By the end of 1919, France had effectively lost all her great allies. Neither Britain nor the United States had ratified the treaties of guarantee which had been attached to the Treaty of Versailles. Russia had collapsed into Bolshevism and civil war. Eastern Europe now contained various medium-sized or small states – Poland, Czecho-slovakia, Rumania, Yugoslavia, which were to become allies of France but could not realistically defend her against a resurgent Germany.

It seemed as though France would have to provide her own security. Superficially, she seemed well able to do so. The French Army was large in numbers (900,000 in 1920) and high in prestige. In 1919 the French Air Force was the strongest in the world. But the Army was tightly stretched to perform its many tasks, and the Air Force was rapidly losing its industrial base: the French aircraft industry employed 200,000 workers in 1919, a mere 10,000 in 1920.[1] More-over, France faced serious economic problems. The franc was weak. In March 1919 the system of wartime exchange controls which had stabilised the value of the franc against the pound sterling and the dollar were ended by the British and Americans – an action much resented in France. The exchange value of the franc at once began to fall, and the French government itself accelerated its decline by refusing to balance the budget, on the ground that 'The Germans will pay'. Each year's Finance Bill included a 'budget of recoverable expenditure', which on paper covered the wide gap between revenue and expenditure, but in fact led to inflation. Since France owed very large war debts to Britain and the United States, calculated in sterling or dollars, this placed her in a weak position in relation to her former allies. Worse still, the British and Americans had the financial power to attack the exchange value of the franc whenever they chose.

The basic elements in the British position were very different. Fundamentally, the British no longer feared Germany. The German

---

1. Jean Doise et Maurice Vaïsse, *Diplomatie et outil militaire, 1871–1969* (Paris, 1987), pp. 267–91.

fleet lay scuttled at the bottom of the harbour at Scapa Flow. The German Empire had vanished. The German menace, so plain to many before 1914, no longer existed. The British therefore recognised no European security problem, and tended to think of the French as paranoiacs, or at best as people who could not see beyond the end of their noses. The fundamental premise from which the French worked thus had no meaning for the British.

The British had their own problems. They were unhappily aware that the balance of economic power had shifted across the Atlantic. They owed the United States heavy war debts, and British commerce had lost many of its markets. Worse still, at any rate symbolically, was the fact that Britain had to accept naval parity with the USA, in the sure knowledge that if the Americans wanted superiority they could take it. The British Empire was larger than ever before, swollen by new mandated territories, but it was also more difficult to manage, with nationalist unrest affecting the Middle East and India. Perhaps above all, the British economy had been gravely weakened by the war, and the system of credit and commerce which underlay British prosperity in the nineteenth century was in ruins.

Most of these problems had in reality no solutions, but so bleak a doctrine found few adherents. Answers had at least to be sought, and two seemed to offer some hope. First, Germany could be restored to economic health, thus reviving the European economy as a whole and providing Britain with a trading partner. Second, Britain could concentrate her remaining energy on developing the Empire and the new Commonwealth which was just emerging, and on cultivating good relations with the United States. The idea of renewing a continental commitment to France against Germany was incompatible with both these courses. The most attractive general solution to British problems appeared to be to secure peace in Europe and across the world with the least possible effort by Britain, whether political or military. A consummation so devoutly to be wished might be achieved through the League of Nations and disarmament, which offered Utopia to the idealists and peace on the cheap to the calculators. It could not be attained by an alliance with France.

So a situation arose where France had one overriding anxiety – security against a German danger, which the British thought exaggerated or unreal. Britain had a series of problems which had little to do with Europe, and in which Germany only figured as part of the solution. The divisions which had so damaging an effect on relations between the two countries followed inexorably from these fundamental differences of outlook. As far as Germany was concerned, each country tended to do enough to obstruct the policy of the other, without arriving at any agreement either to enforce the treaty or to change it. This dreary pattern persisted from 1920 to 1924.

REPARATIONS, 1920–1922

During 1920 and early 1921, the former allies marked time while the Reparations Commission pursued its attempt to calculate a sum which Germany would be expected to pay. A conference at Spa, in Belgium, in July 1920 reached agreement on the proportions of a total figure which were to go to the various countries involved. France was to receive 52 per cent of the total, and Britain 22 per cent.

During this long period of waiting, two events occurred which raised the question of how best to enforce the treaty. First, in March 1920, during the attempted Kapp *putsch*, when there were disturbances all over Germany, troops of the regular German Army entered parts of the demilitarised zone in the Rhineland to impose order there. The French reacted at once by moving forces into Frankfurt and Darmstadt without waiting to consult, or even inform, the British. The British protested, though it is not clear whether they objected to the substance of the French action or to its manner. At the Conference of San Remo, in April, the French agreed to withdraw, and did so by the middle of May. What might have been a salutary warning, and a clear lead on how to enforce the Treaty of Versailles, was weakened by division between the French and British.

Next, in March 1921, an Allied Conference in London agreed to a statement by the French Premier Briand, that the Germans had not yet disarmed to the level fixed by the Treaty of Versailles, and were wilfully delaying the process of reaching a figure for reparations payments. This time, the Allies agreed unanimously to remind the Germans of their obligations by occupying three cities – Düsseldorf, Duisburg and Ruhrort. French, British and Belgian troops combined to carry out this move without delay. On 5 April Briand increased the pressure with a scarcely veiled threat to occupy the Ruhr. When Briand met Lloyd George on 23–24 April, they were both prepared to consider the occupation of the Ruhr; and by the end of the month the Reparations Commission was suddenly able to arrive at a figure to be demanded from the Germans. It was a striking, but rare, example of Allied solidarity.

At the London Conference (29 April–5 May 1921) the Reparations Commission at last produced its figure for Germany's total reparation payments: 132,000 million gold marks (£6,600 million). This debt was divided into three sections, A, B and C. The payment of section C was to be postponed until Germany's capacity to pay had been established, which amounted to indefinite deferment. The adoption of these figures by the London Conference was accompanied by a threat to occupy the Ruhr unless Germany accepted them within six days. Briand emphasised the point by ordering the mobilisation of a class of French reservists, again demonstrating that this famous conciliator could also take a strong line. The Germans, after a change of government, accepted. It appeared that the British and French had finally attained unity on the reparations question, and were prepared to impose their will.

This was not so. During the long delay in producing a reparations figure, British public opinion had shifted decisively against what was now seen as the injustice of the whole Versailles Treaty, and especially the reparations Chapter. Debate about the origins of the war was casting doubt on the simple thesis of sole German responsibility for its outbreak. Documents published by the Bolsheviks in Russia helped to build up a rival theory of a Franco-Russian conspiracy to bring about war, in which Poincaré had played a leading part. The British began to feel that their own country was not guiltless, and that secret British commitments to France had played some part in the coming of the war. All this was combined with what the British liked to think of as their sporting sympathy for the under-dog, which was now Germany. This general shift of opinion was given a decisive impetus by a single book, which caught the public mood. In 1919 the young John Maynard Keynes published *The Economic Consequences of the Peace*. He wrote with the authority of one who had served with and then resigned from the British delegation at the peace conference, and with a clarity, verve and wit which gained him a readership far beyond the bounds of those normally interested in economic analysis. On reparations, his message was that the figures put forward in 1919 by the victorious powers far exceeded the actual damage they had suffered; that Germany would not have the capacity to pay the amounts envisaged; and that the problems of transfer (the means of payment, whether in kind, in gold, in German securities or in foreign exchange) would prove insuperable. Reparations on the scale envisaged were both unjust and unworkable, and if imposed they would make the reconstruction of the European economic and financial system impossible. It was a formidable indictment, brilliantly expressed. The book became an immediate best-seller, and influenced the opinions and sentiments of a generation.

It thus came about that, by the time the British and French governments had finally agreed how much Germany should pay in reparations, British public opinion had come to doubt whether Germany should pay any reparations at all. This conclusion was all the easier to reach because British claims to reparations in kind had already been met. Britain had received a total of 1,653,000 tons of German merchant shipping, without causing any uproar in British opinion or leaving much mark in the history books.[2] French claims to reparations in the form of coal or coke, however, were seen by the British in quite a different light. Ships for Britain made good sense. Coal for France was unjust and unworkable.

The French were aware that there existed a transfer problem, and towards the end of 1921 they took their own steps to deal with it, in what amounted to a direct Franco-German attempt to resolve a part of the reparations question. On 6 October 1921 Loucheur, the French Minister for the Liberated Regions, signed with Rathenau, acting for Germany, the Wiesbaden agreements. These provided that Germany should set up an autonomous organisation to deal with the restoration of the devastated areas in north-eastern France. The French government, or bodies representing those who had sustained damage, would place orders directly with this organisation without going through the Reparations Commission. The organisation would then distribute the orders, whether for finished goods or raw materials, to German firms, which would deliver the goods to France. The German government would then pay the firms involved. It was specifically laid down that deliveries of coal would be made at a price lower than that currently paid by France for British coal. These arrangements offered the Germans the advantage of helping their own economic recovery by setting their industries and mines to work, even though they had to pay the bills themselves. They offered France the actual delivery of material for reconstruction, which had so far been very slow in getting through. The French would also, by dealing directly with Germany, free themselves from the British control over their affairs exercised through the Reparations Commission, and from dependence on imports of coal from Britain. There was thus a very clear anti-British element in the Wiesbaden agreements, which opened up the possibility of wider Franco-German economic co-operation.

The agreements were not actually brought into effect. There was opposition within France, from firms which feared German competition and which would lose contracts for work in the

---

2. Jacques Bariéty, *Les relations franco-allemandes après la Première Guerre Mondiale* (Paris, 1977), pp. 79–80.

devastated areas. More seriously, the agreements were obstructed by the British, who did not want to lose their coal exports and were afraid of the consequences of close Franco-German co-operation. They thought, for example, that the French would use the Wiesbaden agreements to get more than their agreed 52 per cent of the reparations bill. Technically, the Wiesbaden agreements had to be ratified by the Reparations Commission, where the British represent-ative delayed their acceptance until the end of May 1922. By that time events had moved on and nothing was done. Thus a limited but practical method of dealing with the reparations problem was stymied by the British, who at one and the same time complained of French intransigence and thwarted French flexibility.

A Franco-German attempt to ease the problem of reparations thus came to nothing. It was followed by an Anglo-French attempt, partly initiated by Lloyd George in his proposal to link together reparation, security and reconstruction, and partly by Briand, who in December 1921 floated the idea of negotiating a Franco-British alliance. Lloyd George put forward a three-part package. On reparations, France should make concessions and perhaps accept a moratorium; on security, Britain would offer a treaty of guarantee similar to that which had been abandoned in 1919; and on reconstruction there should be a great conference to revive the European economic system. On reparations, the French were unwilling to make any concessions, pointing out that so far the Germans had paid them almost nothing. On a treaty, they wanted, not a guarantee (which was one-sided) but a genuine alliance between equals. They wanted also a firm military commitment to back up an alliance. In meetings between Lloyd George and Briand in London in December 1921 and at Cannes in January 1922, the British refused any guarantee of frontiers in eastern Europe and rejected the idea of a military convention. On 12 January 1922 Briand resigned, after he had foolishly allowed himself to be photographed playing golf with Lloyd George, which seemed to the French press as exposing himself to ridicule. Briand was succeeded by Poincaré, who at once stiffened the French terms for an alliance by claiming that any German breach of the Rhineland clauses of the Versailles treaty should bring it into action immediately, and that France should have the right to forestall any danger of indirect German aggression. In the light of events in the 1930s, these were far-sighted provisions, but there was not the slightest chance of the British accepting them. They amounted to a far tighter commitment than the British government had contemplated, at a time when public opinion was opposed to any continental commitment at all. Poincaré's proposals got nowhere.

The third part of Lloyd George's package, a World Economic Conference, including Germany and the USSR, got under way at Genoa on 10 April 1922. But Poincaré refused to attend in person; the United States was not represented at all; and though the Germans and Soviets participated, they went off by themselves to sign a separate agreement at Rapallo. The conference ended in complete failure. The formula of reparation, security and reconstruction got nowhere in any of its three aspects. Discussions about an Anglo-French treaty stuttered on until July 1922, but there was no life in them.

By the summer of 1922 matters were at a complete deadlock. Attention reverted to the question of reparations, which though at a standstill would not go away. In July the German government declared that it was unable to meet its payments for the previous year, and asked for a formal moratorium for six months. Lloyd George proposed acceptance of a moratorium, and Poincaré agreed, but only on condition that the Allies took the mines of the Ruhr under their control as what he called a *gage productif*, a productive pledge. During August, the British opposed the idea of a 'productive pledge', and Poincaré rejected the proposal for a moratorium. September saw the Chanak crisis in Turkey, which had disastrous effects on Anglo-French relations, and led to the fall of Lloyd George, who was replaced by Bonar Law at the head of a Conservative government. In November 1922 the German government, under Chancellor Cuno, again requested a moratorium; but an Allied conference in London early in December failed to agree. The British were prepared to agree, but the French still stood out for 'a productive pledge'.

OCCUPATION OF THE RUHR

At this stage, in December 1922, Poincaré decided to act without the British. He determined upon the military occupation of the Ruhr, a course which he had been considering since October, and for which plans had been prepared in 1921. He proposed to make this move on the next occasion when Germany failed to make a specific reparation payment. The opportunity arose at a meeting of the Reparations Commission on 26 December 1922. The Commission noted that Germany had not made certain deliveries of timber which had been due in September, and resolved by a majority of 3–1 that Germany was therefore in default and subject to sanctions under the terms of the

Treaty of Versailles. The majority was made up of France, Belgium and Italy. The British representative voted against.

The Commission thus declared Germany to be in default. It was then for governments to decide what to do about it. At a conference in Paris on 2 January 1923 France proposed the occupation of the Ruhr. Belgium and Italy agreed. The British Prime Minister, Bonar Law, protested against this decision and refused to take part in the occupation. The other three went ahead, and the occupation of the Ruhr began on 11 January 1923. The moving spirit in this action was of course France, and the great majority of the troops involved were French; but it was of considerable psychological and political importance that Belgium and Italy also took part, by sending troops and technicians respectively.

It is not absolutely clear what either the French or the British government thought that it was doing. The most learned French historian of this episode, Jacques Bariéty, after careful scrutiny of the archives, was unable to decide whether Poincaré was simply determined to compel the Germans to make the payments which they had not been making, and to extract the coal which the Germans had not been handing over; or whether he also envisaged detaching the Rhineland, as indicated by French encouragement to separatist movements in the autumn of 1923. It may well be that he simply wished to teach the Germans a lesson and exact reparations by force; if other things followed, well and good. As for the British, the government knew what it did *not* want: it did not want to enforce reparation payments, and did not wish others to do so either. But as for positive action, they were uncertain. Economic interests pointed in different directions: the British coal industry would gain from a dislocation in German coal production, but the consequences of a widespread disruption of the German economy would be dangerous. Politically, Britain still needed French support over the Turkish question, and did not wish to provoke a complete breach. There was no wish whatever to risk an armed confrontation between British and French troops in Germany. In effect, the British dissociated themselves from the occupation, but went no further; and they did not question the legality of the French action under the terms of the treaty.

The events of the occupation were dramatic, and might well have ended in serious bloodshed. The German government adopted a policy of 'passive resistance', and was surprised by the massive response which it evoked. The French too were astonished and dismayed by the opposition which they encountered, especially among the industrial workers, whom they had hoped to win over. For a time, the supply of coke, so far from being secured, almost ceased. French furnaces were closed down, coke had to be bought elsewhere at higher prices, iron and steel production declined. But the French stuck to their task. They extended the area of their occupation; put in more troops; and took stern measures against sabotage and violent opposition. They took hostages to put on trains when there was fear of explosions on the line. A total of some 188,000 people were expelled from their homes. There were casualties: 132 Germans killed between January and September 1923, as well as some French and Belgian soldiers. But the most dramatic casualty was the mark. The German government chose to subsidise its industries and finance passive resistance simply by printing money. The consequence was hyper-inflation. On 2 January 1923 the German mark stood at 7,525 to the US dollar; on 1 September at 91,742,250. By November it reached 4,000 million to the dollar.[3]

It was remarkable that this episode ended without more serious bloodshed. The contest remained primarily one of wills rather than of bullets. In this battle of wills the French emerged the victors. By August and September 1923 large parts of the Ruhr were back at work. The railways were running. French and Belgian workers were operating some of the coalmines, and some German miners had voted to go back to work. German industrialists began to talk to the occupation authorities and to pay them the tax imposed on coal production. In mid-August the Cuno government resigned, and Gustav Stresemann became Chancellor. By 25 September he reluctantly concluded that the time had come to surrender; and this was announced in the German press on 26 September 1923.

In these events Britain abstained from any action, and yet exerted considerable influence. At the start, the British abstention was almost certainly crucial. If they had joined in the occupation, the Germans would probably have yielded at once; but division among the Allies encouraged resistance. As the crisis developed, British opinion was itself divided. Labour and Liberals generally opposed the French action. Even those who thought the French had a sound case in principle tended to complain that they were militaristic and aggressive in their methods. There was a good deal of pious talk about not being able to dig coal with bayonets, and reproof for the sterner forms of French action against the civilian population. The Germans found in these aspects of British opinion a hope of support which never actually amounted to anything.

3. Jean-Claude Favez, *Le Reich devant l'occupation franco-belge de la Ruhr en 1923* (Geneva, 1969), pp. 361, 214, 219.

Stanley Baldwin, the new Prime Minister, called in Paris on his return from holiday at Aix-les-Bains and met Poincaré on 19 September. Between them the two said enough to restore some cordiality to Anglo-French relations. They were able to unite in blaming Lloyd George, who was no longer in office, for past difficulties. Baldwin said that British public opinion disapproved of French militarism, and that close co-operation with France would be impossible unless the military character of the Ruhr occupation was modified; but he also said that he was in favour of making the Germans pay, and he did not object to the occupation outright. Poincaré explained that France had occupied the Ruhr because Germany had not paid what was required of her by the treaty, and had done so without Britain because Bonar Law had refused to join in. German resistance must cease. Then France would talk, and in accord with Britain would listen to Stresemann if he made reasonable proposals. A published communiqué emphasised that France and Britain were in agreement, and Baldwin let Stresemann know that there was no hope of British intervention in his favour. So once again British policy had its effect, this time in persuading the Germans that their surrender could no longer be postponed. The British were now taking a stronger line against Germany, probably because they sensed that a surrender was imminent and they did not want to be left out.

There was a twist at the end of the tale. The French occupation had been a hard struggle. Materially speaking, France had spent much without gaining a great deal. Finally, at the end of September 1923, they seemed to have come through. The German government surrendered unconditionally, and Poincaré seemed to hold the fate of Germany in his hands. Determination and the use of force had won, and France had imposed her will while Britain sat on the sidelines and sulked. But then at the end of October 1923 everything changed.

ANGLO-AMERICAN INTERVENTION: HERRIOT SPENDS A NIGHT 'CHEZ CROMWELL'

The American and British – the 'Anglo-Saxons' – suddenly took charge of the game, with the extraordinary acquiescence of Poincaré. In October, President Coolidge of the United States repeated a suggestion which he had made earlier, that the reparations question should be referred to an international committee of experts, on which the USA would be represented. Stresemann intervened on 23 October with a request that the Reparations Commission should re-examine Germany's capacity to pay. On 26 October Poincaré accepted the idea of a committee of experts, which soon emerged as two committees, one on Germany's ability to pay and the other on Germany's monetary difficulties. At the time, this may have seemed simply practical, and Poincaré thought it was better not to leave the proposal for a committee as purely an Anglo-American one. But the result was fatal for France. The initiative was handed to the British and Americans, who took charge of the supposedly 'impartial' committee of experts, and imposed their own view of the reparations question, which was far removed from Poincaré's policy of enforcement.

Why did Poincaré adopt this line, which was destined to lose the advantage gained by the occupation? The answer lay in financial necessity. First, France had forced Germany into surrender on the policy of passive resistance; but if the French were to secure regular payments of reparations from Germany, there would have to be a restoration of the German currency and of some sense in German exchange rates. That restoration could only be brought about by American, and to a lesser extent British, intervention. Second, the French franc was itself in difficulties and losing its value against sterling and the dollar. This process, which had been going on since mid-1919, grew worse during the occupation of the Ruhr, which pushed French prices up and increased the budget deficit. To support the franc, France needed the help of British and American banks and governments. Behind these weighty, if somewhat technical, arguments lay a further psychological fact. If the Germans had been wearied by the effort of passive resistance, so had the French been exhausted by the grind of overcoming it, and by their sense of isolation from Britain and America. Belgian and Italian support was welcome, but not enough. France wanted to get back into the mainstream of great power politics. Moreover, Poincaré's government was nearing its end, and a general election was due in 1924. Poincaré had won the battle of wills with Germany, but his own strength was now beginning to fail.

The consequences of the Ruhr crisis proved long-lasting, and of great importance in relations between France and Britain. The Ruhr proved to be the last occasion when France took the initiative and showed a resolute determination to enforce the Treaty of Versailles, if necessary alone. After that, the initiative passed to the British, in conjunction with the United States. It remained to be seen what they would do with it.

The answer emerged during 1924. That year was marked by two

new developments: the return of the Americans to the European scene, and the appearance of new governments and leaders in Britain and France. The United States took the lead in the committee of experts to consider the German currency and the reparation problem, which met in Paris from January to April 1924. The chairman was an American banker and Director of the US Bureau of the Budget, Charles Dawes. It was plain that only American financial intervention could stabilise the mark. Equally to the point, but less generally obvious, was the fact that only the Americans could save the franc. In March 1924 the French government, still headed by Poincaré, asked the American bankers, J. P. Morgan, for a loan of fifty million dollars. Morgan offered a hundred million, on condition that France introduced tax increases and undertook to bring expenditure into balance with income. Poincaré accepted these conditions, and was thereafter in no position to dissent from the recommendations of the Dawes Committee, which were made in April. These included the stabilisation of the German currency, at the rate of twenty Reichsmarks to the pound sterling, and a new scheme for the payment of reparations. The total sum was left unchanged, but a new schedule of annual payments was proposed, starting at 1,000 million gold marks in the first year, rising to 2,500 millions in the fifth year and thereafter. Payment was to be ensured by the appropriation of certain indirect taxes in Germany, and bonds for the state railways, for that purpose; and the transfer of funds was to be supervised by a Reparations Agency with members appointed by the USA, Britain, France, Italy and Belgium. A loan of 800 million gold marks was to be raised, partly in Britain but mainly in the USA, to back the new currency and to help Germany pay the first annual instalment under the new schedule of reparations payments. These proposals were accepted by Poincaré's government at the end of April 1924, but the whole scheme remained contingent upon the French withdrawing from the Ruhr. It remained to be seen on what terms they would be willing to do so.

The Americans had thus returned, with the influence of the dollar replacing that exerted by the US Army in 1918. The other great development of 1924 was the appearance of new governments in Britain and France. In Britain, Ramsay MacDonald formed the first Labour government in January 1924, becoming Foreign Secretary as well as Prime Minister. He had never held government office of any kind before. He had been a member of the Union of Democratic Control, which had never accepted the thesis of sole German responsibility for war in 1914. He had opposed British entry into the war, and denounced the secret diplomacy and alliances which he believed had brought it about. He had opposed the Treaty of Versailles as excessively harsh, and argued that Germany should not be crushed or treated as a pariah state. He denounced guarantees and alliances of all kinds. It was not clear how much of all this he would put into practice on taking office, but from a French point of view it was an unpromising record. There was a hopeful sign when MacDonald wrote a long letter to Poincaré (21 February 1924) surveying the state of Anglo-French relations and suggesting a joint review of the questions of reparations and war debts. Poincaré replied politely, pointing out that France wished (not for the first time) to link the issue of reparations with that of security. It seemed that the two statesmen would at least be willing to talk to one another.

In May 1924 French legislative elections were won by the Cartel des Gauches. Poincaré resigned on 1 June, and Edouard Herriot became Premier. The Cartel des Gauches was a coalition of Radicals, who had in general supported the Treaty of Versailles, and Socialists, who had opposed it. It was therefore not easy for them to agree on a policy towards Germany. During the election they had made do with phrases about peace, understanding, justice and co-operation which were as vague as anything produced by MacDonald, and might well fit in with the Labour government's ideas. The leader of the Cartel, Herriot, had little more experience of office than MacDonald – he had been a minister for four months in one of Briand's wartime governments. He had no experience of foreign policy, and not much of finance except as Mayor of Lyons. It appears that he actually believed that relations with Britain could be cleared up by a simple change of approach. He would abandon the sterile diplomacy of notes and telegrams, and resolve all difficulties in face-to-face conversation with MacDonald, a man of the Left with the same ideals as himself.

Herriot spent a few hectic days forming his government, and then, as soon as he could, on the morning of 21 June 1924, he took the train from Paris to London. He had made almost no preparations. A senior official from the Quai d'Orsay, not expecting to accompany Herriot to England, got into the train at the Gare du Nord for last-minute discussions, and that evening found himself having dinner at Chequers. The French Ambassador in London, who had prepared an analysis of the situation for Herriot's guidance, was left behind when Herriot went to Chequers, and his memorandum was discarded. Instead, Herriot jotted down, in the course of his train journeys, what he loosely called his plan.

The essence of this lay in the terms on which he was prepared to give up the French military occupation of the Ruhr. He wanted to secure a written agreement with Britain to co-operate in face of any future German breaches of the Treaty of Versailles; a technical arrangement about the reparations debt, called 'commercialisation', which would enable France to gain capital from the debt at once; and an agreement with Britain on the question of their war debts to the United States. Together these would have made a satisfactory package for France.

The British position was completely different. Fundamentally, the British had ceased to believe in the German menace, and saw themselves as standing above the struggle between France and Germany, acting as the impartial friend of both. They had begun to adopt this lofty stance some time before – there were signs of it in Lloyd George's Fontainebleau memorandum. But Lloyd George had been Prime Minister in the war, and he retained the habit of contact with the French. MacDonald had opposed the war, and was emotionally sympathetic to Germany as the victim of French vindictiveness and militarism. He brought a new attitude of mind to the conduct of policy. In this he was supported by Foreign Office officials, not for reasons of emotion but from calculations about the balance of power. France was now the strongest single power in Europe, and traditional British policy, operating from a position outside the continent, was to redress the balance. In the conversations at Chequers, MacDonald was supported, and sometimes led, by Eyre Crowe, the Permanent Under-Secretary at the Foreign Office. Long ago, on 1 January 1907, Crowe had been the author of an influential memorandum analysing the German danger to Britain. He now set himself to argue the case for bringing Germany into negotiations as an equal partner. So for a time MacDonald's vague idealism chimed in with Foreign Office concepts of power politics. Herriot found the combination overwhelming. In 1930 Georges Suarez published a book about these talks at Chequers, under the title *Une nuit chez Cromwell*. Rarely if ever have British writers seen MacDonald as being inspired by the spirit of the great Ironside, but so he appears in this French account. We can see why.

Through a combination of inexperience, lack of preparation, and the effects of a long journey and a sleepless night, Herriot failed to secure any of the points sketched out in his plan. When he put forward a proposal for a written Franco-British undertaking to take action against German default on reparation payments, MacDonald refused, and Herriot let the matter drop. Herriot proposed the commercialisation of the reparations debt; MacDonald said that under the Dawes proposals this would not be necessary. Herriot suggested the linkage of the payment of war debts to the payment of reparations (something which British governments had often advocated, and MacDonald himself had supported), but MacDonald simply rejected the idea without discussion. Thus all the points which Herriot meant to gain in return for the evacuation of the Ruhr were abandoned. Yet when MacDonald pressed for French military withdrawal from the Ruhr, Herriot agreed to accept what he called 'an invisible occupation', which amounted to no occupation at all. On the other hand, the British pushed forward their own demands with persistence and success. They wanted to achieve the French evacuation of the Ruhr without giving anything in return, especially in the form of British commitments. They wanted to introduce the idea of a conference to endorse the Dawes Plan, in which Germany would take part as an equal. Herriot balked at the proposal, but eventually accepted a conference in two phases: first of the wartime allies, and next with Germany as a member. The British also insisted that, when the Dawes Plan was accepted, there should be provisions to ensure that there would be no sanctions against Germany in the event of default. The reasoning behind this was that British and American banks would not make loans to Germany, on which the whole operation depended, if they were afraid that some repetition of the Ruhr occupation would wreck the German economy and destroy the mark yet again. The French for their part had sought to provide *for* sanctions in the event of default. At the time, this question was left open; but the French later accepted the British proposal. It meant in effect the end of the policy of enforcing the Treaty of Versailles, because although in principle it applied only to reparations, once the precedent was set it was only too easy to extend it to other sections of the treaty.

A final proposal by Herriot for a general European security pact, which he claimed was vital for the safety of France, was dismissed by MacDonald as being out of the question for Britain. General disarmament and *détente* across Europe would lead to security. Herriot launched into an emotional speech. What would happen if, in ten or fifteen years, the League had not provided any means of security, and Germany freed herself from her treaty obligations by force? He would prefer France to forfeit reparations rather than to forfeit her security. 'If there were to be another war, France would be wiped off the map of the world.' Sixteen years later this very nearly came about. But Herriot's appeal was brushed aside. MacDonald said that they must proceed step by step: first the Dawes Plan, then the question of war debts, and finally security. Herriot gave up, and said that the most important result of their meeting was that a 'sort of moral pact of co-operation still exists between us'.[4] A moral pact, however, was of no value. France emerged from these discussions the loser. It was British policy that prevailed.

At this meeting at Chequers, Herriot accepted the British proposal for an international conference to discuss the Dawes Plan. This conference met in London, in two stages. There was first an Allied conference (16 July–2 August 1924), at which the main participants were Britain, France and the United States, though Italy, Belgium and other former allied belligerents were also present; and an international conference with the Germans as full members (5–15 August). The American influence at both conferences was strong, not least through the unofficial pressure of American bankers, who would have to supply the loans which alone would make the Dawes proposals work. They continued to insist that there must be no further threat of sanctions against Germany, and in this they were supported by the British. The Anglo-Saxon partnership was at work again.

The main issue at the conference was French withdrawal from the Ruhr, and despite Herriot's surrender on this question at Chequers the French put up a fight about conditions for their evacuation. MacDonald broke the deadlock by almost openly adopting the German position: that an unconditional withdrawal was necessary in order to satisfy German public opinion and to allow Stresemann to get the legislation needed for the Dawes Plan through the Reichstag. This put Herriot on the spot. If he refused, France would be held responsible for the failure of the conference and of the Dawes Plan, and would be isolated in her intransigence. If he accepted, the vital concession of evacuation would be made, without France gaining anything in return. In fact, he had almost no choice. He had already conceded the principle of withdrawal at Chequers; and the franc remained dependent on American support. To risk a solitary defiance in such circumstances would have tested the will-power of even Clemenceau or de Gaulle. Herriot was not cast in that heroic mould. He agreed on evacuation, with the sole condition that its actual execution should be put off for a year. The Germans were then invited to join the conference, and the details of the application of the Dawes Plan were worked out.

The loans were raised without difficulty in October 1924, rather more than half in the United States, a quarter in Britain, and the rest in various western European states. The Germans then made regular reparations payments according to the terms of the Dawes Plan,

4. Bariéty, *Relations franco-allemandes*, pp. 407–8.

starting in 1925. The French evacuated the Ruhr in July and August 1925. The long and arduous dispute between France and Britain over reparations and the occupation of the Ruhr came to an end.

In 1923, France took independent action by the military occupation of the Ruhr. She won a victory over German passive resistance, but at a high cost in both financial and psychological terms. The weakness of the franc pushed France into dependence on American and British bankers. Weariness and doubt eroded her will to take any further action alone. British policy evolved towards revising Versailles to meet German requirements on the reparations question, and in 1924, with American intervention, this was achieved. An Anglo-Saxon coalition, with the Americans as senior partner, imposed its will on the French. Equally important, the British no longer saw themselves as an active partner with France, but as an outside mediator between France and Germany, standing above their disputes and being fair to both sides – which, since France was in the stronger position, usually meant supporting Germany. This was an attitude which was to persist right into the so-called disarmament negotiations of the early 1930s.

RECONCILIATION: LOCARNO AND AFTER

The year 1925 was to see an apparent settling down of the triangular relationship between France, Britain and Germany into mutual reconciliation and even amity. At the end of 1924 MacDonald's Labour government fell, and was replaced by a Conservative administration with Baldwin as Prime Minister and Austen Chamberlain as Foreign Secretary. Austen Chamberlain was strongly Francophile. He had studied in both France and Germany, and returned with an abiding affection for the one and a deep dislike of the other. In April 1925 there was a change of government in France, bringing Aristide Briand back to office as Foreign Minister. Chamberlain rapidly developed a liking and admiration for his French opposite number. Over the next four years the two developed a friendship which made a refreshing change from the personal friction between Curzon and Poincaré. Chamberlain also realised that British interests were bound up with the continent, and believed that it was in Britain's power to settle the fundamental question of war and peace in Europe by resolving the problem of French security.

Chamberlain was right to think that this was within Britain's capacity. An outright, copper-bottomed guarantee of support for

France in the event of war with Germany, together with some visible means of carrying it out, would have settled the issue. Chamberlain himself was in favour of giving a firm commitment to France, but a number of his colleagues were not. Churchill believed that to conclude a treaty with France would be too risky, and he refused to accept that Britain's fate was necessarily bound up with that of France. Moreover, the cast of mind which predominated in MacDonald's negotiations in 1924 still prevailed, despite the change of government. The British still saw themselves as standing above the Franco–German problem, and the only proposal that Chamberlain could persuade the Cabinet to accept was a mutual security pact between France and Germany, with Britain acting as an outside guarantor.

It was in fact Stresemann who in January 1925 first suggested the idea of a mutual security pact, but it was Chamberlain who in four months of negotiation carried it through to success. The Treaty of Locarno, initialled on 16 October 1925 during a conference at that attractive Swiss resort, and then formally signed in London on 1 December, was a limited but significant agreement. The Franco–German and Belgian–German frontiers as they existed at that time (i.e. the frontiers established in the Versailles Treaty) were accepted by the three powers concerned, with an external guarantee by Britain and Italy. The demilitarised zone in the Rhineland was accepted and guaranteed in the same way. In a strict sense, this changed nothing, because the frontiers and the zone already existed. The new element, to which the greatest psychological significance was attached, was that the German government accepted the frontiers and the demilitarised zone by a treaty freely negotiated between equals, rather than being imposed by what the Germans always chose to call the *Diktat* of Versailles. It was this symbolic act which gave Locarno its aura of reconciliation between former enemies.

A word frequently attached to Locarno is 'honeymoon'. Austen Chamberlain, during the conference itself, wrote: 'I rub my eyes and wonder whether I am dreaming when the French Foreign Minister invites the German Foreign Minister and me to celebrate my wife's birthday, and incidentally talk business, by a cruise on the Lake in a launch called *Orange Blossom*, habitually used by wedding parties.'[5] Orange blossom soon fades, and honeymoons come to an end. In any case, the analogy is a dangerous one, because what was being attempted at Locarno was a *ménage à trois*. What was the reality which lay behind the radiant appearance?

5. David Dutton, *Austen Chamberlain: Gentleman in Politics* (Bolton, 1985), p. 230.

The important gain from the French point of view was the British guarantee of their frontier with Germany and the demilitarised zone. This was something which the British had avoided giving ever since 1919, when the treaties proposed by Lloyd George and Wilson to accompany the Treaty of Versailles had lapsed. But what did this commitment amount to? The British guarantee was limited to cases in which there was a 'flagrant breach' of the treaty, and 'unprovoked aggression' by one of the powers; and the British government was to judge whether these conditions had been met. Austen Chamberlain himself told the Committee of Imperial Defence that he regarded the Treaty of Locarno as a diminution, not an extension, of British liabilities. His biographer, David Dutton, has emphasised that Locarno marked not the beginning of British participation in the affairs of western Europe but the limit of that involvement.[6] Moreover, the guarantee was treated as being purely a matter of form. The British provided no specific military force to carry it out, and continued to organise their army as though they had no European commitments at all. When the Chiefs of Staff reviewed Imperial defence policy in July 1926, they concluded that Locarno had simplified their tasks. With a friendly France, the Rhine had become Britain's strategic frontier on land. There was thus less need to prepare home defences against air or sea attack, and the Territorial Army could be reduced. The implication of this was clear. So far from the British defending France, France would now defend Britain, and the British could reduce their own armed forces. This stood the idea of a guarantee to France on its head.

All this presupposes that the Locarno guarantees by Britain and Italy were in fact extended to France against Germany, but of course the form of words used in the Treaty was entirely impartial. Germany was guaranteed against France as well as *vice versa*. This was more than merely a form of words. It emphasised the way in which the British now thought of themselves, as standing outside the affairs of western Europe and above the Franco-German dispute.

The British guarantee given to France at Locarno was thus valueless except as a gesture. Its true purpose was to create an atmosphere of confidence in which Franco-German reconciliation could develop. The spirit of Locarno was to guide western Europe to the promised land. The period after Locarno was indeed one of hope in Franco-German relations. During a meeting at Thoiry (17 September 1926), Briand proposed to Stresemann a far-reaching arrangement which would have brought an early end to the military occupation of

6. Ibid., p. 259.

the Rhineland and the return of the Saar to Germany, in return for a large capital payment by Germany in lieu of certain reparation payments. Briand also remarked during this meeting that French officers were always bringing him masses of paper about German evasion of the disarmament clauses of the Versailles Treaty, but he was not interested in such details. In the event, nothing came of these proposals; but they showed how far Briand was willing to go in concessions to Germany, and how much he was prepared to ignore.

In the same month as the Thoiry meeting (September 1926) an International Steel Agreement was signed between steel producers in France, Germany, Belgium, Luxembourg and the Saar. This was largely arranged by a Luxembourg industrialist, Emil Mayrisch, whose firm operated in France, Belgium and Germany as well as in his own country. It regulated annual steel production in the five territories, and allocated fixed proportions to each of them (43.18 per cent to Germany, 31.18 per cent to France). This was yet another precursor of the Coal and Steel Community of 1950, this time including four of the ECSC's six members. It was a private, not a government, venture, but Briand approved of it. This was also a time of great activity for the Franco-German Committee, which originated with a small group of writers, politicians and businessmen drawn from both countries. French and German ex-servicemen's organisations arranged meetings in each other's countries, and joint visits to the battlefields of 1914–18. Reconciliation was in the air. If it were to take permanent shape, then the guarantees set out in the Treaty of Locarno would never be needed. The gesture alone would have sufficed.

This scenario might have worked out. Under the Dawes Plan, Germany paid reparations regularly. Of the payments made to France, rather over 60 per cent were made in kind (notably coal, timber and chemicals). This proved to be compatible with a general recovery in European commerce and industry. Even before the Dawes settlement, in 1924, the index of industrial production in France passed the level of 1913. The German index followed in 1926. Trade between the two countries flourished. French imports from Germany increased by 60 per cent between 1926 and 1930, and the French industrial growth which marked these years was closely linked to that of Germany. Currencies – sterling, the franc and the mark – were stabilised and returned to the gold standard, which restored confidence and promoted international trade. If these economic developments had continued, and if Franco-German reconciliation had truly struck root and flourished, then Anglo-French relations, which were so much influenced by the German question, might well have become of secondary importance. France and Germany would have settled down in partnership, and Britain would have been content with her semi-detached position, cultivating her Commonwealth and Empire, and intervening in Europe as little as possible.

It is possible to see here a dim outline of what in fact was to happen from 1950 onwards, which makes those later developments less surprising than they sometimes appear. But at the time events turned out very differently. With the great crash on the New York stock market in 1929, the world-wide economic depression which followed, and the rise of Hitler to power in Germany, things fell apart.

CHAPTER 9

'Providence has made us an island'

Conflicts of policy at the Paris Peace Conference and during the 1920s were reflected in the views which the British and French took of one another during the same period. These were generally negative, and sometimes bitter.

Some of the old appearances were kept up. Early in 1929 Marshal Foch died, full of years and honours. His funeral was on 26 March, and Jean Autin, later Foch's biographer, witnessed the cortège as a boy of seven. He was astonished and delighted by the British contingent – the Guards with their busbies and the Highlanders with their kilts and bagpipes. Here was the memory of comradeship in arms, and a mark of respect to the old Allied Supreme Commander. It was by its nature backward-looking. The contemporary scene was very different. Denis Brogan, whose knowledge of France was deep and affectionate, reflected that in the 1920s France was subject to three main intellectual, cultural and political influences. In philosophy, the German school of Kant, Nietzsche and Hegel was predominant; and in every *lycée* philosophy was a compulsory subject. In cultural life, the craze was for things American – this was the jazz age, and the time of the American literary exiles in Paris, often gathered round Gertrude Stein. Despite political hostility to the United States, many French intellectuals looked ardently to America. Others looked to the Soviet Union. The Bolshevik Revolution, which had received at best an ambiguous welcome when it occurred in the midst of war, now took on some of the glories of 1789 and the glow of the French revolutionary tradition. Intellectuals turned in force to the great light in the east, and Marxism as preached by Lenin became an established orthodoxy in French intellectual life. None of these influences came from Britain, or induced much sympathy for the British way of life.

The Marxist influence, on the contrary, was deeply hostile to Britain as the standard-bearer of capitalism and imperialism.

In Britain, intellectuals and writers had much less influence than in France, but during the 1920s their struggle to come to terms with the Great War probably made them more important than usual. In effect, that struggle was an inward one. The dugout in R. C. Sheriff's *Journey's End* is somewhere in France, but its occupants are English public school officers, and their conversation is thoroughly insular. The stream of anti-war novels and poetry which ran strongly in the 1920s brought with it a revulsion against the whole circumstances of the Great War, including France and the French. Outside literary circles, if people were concerned with 'abroad' at all, it was with America, the Dominions or the colonies. This was the jazz age in Britain every bit as much as in France, and even more the age of the American movie – a mass cinema audience grew quickly in Britain, but not in France. This was also the time when some of the young men who had come through the trenches went off to Australia to raise sheep, or like H. W. Tilman, later famous as explorer and mountaineer, went to Kenya to grow coffee. For the British elites, admiration for French culture and the French way of life never completely vanished, but it seems at least to have been in abeyance.

THE TUNNEL – AGAIN

It was almost as though the two countries were averting their gaze from one another. Did they in fact want close contact with one another, after the exceptional proximity imposed by the events of war? Not for the first or last time, the Channel Tunnel provided a test case. The project was revived during the war, and discussion intensified after it ended. On the French side, there was strong pressure to get the project under way on both strategic and commercial grounds. The French Ministry of Public Works set up a committee on the Channel Tunnel at the end of September 1918, not as a means of shelving the matter but in order to get to work on it. A technical report was quickly produced on a new method of removing the spoil while the tunnel was being dug. Albert Sartiaux, a long-standing advocate of the Tunnel, published an influential article on the project in 1919. On the military side, Sartiaux calculated that it would take at most 150 trains to move some 30–35,000 troops through the Tunnel. In 1914, this would have meant that the BEF could have been transported to France within three days instead of three weeks. The strategic value of the Tunnel, he concluded, was now obvious. As for commerce, he believed that there would be a big passenger market, and great advantage for the transport of perishable goods and commodities of small bulk but high value – his prize example was fashionable Parisian hats. Within the French Foreign Ministry, the *Bureau d'Etudes Economiques* produced a paper arguing that the wartime shipping crisis, submarine warfare, and the general difficulties of sea transport had demonstrated the advantages of a tunnel as against the Channel crossing. Previously, Britain had been opposed to the project. 'She imagined that she would in some way lose the advantages of being an island.' But the war had changed all that, and in future England could only gain by a rail link which would make London the starting-point for Brindisi, Constantinople and Baghdad.[1]

The committee set up by the Ministry of Public Works reported to the Ministry, and the Ministry to the Council of Ministers. The Minister for War (who was still Clemenceau, doubling the post with that of Premier) was consulted. Clemenceau in turn spoke to Foch, and between them they produced one of the shortest documents in a thick file, concluding that in the event of a war in which the British Army was co-operating with France communications would be much assisted by a tunnel, and if the two countries were not co-operating there would be no danger to France. The Minister of Public Works wrote to the Foreign Minister on 28 March 1919, asking him to approach the British and embark on a joint study on how to build a tunnel. The French Embassy in London approached Lord Curzon, who at once applied the brakes. He assured the French that the British government was following the question with particular attention. Public opinion was now favourable to the project, but the military and naval authorities must be consulted, and many of the persons involved were away in Paris. The question could therefore not be pursued actively at once, but it would be closely examined, and Lord Curzon would keep the ambassador informed. It was a reply of which any prevaricating civil servant would have been proud.

The French Ministry of Public Works and the Paris Chamber of Commerce were unwilling to be deterred, and reactivated the Foreign Ministry in August. The Ambassador tried again, only to be told by a Foreign Office official that the British government could not as yet designate a responsible ministry which could confer with the French

1. MAE, Série Z. Europe 1918–1940, Grande-Bretagne 115. Memorandum, 4 January 1919, 'Le Tunnel sous la Manche'.

on the subject. In September a further reply was given, again by an official: 'The matter is one of the greatest importance and the several Departments of His Majesty's Government concerned are now engaged in considering from every point of view the complicated considerations to which it gives rise.' Some time might yet elapse before there could be any response to the French enquiry about the Tunnel.[2] The sound of feet being dragged was audible.

Why was this? At the Paris Peace Conference, while raising the idea of a guarantee to France, Lloyd George had himself introduced the idea of the Tunnel into the discussions, arguing that it would assure the French of rapid British military assistance. Later that year, Sir Arthur Fell, the Chairman of the House of Commons Channel Tunnel Committee, began to revive the committee's activities. He secured an indication of support for a tunnel from 310 MPs (a comfortable majority of the 550 sitting members); 236 made no reply or did not know, and only four were opposed outright. On 11 November 1919 Lloyd George received a delegation from the committee, led by Fell, who set out the case for the project. There was a hopeful prospect of goods and passenger traffic, promising a return of perhaps 5 per cent on capital invested. The tunnel would be a great enterprise, appealing to the imagination as well as stimulating employment. It would unite Britain with France through trade, and be an advantage if war should break out again. As to possible military dangers, much had now changed since previous discussions of the project, and Fell hoped that the government would no longer obstruct its passage. The case for a tunnel thus had substantial support in Parliament, and Lloyd George himself had favoured the idea earlier in 1919.

In the Cabinet on 10 November there was almost no opposition to the project, but the Secretary, Maurice Hankey – a fierce opponent of the Tunnel – drafted the minutes in such a way as to avoid registering agreement. He then persuaded Lloyd George and Bonar Law that it would be unsafe to go ahead without fuller enquiry. When the Prime Minister met Fell's delegation, he explained that Ministers had changed their attitude since the pre-1914 discussions and would be prepared to support the scheme, but only subject to naval and military advice. He then added:

Providence has made us an island – I think for a great purpose in the history of Europe and of the world. The fact that it is an island has been the means of saving the liberty of Europe many a time. I do not want it

2. Ibid., Cambon to Pichon, 23 September 1919.

> to cease to be an island, and I want to be quite sure before I commit myself – and I think my colleagues take the same view – that our action will not deprive the country of any advantage in that respect.

If he could be reassured on that point, then Lloyd George thought that there was everything to be said for the Tunnel, an imaginative project which would improve links with France, 'with whom we have linked our fortunes'.[3]

From this meeting three issues stand out. One was strategic: the use of the Tunnel in war and whether it posed a threat of invasion. The second, closely linked, was the question of relations with France. The third was Lloyd George's reference to emotions – intangible yet crucial – about Britain as an island.

In the ensuing discussion, all of these questions were debated further.[4] On the strategic aspects, the Admiralty did not oppose the project, but had lost confidence in the fleet's ability to control the sea in the Straits of Dover and so to destroy the approaches to a tunnel by naval gunfire at any time. This increased the danger that the Tunnel would be used for an invasion. The War Office spoke with different voices. Churchill, the Minister, was whole-heartedly in favour of the Tunnel, though he chose to stress its commercial rather than its military advantages. Henry Wilson, now Chief of the Imperial General Staff, favoured a tunnel if Britain adopted a policy of alliance with France; but if an alliance was ruled out, then he would oppose the Tunnel. One of his memoranda, on 16 December 1919, contained a sentence which was in itself almost enough to kill the project.

> Unless we are prepared to intervene on the Continent and on a continental scale, the military advantages of the Tunnel do not outweigh the military disadvantages; that is to say that for an offensive war on the Continent we want the Tunnel, but for a defensive war in England we do not.[5]

It is unlikely that anyone could have been found (except Wilson himself), willing to make plans for an offensive war on the continent,

---

3. Channel Tunnel Committee, *Deputation to the Prime Minister, Wednesday, 12 November 1919, Official Report of Proceedings*.

4. Alan Sharp, 'Britain and the Channel Tunnel, 1919–1920', *Australian Journal of Politics and History*, vol. XXV, No. 2, 1979, pp. 210–15, provides a valuable review of the subject. See also Keith Wilson, *Channel Tunnel Visions, 1850–1945: Dreams and Nightmares* (London, 1995), ch. 5.

5. FO 371/3765, 187041, memorandum by CIGS, 16 December 1919.

and on a continental scale, at that particular time. There would surely
not have been a single minister prepared to put such an idea to the
country.

As to relations with France, Hankey, the Secretary to the War
Cabinet, warned the Cabinet that, though relations with France were
at present good, a tunnel would last for centuries. It was a mere
twenty-one years since the Fashoda crisis, and the political climate
could change rapidly. A memorandum by Lord Hardinge, endorsed by
Curzon as representing the considered view of the Foreign Office
(1 May 1920), was even sterner. If we could be certain that there
would be perpetual friendship with France, there would be distinct
advantage in a tunnel. But Hardinge was convinced of no such thing.

> It must be remembered that until a century ago France was England's
> historic and natural enemy, and that real friendship between the
> inhabitants of the two countries has always been very difficult owing to
> differences of language, mentality and national character. These differences
> are not likely to decrease. The slightest incident may arouse the
> resentment or jealousy of the French and fan the latent embers of
> suspicion into a flame. Nor can Great Britain place any reliance upon
> public opinion in France being well balanced and reasonable.

Hardinge went on to recall earlier Franco-British disputes, and
predicted that there would be others in the future.

> Nothing can alter the fundamental fact that we are not liked in France,
> and never will be, except for the advantages which the French people
> may be able to extract from us.

And he concluded:

> . . . our relations with France never have been, are not, and probably
> never will be, sufficiently stable and friendly to justify the construction of
> a Channel tunnel.[6]

It would be difficult to be more emphatic than this last sentence,
which assumes its full force when we remember that its author had
been one of the advocates of the *entente* with France before 1914 and
was to be appointed as the next Ambassador to Paris.

That leaves the instinct of insularity, and the sense of security which

6. Ibid., memorandum by Hardinge, undated, endorsed by Curzon in a note dated
1 May 1920; partly quoted in Sharp, p. 213.

was bound up with it. Balfour, who had been Prime Minister when the *entente* was concluded in 1904, and was now very much an elder statesman, argued that it was of the first importance that the country should be secure from invasion, and almost equally important that it should *feel* itself to be so. It might come about, some time in the future, that the command of the sea would be useless as a means of defence, and a tunnel would not matter. 'It may be so', wrote Balfour, 'but let us wait till it is so, and as long as the ocean remains our friend do not let us deliberately destroy its power to help us.'[7]

Finally, Geddes, the President of the Board of Trade, opposed the Tunnel on the grounds that it would be madness to lock up some £60,000,000 of capital in an enterprise which could not yield any adequate return for years.

THE FADING ENTENTE

The views of France, and of Britain's general relations with Europe, elicited by the Channel Tunnel project were part of a wider picture. The British believed that France was suffering from an inferiority complex; that her fears of Germany were exaggerated and neurotic; and that she was militarist and aggressive. They regarded France as the real danger in Europe.

The collective wisdom of the British Embassy in Paris for the year 1921 was that the French resented the weight of British influence in Europe, her superior financial position, and the extent of French dependence on the British. In their resentment, the French people refused to acknowledge the immense debt which they owed to the British for saving them from defeat and driving out the German invader. The Ambassador's annual report was condescendingly indulgent towards these failings. 'It is easy to accuse the French of ingratitude, but they have suffered so heavily that some excuse must be made for the distortion of their political vision.'[8] Spears, in reports to the War Office in 1919 and later in his book *Liaison 1914*, made very similar comments on French reluctance to acknowledge the importance of British help during the war. The British were conscious that this 'inferiority complex' arose from fears of Germany, but they

7. Ibid., memorandum by Balfour, 5 February 1920, quoted in Sharp, p. 213.
8. FO 371/8625, W/1389/1389/17, Hardinge to Curzon, 11 February 1922, enclosing Annual Report for 1921.

160

believed firmly that those fears were exaggerated, nightmare visions which distorted the facts. Even Lord Derby, Ambassador in Paris before Hardinge, who was fundamentally sympathetic to the French position, still used language which betrayed his irritation. 'The French are still in a mortal funk over Germany', he wrote in March 1919.[9] The implication is one of childishness: mortal funk is something which a grown-up ought not to show.

Almost paradoxically, the British also believed that the French were in a mood of aggressive militarism. This was shared across the whole spectrum of opinion, from professional diplomats to those whom A. J. P. Taylor called the Dissenters, the radical opponents of all professional diplomats. The Paris annual report for 1921 described French foreign policy as 'nervous, restive and aggressive', and sensed 'an atmosphere of militarism pervading the Government'. E. D. Morel, the founder of the Union of Democratic Control and aspirant to the post of Foreign Secretary in the first Labour government, wrote of France at the end of 1920 as 'a state, traditionally militaristic, which enjoys today a domination over Europe unequalled for a century'.[10] H. N. Brailsford, another radical, wrote (also in 1920) that 'France has recovered the military predominance which she enjoyed under the first Napoleon', and returned to 'the persistent military tradition of this most nationalist of peoples'. Taylor commented that 'all Dissenters held these views about France'.[11]

The basis for such views was to be found in the size of the French Army and the extent of its influence – French troops and military advisers were active in Poland and Czechoslovakia, as well as in the occupied zone of Germany. The French Air Force, though in fact in headlong decline, still retained large numbers of aircraft, which in 1922 so alarmed the Committee of Imperial Defence that it recommended a large increase in the Royal Air Force to guard against a French attack. In a memorandum for the committee (29 May 1922) Balfour claimed that the French could drop on London 'a continuous torrent of high explosives at the rate of 75 tons a day for an indefinite period'. The Cabinet agreed to provide twenty extra squadrons of aircraft for home defence. But this was not enough. In June 1923, the Salisbury Committee on Home and Imperial Defence estimated that the French could drop 168 tons of bombs on London in the first 24 hours of a

---

9. M.L. Dockrill and J.D. Goold, *Peace without Promise* (London, 1981) p. 36.

10. Report cited in n.8, above; E.D. Morel, Preface to H.M. Swanwick, *Builders of Peace* (1924), quoted in A.J.P. Taylor, *The Trouble Makers* (London, 1957), p. 177.

11. H.N. Brailsford, *After the Peace* (London, 1920), pp. 70, 79, quoted ibid., p. 177.

war, followed by 126 tons in the next 24 hours. They could then settle down to a steady 84 tons per day for an indefinite period. The Committee recommended a Home Air Force of 52 squadrons, so as to deter an aggressor (i.e. France) by the threat of 'unacceptable and inescapable destruction'.[12]

It is a well-known principle in the Service departments that, to secure funds, one must frighten the Treasury; and it may be that these startling projections about French bombs raining down upon London should not be taken entirely seriously. But the scare lasted for two years, and substantial sums were voted for the RAF at a time of severe economies. Such an outcome would have been impossible if a number of responsible men had not seriously considered France as a possible, or even a likely, enemy.

The picture of France was cumulatively depressing. Ministers and officials opposed the Channel Tunnel because they did not believe good relations with France would last. There was a general impression that the French were neurotic, ungrateful and militaristic, all at the same time. Senior politicians had nightmares about French bombers over London. When Lord Derby, after giving up the embassy in Paris in November 1920, publicly advocated an alliance with France, he was swimming against a very strong current. Not surprisingly, he got nowhere.

French observers too looked on the fading *entente* with Britain with a jaundiced eye. Paul Cambon, who had devoted so much care to the nurturing of the pre-1914 *entente* in the ambience of the old secret diplomacy was afraid that his handiwork would not survive in the new world of Wilsonian idealism. Existing agreements, he wrote in July 1919, were being dissolved: '. . . all that becomes a mess, on which, according to President Wilson, we are building a new structure which will have no foundation other than justice'.[13] His brother Jules wrote wearily in December 1919 that Lloyd George, with his anarchic mind and false idealism, was reducing Europe to a wreck; 'and nothing will remain of our victory – we shall have lost everything'.[14]

Before the war, Jacques Bardoux had promoted the *entente* by his journalism and books, presenting a generally sympathetic picture of Britain to his readers. After war service and a spell on Foch's staff at the Paris peace conference, he returned to his studies of the British,

---

12. Stephen Roskill, *Naval Policy Between the Wars*, vol. I (London, 1968), pp. 382–3; Kenneth Young, *Arthur James Balfour* (London, 1963), pp. 437–9; Brian Bond, *British Military Policy between the Two World Wars* (Oxford, 1980), pp. 72–3.

13. MAE, Papiers Jules Cambon 43/101, Paul Cambon to Jules, 11 July 1919.

14. Ibid., 43/100, Jules Cambon to Paul, 10 December 1919.

publishing in 1923 a book on *Lloyd George et la France*. He found many things unchanged from before 1914. The same rituals surrounding the monarchy were observed. He thought that Puritan influence was still strong – a belief which coloured many of his views, especially (though mistakenly) of Lloyd George. In his club, the old rules were still observed. 'It is better not to speak. It is quite in order not to think.' This barbed remark illustrates one of his main themes. Bardoux found the English carapace of self-satisfaction – *'l'armature psychologique'* – far too thick. England was more shut in on itself and more insular than before the war.[15]

Bardoux was impressed by the parallels between the British reactions to the Great War of 1914–18 and the Napoleonic Wars a century before. An immense weariness and desire for peace led the British people to try to shut out the rest of the world. Among their political leaders, just as after 1815, conservatives were dismayed by the strength of Britain's wartime allies, while radicals were moved by the pleas of the vanquished. The Foreign Office too followed the same pattern, seeking a free hand and avoidance of commitments, and falling back instinctively on a policy of balance. After 1815 it was France, the defeated power, which had benefited from these reactions; after 1918 it was Germany. Bardoux quoted Palmerston: England had no eternal allies and no eternal enemies; only her interests were eternal. There was a warning here for France.

Bardoux spent much effort in trying to understand Lloyd George – an intriguing if often fruitless quest. He compared him with Canning: both fertile in ideas and great orators, but neither capable of remaining a gentleman for more than two hours together. Lloyd George was an improviser, a master of manoeuvre, and a gambler. His position was unprecedented in British politics: personal authority, virtually unrestrained by the old party system or the norms of Cabinet government. Repeatedly he used this authority against the interests of France: in the Middle East and Turkey, and above all in his German policy.

Bardoux looked beyond the personality of Lloyd George to the deeper movements of politics and opinion. The extension of the franchise to near-universal suffrage in 1918 had contributed to the growth of the Labour Party, and strengthened the current of British radical opinion. Historically, this movement had always opposed involvement in European affairs, and now advocated the revision of the Treaty of Versailles, especially its reparation clauses. Morality,

---

15. Jacques Bardoux, *Lloyd George et l'Angleterre* (Paris, 1923), p. 12.

sentiment and commercial interest all came together in an alliance of economics and self-righteousness. (Bardoux believed that Lloyd George was still subject to Puritan, Nonconformist influences, which were often dangerous to France.)

Bardoux's message to his fellow-countrymen was bleak. The strong threads of continuity in British policy, stretching back to 1815, were drawing the country into isolation and a policy of the balance of power directed against France. The new factors – Lloyd George's personal ascendancy and the rise of Labour – pulled in the same direction. The foundations of the *entente* on the British side were being rapidly eroded.

Bardoux had long been an Anglophile, and his analysis was still tempered by a continuing affection for Britain and the British. Jacques Bainville, the royalist historian and political commentator for *Action Française*, had no sentimental attachment to Britain (though he admired its monarchy). But his own brand of political scepticism led him to much the same conclusions. He too found the key to British policy in the doctrines of radical Nonconformist liberalism, which combined a peace-loving idealism with commercial interest. Manchester, with its famous *Manchester Guardian*, was the Rome of this orthodoxy. In 1919 the policy of Manchester was to be lenient towards Germany, and to resume business with her rather than ruining her, thus combining compassion with profit. Bainville's comment was far-sighted: compassion for Germany today would mean orders for British industry tomorrow, but a powerful German menace the day after.

Bainville was no better pleased with Austen Chamberlain and Locarno. He thought that Chamberlain was trying to please everyone: to reassure the British that the Pact did not commit them to European wars; to persuade the French that England was concerned about the Rhine; and to show the Germans that they were being treated as equals. He saw clearly that for Chamberlain the guarantee to France existed only in theory, not backed by an Anglo-French military agreement – which would in any case, on grounds of equality, have to be matched by an Anglo-German agreement.

Yet Bainville believed that there was still a basis for a Franco-British alliance, and that it was possible to find the point where the interests of the two countries coincided. He wrote in February 1920 that it could be demonstrated – even to a hypothetical British Labour government – that Britain needed France, and that the British were mistaken if they believed that the problems of Europe had either been resolved or were unimportant. The basic truth was that if France did not stand guard on the Rhine and the Danube, then the Straits and

Suez would not be secure. If this was not recognised, then the alliance would become a mere memory. Bainville argued that this would damage France as well as Britain, and that it was not just a European matter. Outside Europe, the fates of the two empires were bound together. They had been built up against one another, but they would stand or fall together. Bainville reproved those of his countrymen who looked forward to seeing the British driven out of India. 'India without the English would swiftly be Indo-China without the French.' Bainville's phrases were cutting, and his arguments powerful, but his prevailing tone was pessimistic. He had little real hope that either the British or the French could be persuaded to recognise the community of interests between the two countries.[16]

There was little sympathy in France for the British Empire. On the contrary, there was a general belief that French imperialism was benevolent and civilising, while the British were harsh and brutal. Henri Béraud published two novels, *Le Vitriole de la lune* (1921) and *Le Martyr de l'obèse* (1922), which were jointly awarded the Prix Goncourt in 1922. Both were anti-British, and the latter drew together in one condemnation the iniquities of British rule in Ireland and India. (Béraud was to ask in a pamphlet of 1935 whether England would have to be reduced to slavery.) Pierre Loti, a colourful and popular novelist, wrote about British misdeeds in India, while André Malraux, who was very different in style and politics, turned his novel *Les conquérants* (published in 1928) into an attack on British capitalism in China. The British Empire was a target for both Right and Left.

In October 1923 Jules Cambon wrote gloomily to his brother Paul, who had been one of the principal architects of the Anglo-French *entente*: 'The English Liberal Party and the Socialists are obviously against us: I doubt whether we can keep up the fiction of the *entente cordiale* for long.'[17] Such sentiments had some basis: British radical opinion was indeed anti-French. But the conclusion was very much premature. The fiction of the *entente* could be kept going almost indefinitely, and even the reality had a good deal of life in it. We have seen that the Treaty of Locarno and the friendship between Austen Chamberlain and Briand restored cordiality to Anglo-French relations; and the 1930s were to show that, despite much friction, the two countries still had much in common.

Even so, the 1920s ended with a cloud, so far no bigger than a man's hand, but – as we now know – full of ill omen for relations

---

16. Jacques Bainville, *L'Angleterre et l'Empire britannique* (Paris, 1938), p. 193; the original appeared in *Action Française*, 6 March 1931.

17. MAE, Papiers Jules Cambon 43/100, Jules Cambon to Paul, 13 October 1923.

between France and Britain. In a speech to the Assembly of the League of Nations in September 1929, Aristide Briand (still French Foreign Minister) made a somewhat vague proposal for a European federation. In May 1930 he put his plan into more definite shape in a memorandum, in which there appeared the words 'common market'. The British Foreign Office, taken aback by these visionary proposals and not knowing quite what to make of them, concluded after much discussion that the British attitude should be one of 'caution, but cordial caution'. At the time, nothing came of Briand's ideas. Briand himself fell ill and died not long afterwards. In the 1930s, economic nationalism, ideological strife, aggression and war pushed thoughts of federation or common markets to the side-lines. But in this strange episode of the Briand Plan it is as though there was a gap in the curtain of time and we see a glimpse of the future.[18]

18. For this episode, and the lovely phrase 'cordial caution', see Ralph White, 'Cordial Caution: the British response to the French proposal for European Federal Union of 1930', in A. Bosco, ed., *The Federal Idea*, vol. I, *The History of Federalism from the Enlightenment to 1945* (London, 1991), pp. 237–62.

CHAPTER 10

Things Fall Apart, 1929–1934

COPING WITH THE DEPRESSION

1929 was the year of the onset of what is still generally called 'the great depression'. The cumulative effects of that depression were formidable. World trade almost collapsed. The value of the imports of 75 countries, calculated in US dollars, fell from approximately 2,998 million dollars in January 1929 to 992 million in January 1933.[1] That represented a fall of two-thirds, and since every country's import was another's export, the collapse of international trade was catastrophic. The effects in all countries, but more especially those which were heavily dependent on international commerce, were severe. There was a fall in industrial production, and therefore in demand for raw materials. Prices for all commodities fell, business profits declined or vanished, share prices collapsed. Demand for services dwindled. Unemployment increased rapidly. Banks and other creditors were unable to recover loans. The Kredit-Anstalt in Vienna failed. On 13 July 1931 all German banks closed, and when they reopened they suspended payments on all foreign credits. With this, the confidence which sustained the system of credit collapsed, with far-reaching effects on international currency exchanges. The rush to withdraw gold from the banks confronted governments with the question of whether to take their currencies off the gold standard, which would break up the monetary unity and stability, based on equivalence with gold, which had been painfully (and perhaps mistakenly) restored in the mid-1920s.

Britain and France responded to the onset of the economic crisis in

1. Charles P. Kindleberger, *The World in Depression, 1929–1939* (London, 1973), p. 171.

different ways. At the end of 1929 and early 1930, the British Labour government, with Snowden as Chancellor of the Exchequer, tried to develop a free-trade answer to the rapid contraction of international commerce. They tried to secure general agreement not to impose quotas or embargoes, and to negotiate a 'tariff truce'. This policy had little chance of success in face of the instinct for self-defence felt in all countries, and in fact elicited little response. The French sought a protectionist and European response to the crisis. Briand's plan for some form of European federation, launched in September 1929 and repeated in May 1930, was strongly economic in its emphasis, and aimed at creating a European market and trading bloc.

The French opposed the British schemes as unrealistic; the British denounced the French policy as tending to create antagonistic trading blocs and so in the long run to make things worse. Each, according to its own lights, was correct. The same was true in another Franco-British dispute in June 1931, over the old question of reparations in the new context of the great depression. On 20 June 1931 President Hoover of the United States proposed a one-year moratorium on all inter-government debt payments, including reparations and war debts. His purpose was to take pressure off the German mark by allowing the German government to retain the reserves which would otherwise be used to pay reparations, and so perhaps save the German banking system. This proposal was at once welcomed in London, where British banks had made large loans to Germany which they were in grave danger of losing. France, on the other hand, had made few loans to Germany, and was still receiving the major share of reparation payments. The French therefore held out against the Hoover proposals for a fortnight, trying to safeguard at least the principle of reparation payments. During that fortnight, the run on the German banks accelerated, so that they had to close on 13 July. In consequence, the British government and bankers blamed the French for their stubbornness, claiming that immediate acceptance of the Hoover moratorium would have saved the day. The French complained that they had lost their reparations to no purpose.

In the event, nothing was saved. The German government suspended most foreign payments in mid-July 1931. The British government took sterling off the gold standard in September, and by the end of the month the pound had fallen by 30 per cent in its exchange rate against the dollar. France, on the other hand, kept the franc on the gold standard, and emerged as the leading country in the so-called 'Gold Bloc', which included the Low Countries, Switzerland and Italy. The monetary policies and interests of Britain and France thus diverged sharply, and the same came to be true of their economic policies and general responses to the depression.

British policy followed two main lines. First, sterling was managed so as to retain an exchange rate of around $3.80 to the pound, which was favourable to British exports to countries which stayed on the gold standard. Interest rates were kept low. Second, the government adopted a policy of protective tariffs and imperial preference. In February 1932 Britain introduced a duty of 10 per cent on all imports except food and a number of raw materials. In April the import duty on all manufactured goods was increased to 20 per cent. At the Ottawa Conference in July–August 1932 the principle of Imperial preference was adopted: Britain gave preference to foodstuffs from the Dominions, in return for Dominion preference for British manufactured goods. These preferences were usually achieved by raising the rates on foreign goods rather than by lowering them on exchanges between Britain and the Dominions. These arrangements had far-reaching effects on the direction of British trade. Britain moved towards greater self-sufficiency within the Commonwealth and Empire, at the expense of trade outside it, and a pattern of trade was built up which was to last for a quarter of a century. Between 1935 and 1939 50 per cent of British exports went to the Empire–Commonwealth, and 40 per cent of imports came from it. The comparative figures for the period 1910–13 had been 35 per cent and 25 per cent respectively.[2]

A substantial economic recovery followed these measures. The effects of devaluation on exports were useful though short-lived, being overtaken by retaliatory measures by countries in the Gold Bloc (including France) and by American devaluation in 1933. Tariffs, Imperial preference and low interest rates assisted British industry, and by the end of 1934 Britain became the first major country to surpass 1929 figures for industrial production. Unemployment, which reached an average of just over 2.8 million in 1932, declined to just under 1.5 million in 1937.[3]

Doubtless assisted by this recovery, but reflecting also the strength and stability of British traditions, the country's political institutions continued to work normally. There was some slight movement towards extreme opinions. The Communist Party won a Parliamentary seat in

2. Brian Porter, *Britain, Europe and the World, 1850–1982: Delusions of Grandeur* (London, 1983), p. 94.

3. G.C. Peden, *British Rearmament and the Treasury, 1932–1939* (Edinburgh, 1979), p. 208; Carlo M. Cipolla, ed., *Fontana Economic History of Europe*, vol. 6, Part 2 (London, 1976), p. 667.

the general election of 1935, and a considerable number of fellow-travellers expressed their admiration for Soviet planning as against capitalist breakdown. On the other wing, Oswald Mosley's British Union of Fascists gained some notoriety without coming near to winning a seat in Parliament, and a number of fellow-travellers of the Right looked hopefully towards Nazism or Fascism. But the general election of 1931 produced a landslide victory for a Conservative-dominated coalition (or National) government, and the next election in 1935 again returned a solid Conservative majority. Despite some bitter divisions arising from the depression, Britain confronted the traumas of the 1930s with a basic political steadiness which contrasted sharply with the turbulence and flight to authoritarian doctrines on the continent of Europe.

The economic course followed by France was in some ways different. At first, France was given a new sense of confidence and strength by the crisis of 1929–31. The French franc was kept on the gold standard, and for some time Paris, as the centre of the Gold Bloc, was in a stronger monetary position than either London or New York. Moreover, the French economy was in many ways self-sufficient, and depended much less than Britain on foreign trade – Britain, for example, was heavily reliant on imports of food, while France was not. But it was impossible for France to escape all the consequences of the depression, or of the steps taken by others to deal with it. The strength of the franc and British devaluation meant that British exports to France became cheaper, which France countered by the introduction of quotas on British goods. French exports to countries outside the Gold Bloc were highly priced, and fell off, leading to difficulties in paying for imports. French governments met this problem by introducing, during the latter part of 1931, import quotas on nearly all agricultural commodities, followed later by quotas on a number of industrial products. This system reduced imports from foreign countries, and it was accompanied by a system of imperial preference which was stricter than the British equivalent, because the French were dealing in every case with colonies, not with largely independent Dominions. There were great advantages in this system. There was little competition, and all payments could be made in French francs, which eliminated problems of foreign exchange. The consequences for the direction of French exports were much the same as for British. Between 1930 and 1936, the Empire took on average 50 per cent of French exports, and within this average figure some industries (including motor manufacturers) sold more than half their production to the Empire.[4] The French thus built up a system of tariffs, quotas

4. Hubert Bonin, *Histoire économique de la IVe république* (Paris, 1987), pp. 24–5.

and imperial self-sufficiency which was largely separate from, and sometimes in competition with, the similar British system.

The form of insulation achieved by the Gold Bloc and imperial self-sufficiency deferred and cushioned the impact of the depression on France, but could not avert it altogether. As Britain recovered, the French economic position declined. By 1935, French foreign trade was down to less than half of its level in 1930. Industrial production reached low points in 1932 and 1935, and unemployment was at its worst at the beginning of 1935. At a mere half-million, unemployment was slight in relation to that in Britain, but the figures were hard to compare, because the French total was kept down by conscription for the Army and by the habit of many townsfolk of going to live with relatives in the country rather than registering as unemployed. In general, the depression hit France later than Britain, diminishing French freedom of action in the mid-1930s. Keeping the franc on the gold standard also meant that much of the energy of French governments had to be devoted to the increasingly uphill task of 'saving the franc', not abandoned until September 1936.

Politically, France suffered severely from the country's economic problems. Government revenue fell as a result of declining foreign trade and low prices at home, and yet fiscal orthodoxy and the defence of the franc demanded a balanced budget. This meant reducing government expenditure, which was easy to agree on in principle but impossible to put into practice without harming some important group – civil servants and teachers, for example, or even worse the wounded soldiers and other pensioners from the Great War. The result was that successive Ministers of Finance proposed reductions in government expenditure, only to see them defeated in the National Assembly. One government after another was brought down in this way. There were three changes of government in 1932, four in 1933, two in 1934 and two in 1935 – a total of eleven in four years. The combination of economic difficulties and governmental instability produced a marked movement towards the extremes on Right and Left. The conservative and neo-fascist Right flourished in the mid-1930s, and showed its strength in street riots on 6 February 1934. In 1935 the Communist Party revived after a period in the doldrums, and launched the successful slogan of the Popular Front against Fascism. The middle ground, on which the parliamentary regime depended, was eroded on both flanks.

The economic depression thus produced divergent, and sometimes contrasting, effects in Britain and France. Even when the two countries adopted the same strategy – imperial self-sufficiency – the consequences led to separation. The British devaluation and the French

171

adherence to the gold standard set the two countries on opposite monetary courses. By 1935 the British recovery stood in contrast to the French low point. From 1932 and 1935, British political stability was the converse of French turmoil and division.

THE GENEVA DISARMAMENT CONFERENCE

While the effects of the economic depression were working themselves out, the League of Nations Disarmament Conference (1932–34) was meeting at Geneva. The two sets of events were connected in the eyes of both the British and the French governments. At the time, neither took the view that rearmament would be a way out of depression, which would have been thought immoral as well as impractical. On the contrary, they both sought to restrict military expenditure as a means of balancing the budget, and both considered the manufacture of arms as an unproductive use of national resources. To that extent they thought in the same terms. The two governments were also under the same pressure from a disarmament-minded public opinion. In Britain the linked causes of the League of Nations and disarmament formed the leading political sentiment of the early 1930s. In France, support for the League was less strong than in Britain, but pacifism was powerful, sometimes in the form of an absolute rejection of force, more often a general revulsion against war. The League and disarmament seemed to offer a combination of security and peace which was particularly seductive to the Left. J.-B. Duroselle described Herriot and Paul-Boncour in 1932 as 'men of the Left, patriotic but under the spell of collective security and disarmament'; and as such they were characteristic of a type.[5]

At first sight, there seemed enough common ground for a joint Anglo-French approach to the Disarmament Conference of 1932–34. This was not so. In practice, the British adopted the same attitude that we have already seen taken by Ramsay MacDonald in 1924: that of a mediator between France and Germany. Sir John Simon (the Foreign Secretary) explained his view of the situation in February 1932, two months before the Conference opened: 'The role of Britain at the Conference was to do all that she could to promote practical disarmament and to act as a sincere friend to both sides, desiring to promote appeasement between France and Germany.'[6] In effect, this

5. J.-B. Duroselle, *La Décadence, 1932–1939* (Paris, 1979), p. 41.
6. Simon to Rumbold, 30 March 1932, *DBFP*, 2nd series, vol. III, No. 239.

meant that Britain proposed a series of concessions to Germany, and put pressure on France to accept them.

This process began in August 1932, when the German government (with Brüning as Chancellor) announced that it would cease to attend the Conference until its demand for equality of status was conceded. 'Equality of status' meant that Germany should not be subject to one-sided restrictions on armaments, imposed by the Treaty of Versailles, but be treated in the same way as other countries. The Germans insisted that they sought only a change of status, and not in their actual level of armaments. Churchill commented that 'All these bands of sturdy Teutonic youths marching along the streets and roads of Germany . . . are not looking for status. They are looking for weapons.'[7] But the British government was more optimistic. Simon proposed in November 1932 to give Germany the right to have the same types of weapons as other countries, but not in the same numbers. In December a formula was found which balanced a reference to equality of status against another to security for all nations, and Germany returned to the Conference.

In March 1933 the British put forward a draft convention on armaments, called the MacDonald Plan because the Prime Minister himself went to Geneva to present it. Germany was to be allowed an army of 200,000 men (twice the size permitted by Versailles), equipped with weapons previously forbidden, and to be raised in part by conscription, prohibited under the Treaty of Versailles. These were substantial concessions, though Germany was still to have no Air Force. The French felt that they could not afford to reject these proposals, and agreed to accept them subject to a system of verification and provision for a trial period before France made any substantial reductions in her own armaments.

In the middle of these discussions, Hitler came to power in Germany on 30 January 1933. On 14 October 1933 the new German government announced that it was leaving the Disarmament Conference and resigning from the League of Nations, which might have caused great offence among the League-minded in Britain. It did not do so. Simon refrained from criticism of the German actions, and insisted that Britain would continue to seek a disarmament agreement. As before, this meant moving steadily towards the German position. On 24 October 1933 Hitler proposed that the German Army should expand to 300,000 men (though without tanks or heavy artillery), and that later Germany should have an Air Force (though without

7. Hansard, *H.C. Deb.*, 5th series, vol. 272, col. 81.

bombers). In January 1934 the British accepted most of these demands, though seeking to postpone the creation of an Air Force for two years. In February, Anthony Eden (then Under-Secretary at the Foreign Office) visited Berlin, and was told that Germany wanted an Air Force without delay. Eden thought this would have to be accepted; Simon and MacDonald at first did not. But by the end of March 1934 they changed their minds. They proposed to accept all the German demands, and urged the French to do so as well.

At this point the French drew the line. The latest proposals would concede to Germany an army of 300,000 men, as against the 200,000 of the MacDonald Plan and the 100,000 of Versailles, and an Air Force which had previously been denied altogether. The idea of a trial period and inspection had disappeared. Moreover, on 22 March the German government publicly introduced a large military budget for the year ahead, showing that it intended to press ahead with rearmament whatever the circumstances. Under the impulse of Louis Barthou, a tough-minded Right-winger and advocate of power politics, who became Foreign Minister in February 1934, the French told Britain in a note of 17 April that they could no longer pursue these useless negotiations. France must look to her own safety: 'Her wish for peace must not be confused with abdicating her own defence'.[8] This phase of British 'mediation' between France and Germany, which in fact meant the acceptance of successive German demands, was thus brought to an end.

The arguments used by the French and British during these so-called 'disarmament' negotiations of 1932–34 were revealing of national attitudes. The French were straight-forward in their diagnosis of the problem. From the beginning they maintained that the German claim to equality of status would in fact mean Germany's return to the dominant military position which she had held in 1914. In October 1932 Herriot told MacDonald and Simon that, while German claims 'seemed to have a moral character which made a great appeal . . . what they really wanted was rearmament'.[9] Moreover, the Germans would always put up their demands. After rearmament would come the Polish corridor, the Saar, and the return of German colonies. Herriot thought the British were blind not to recognise this, and yet he was himself largely under the spell of disarmament incantations, and very much afraid of acting in isolation. He analysed the problem, but could offer no solution.

8. Duroselle, *Décadence*, p. 97.
9. Record of conversation, 13 Oct. 1932, *DBFP*, 2nd series, vol. IV, No. 153.

The British diagnosis was different, because they took a different view of Germany. It was now widely accepted in Britain that Germany was not solely responsible for starting the war of 1914, and French warnings about future German intentions were dismissed as scare-mongering. Hitler's advent to power did not alter this basic view because nearly everyone hoped that Hitler would prove better than he seemed. Phipps, the Ambassador in Berlin from May 1933, advocated binding Hitler 'by an agreement bearing his signature freely and proudly given', which he thought that 'some odd kink' might impel him to honour.[10] Eden, meeting Hitler for the first time in February 1934, was impressed by his sincerity, and believed that he really wanted a disarmament agreement. The key to British thinking lay in their belief that the choice lay between an arms agreement and an arms race, which in turn meant war. The belief that a combination of arms races and alliances had produced the Great War was now widely accepted, and both were to be avoided. As MacDonald put it in March 1933, 'There was no sense in rushing into alliances and making Germany feel that she was being threatened.'[11]

There were some limitations on the British desire for a disarmament agreement, but these were not likely to cut much ice with the French. At the very time when MacDonald was putting forward his plan to bring about equality between the German and French armies, he told the Americans with artless simplicity that 'There were certain things which we could not do, even to bring about equality with Germany, e.g. scrap the British fleet . . .'[12] To MacDonald this was doubtless the merest common sense. To the French, it would have been a further demonstration that the British were willing to pursue a righteous cause at someone else's expense rather than their own.

DIFFERING ASSUMPTIONS AND CROSS-PURPOSES

The divergent policies followed by France and Britain on economic matters and disarmament were symptomatic of their different assumptions about international affairs and their deeply ingrained casts of mind. These assumptions, which influenced British and French actions for most of the 1930s, are worth pausing to examine.

The British took for granted the overriding importance of the

10. Phipps to Simon, 21 November 1933, ibid., vol. VI, No. 60.
11. Record of conversation with Benes, 13 March 1933, ibid., vol. IV, No. 298.
12. Record of conversation, 11 March 1933, ibid., No. 294.

Empire. Among Conservatives, it is true that Baldwin was not an ardent imperialist (but then he was not unduly ardent about any aspect of overseas affairs). Neville Chamberlain, who provided much of the energy and drive in the National government, was heir to his father's imperial sentiment. Halifax was a former Viceroy of India, and Hoare served a long and arduous spell as Secretary of State for India. Labour was in theory opposed to imperialism, but in practice did little to dismantle the empire of which it was supposed to disapprove. The Ottawa agreements of 1932 placed the Empire, and especially the Dominions, at the centre of British commercial policy. Strategically, the Admiralty always recognised that one of its tasks was to protect Australia and New Zealand, far away on the rim of the Pacific. But this was not one-way traffic. The lesson of the Great War was that, in the event of another conflict, Britain would need the help of the Dominions.

The Imperial–Commonwealth presence was also all-pervading in other ways. Empire Day was marked in schools. The Round Table group worked for imperial federation. Lord Beaverbrook's *Daily Express* was an Empire paper, and Beaverbrook himself was a Canadian. Many British families had relatives in one other of the Dominions. Cricket was a powerful bond. The immensely popular fiction of John Buchan was full of references to the Empire; his hero Richard Hannay was a Rhodesian; and Buchan himself ended his life as Governor-General of Canada.

The League of Nations shared pride of place with the Empire in the Pantheon of British opinion. The League of Nations Union was under royal patronage, its committee included the leaders of all three major political parties, and unusually among political organisations it was allowed to be active in schools. In the so-called 'Peace ballot' of 1935 the Union organised a vast questionnaire, in response to which some 11.5 million people declared their support for the League. This sentiment was deep-rooted and persistent. As late as June 1936 Duff Cooper, then Minister of War, made a speech to the *Association France–Bretagne* in Paris, in which he declared that friendship between France and Britain was not a matter of sentiment but of life and death; their frontiers and their ideals were both in mortal danger. On 29 June the Leader of the Labour Opposition, Clement Attlee, attacked this speech in the House of Commons on the ground that it made no reference to the Covenant of the League of Nations, but appeared to advocate a military alliance with France, which the Labour Party would in no way accept. For the government, Simon replied lamely that Duff Cooper had advocated Anglo-French understanding, but not at the expense of Germany, and that nothing derogatory to the League was implied. The episode is almost startlingly illuminating. By June 1936 the League was effectively defunct, killed in Ethiopia (as we shall see in the next chapter). Yet Attlee insisted that it should be referred to, and the government – whatever it really believed – did not dare to say that they were talking about a corpse.

The consequence of this cast of mind was to inhibit any realistic discussion of European policy or relations with France. Correlli Barnett has put it with characteristic vigour: 'They [British governments] did not dare to expose the League of Nations as the sentimental myth it was. . . . It was an essential aspect of the British tragedy then [1932] and later that public discussion on world affairs was almost wholly conducted in terms of idealistic humbug rather than in terms of uncomfortable and unlovely reality.'[13] This judgement is severe but accurate. There was a gap between the League mentality and the realities of international politics which could not be crossed. This situation was not new: the League provided a natural home for the Gladstonian tradition in British politics, which had long regarded foreign policy as a matter of morality rather than power.

The Empire–Commonwealth and the League of Nations were both world-wide in scope, and one result of their influence on British opinion was to prevent any sharp focusing of attention on European affairs, and even more on specific relations with France. But Europe was still there, and the British, whether they liked it or not, were still confronted by Germany and France.

The new Germany under Hitler presented some particularly difficult questions, and the British groped uncertainly for answers. There were a few who still thought in terms of a long-standing German menace, of which Hitler represented a new and ugly form. To Vansittart, the Permanent Under-Secretary at the Foreign Office, Germany was still 'the old Adam'. Warren Fisher, the permanent head of the Treasury, wrote in April 1934 about 'these Teutonic tribes, who century after century have been inspired by the philosophy of brute force', and thought that the British would be unusually stupid to assume that they had now been converted to the tenets of the Sermon on the Mount.[14] In January 1936 the aged Rudyard Kipling wrote that Germany 'has been explaining what she is arming for for 5 or 6 years – as she did for 6 or 7 before the war. In these matters I have noticed that she keeps her word.'[15]

13. Correlli Barnett, *The Collapse of British Power* (London, 1972), p. 303.
14. A.P. Adamthwaite, ed., *The Making of the Second World War* (2nd edn, London, 1979), Document No. 10.
15. Frank Field, *British and French Writers of the First World War* (Cambridge, 1991), p. 173. The chapter on Kipling is particularly striking.

But Kipling was by then discredited, and the extreme language used by Vansittart and Fisher made them appear unbalanced. Conventional wisdom was very different. The Treaty of Versailles had been far too harsh on Germany, and in the 1930s 'revision' was still the watchword. This belief in the injustice and errors of Versailles was held right across the political spectrum. Hitler's advent to power did not alter these basic assumptions. After all, a policy which was morally right and politically sensible before January 1933 did not cease to be so after that date. There was little active support for the doctrines of National Socialism, but Hitler himself succeeded in charming a string of visitors. The British were a profoundly non-ideological people, and among those who conducted foreign policy it was a long-standing tenet that the internal politics of another country were its own affair. In the light of common sense, it was clearly impossible to run a foreign policy which did not deal with dictators: Europe contained far too many of them. It was natural to assume, therefore, that the existing and acknowledged German grievances remained justified, and should be remedied, even though the German regime had changed. This was the essence of the policy which came to be called 'appeasement'.

Where did France fit into these British assumptions? J.-B. Duroselle, in his massive history of French foreign policy in the 1930s, argued that the National-Conservative majority which governed Britain from 1931 to 1940 was profoundly Francophobe. All three Prime Ministers (MacDonald, Baldwin and Neville Chamberlain) and most of the Foreign Secretaries (Simon, Hoare and Halifax) were unsympathetic to France. Only Eden was a Francophile. There is much truth in this.[16] MacDonald, Prime Minister of a Labour government in July 1931, blamed France for delaying the acceptance of the Hoover moratorium on debts and reparations: 'France has been playing its usual small-minded and selfish game over the Hoover proposal. . . . So Germany cracks while France bargains.'[17] Three and a half years later, in January 1935, the same MacDonald, now Prime Minister of a National government, was writing: 'France the cause of the later evolution of German policy is steeped in the militarist mind. Had there been no Tardieu there would have been no Chancellor Hitler.'[18] It was a standard accusation that France had missed one opportunity after

16. Duroselle, *Décadence*, p. 201; cf. R.A.C. Parker, *Chamberlain and Appeasement* (London, 1993), p. 11.
17. MacDonald diary, 5 July 1931, ibid., p. 16.
18. MacDonald diary, 9 January 1935, Nicholas Rostow, *Anglo-French Relations, 1934–36* (London, 1984), p. 85.

another to come to terms with Germany, particularly on the question of armaments. In March 1936, at the time of the German occupation of the Rhineland, Baldwin, by then Conservative Prime Minister, said that hopes had been blighted time after time by the French missing opportunities of accepting a German offer. Hugh Dalton, the Labour spokesman on foreign policy, said 'It is true that Hitler has broken treaty after treaty. It is also true that the French government have thrown away opportunity after opportunity of coming to terms with him.' Vansittart (who was in many ways a Francophile) commented in private that it was through French blindness that one opportunity after another to come to terms with Germany had been lost.[19]

Even Eden, when he visited Paris in February 1934, described the French Foreign Minister, Louis Barthou, as 'bristly and foxy. I should think a nasty old man at heart.' One of Eden's most sympathetic biographers, Robert Rhodes James, comments: 'Just as Eden loathed Prussian arrogance and brutality, so also did he despise the merciless Clemenceau generation that had been resolved to ruin and humiliate Germany and its fledgling democracy. In the front rank of that generation stood Barthou.'[20]

Moreover, British politicians looked back with dismay on what they regarded as the errors which had led to war in 1914. MacDonald's background lay in the Union of Democratic Control, which opposed secret diplomacy and argued that the military conversations with France before 1914 had dragged Britain into an unnecessary conflict. As Prime Minister, MacDonald retained some of these instincts, and in any case the standpoint of the Union of Democratic Control had become the accepted wisdom of the next generation. Military conversations were dangerous; the whole alliance system had been a major cause of the Great War. One great virtue of Locarno was that it was not an alliance, but a Franco-German agreement with outside guarantors. The name retained its magic ten years after, and in 1935 the British were anxious to secure an 'Air Locarno', by which the Locarno powers would guarantee one another against air attack.

Alliances and military conversations with the French had led Britain into the calamity of the Great War. 'Never again' was still the watchword of British opinion. In November 1934 the Committee of Imperial Defence estimated that there might well be a war with Germany in five years' time, which proved an uncommonly accurate forecast. But the Committee's minutes warned its members, and those

19. Quotations in this paragraph, Parker, *Chamberlain*, pp. 18, 63.
20. Robert Rhodes James, *Anthony Eden* (London, 1986), pp. 134–5.

who prepared its documents, that neither in confidential papers nor (*a fortiori*) in public should they use the words 'Expeditionary Force'. Memories of the Somme and Passchendaele cast a long, dark shadow.

All this added up to a deep distrust of France. The predominant impression was that the French were obstinate and obscurantist, vengeful in the 1920s and still in the 1930s missing one chance after another of coming to terms with Germany. These feelings were compounded by the extreme instability of French politics in the early 1930s, when governments succeeded one another with bewildering rapidity. In January 1934 the Stavisky scandal came to light – a sordid affair of fraud, involving about half-a-million francs worth of bonds issued by the *Crédit Municipal* of Bayonne. Stavisky was a flashy crook of no great importance, but his activities had involved deputies and even ministers, and the affair led to the fall of a government and eventually to the great riots of 6 February 1934, in which a Right-wing crowd came near to storming the Chamber of Deputies. These events naturally made a stir in the British press – Alexander Werth wrote particularly vivid accounts of the rioting for the *Manchester Guardian*. The Embassy in Paris, though firmly of the view that there was no serious Fascist movement in Paris, was badly worried. There was a dangerous breach between the people and the Assembly, and between Paris and the provinces. The parliamentary system had fallen into disrepute, of which the Stavisky affair was a symptom; and the younger generation had been affected by the anti-democratic current which was running through Europe. 'Democracy is now on trial here', pronounced the Ambassador on 20 March; and he thought that there would be few who would man the barricades to defend the present parliament.[21]

There was thus plenty to dismay the British in the France of the early 1930s. And yet, at bottom, the British still thought that they and the French were on the same side. It was *because* France was a parliamentary democracy, like Britain, that the riots of 6 February 1934 were disturbing. Even Baldwin knew that the frontier of British security lay on the Rhine – though it was not something that he liked to think about too much. There was a deep and disquieting discrepancy between the British carping about French policy and French politics and the feeling that, in case of necessity, the two countries would have to stand together.

The French for their part had some difficulty in focusing their vision of Europe and of relations with Britain. The time and energy of

21. FO 432/1, ff. 67–9, 118–20, 123–4. The quotation is from Tyrell to Simon, 20 March 1934, C1839/125/17.

governments were much taken up with parliamentary manoeuvres. Budgetary problems and the state of the franc dominated policy. Public opinion was confused, and foreign policy hamstrung, by ideological divisions. On the Right, Charles Maurras's *action française*, monarchist in inspiration, was now flanked by a crop of new organisations. Colonel de la Rocque's *croix de feu* was by far the strongest, and held impressive torch-light parades. The British Embassy was surely correct in diagnosing that Fascism had no serious hold in France, but near-Fascist groups were noisy and conspicuous. It was ominous that the crowds on 6 February 1934 were well dressed and middle-class. On the Left the Communists had fared badly in the elections of 1932, but recovered strongly in 1934 and 1935, benefiting from a reaction against the Right. They were well disciplined, and had the prestige of support by prominent intellectuals.

These groups on the extreme Right and Left looked abroad for their models, support, or even orders. The fascist-style groups and the *action française* looked to Mussolini's Italy with admiration, sometimes reinforced (as in the case of the *francistes*) by Italian funds. Attitudes towards Hitler and the Nazis were less clear-cut, because the French Right was divided between its traditional opposition to Germany on patriotic grounds and its admiration for a strong, anti-Bolshevik regime. A number of ex-servicemen's organisations, from the best of motives, became apologists for the Nazi regime. As for the Communists, they were ostentatiously Stalinist and clandestinely controlled and financed from Moscow. Sections of French opinion, whether of the Right or the Left, thus identified themselves with foreign powers in a way unknown in the simpler and more coherent Europe of before 1914.

Despite all these problems, the fundamental question for French foreign policy remained the same: how to achieve security in relation to Germany. In the late 1920s there seemed a good chance that this could be secured by Locarno, the League and goodwill. If all these failed, the French Army was strong in numbers and high in prestige, and France could rely on her own strength. During the early 1930s, all this ceased to be true. The advent of Hitler to power in Germany destroyed the notion of goodwill. German rearmament, which was clandestinely under way before the Nazis took power and advanced with greater speed and boldness thereafter, rapidly diminished French military superiority. The security of France was directly menaced, in a way unknown in Britain. What was to be done?

One answer was to revive a system of alliances. Louis Barthou, Foreign Minister from February to October 1934 (of whom Eden took such a poor view) believed that the policy of reconciliation with Germany practised by Briand had failed and must be abandoned. During his few months in office, he visited eastern European capitals to try to revive France's alliances with Poland, Czechoslovakia, Yugoslavia and Rumania. He sought an alliance with the Soviet Union, disregarding ideological considerations. What counted for him was the safety of France, which required the revival of the pre-1914 Russian alliance; and his secret negotiations ultimately resulted in the Franco-Soviet treaty of May 1935.

This policy encountered stiff opposition from Britain. The British deplored alliances, which would divide Europe into hostile camps and make the Germans feel threatened. Equally, they wanted no truck with the Soviet Union, which was Bolshevik and anti-imperialist. But Barthou, acting with an independence which had not been seen since the days of Poincaré, was willing to disregard the British complaints and take his own line. Whether he could have succeeded can never be known. On 9 October 1934, in pursuit of his alliance policies, Barthou welcomed King Alexander of Yugoslavia at Marseilles. Croat terrorists assassinated the King, and Barthou, riding in the same carriage, died of his wounds.

Barthou's successor as Foreign Minister was Laval, a shrewd and effective politician, with his roots in the provinces but at home in the intrigues of the capital. He dealt with foreign policy in the same way as with domestic politics, by keeping his options open and making as many agreements as he could. He visited Mussolini in January 1935, and later developed a series of military agreements with Italy. He went to Moscow to meet Stalin in May, after signing in Paris the Franco-Soviet treaty which Barthou had worked for. His fundamental approach to foreign policy was different from that of Barthou. Each sought to secure France from the German menace, but by opposite methods. Barthou tried to make alliances *against* Berlin; Laval wanted to use alliances in order to come to an agreement *with* Berlin. His attitude to Britain was ambiguous. Since Britain too wanted agreement with Germany, he became almost a rival suitor with the British for German favours. But at the same time, he believed that the British connection would always be there as a last resort. In this confidence, and relying boldly on his political dexterity, he was willing to take great risks in his relations with the British, with dangerous results.

This view of the British as a reliable last resort in French policy was of crucial importance. From the point of view of power politics, the Franco-Soviet alliance seemed to offer more advantages. So, in a different way, did an agreement with Italy, which secured France's

Alpine frontier. But from the point of view of French domestic politics and ideology, the Soviet and the Italian options aroused dissent and sowed confusion. An alliance with Moscow pleased the Communists and the realist Right; but it offended many on the Left because it was an alliance, and many on the Right because it was with Moscow. An alliance with Fascist Italy pleased the Right, whether for military or ideological reasons, but offended the whole of the Left. The result in both cases was an arrangement which made much sense in terms of pre-1914 foreign policy; but unhappily 1914 was long ago and the ideological confusion in France was such that no French statesman, however hard-headed or cynical, could operate simply on the basis of power politics. From this impasse Britain might still offer an escape. At least the British were neither fascist nor communist, and even though the record of their policy towards Germany in the 1920s was distasteful to France, there was a feeling that ultimately they would be on the same side. It was not far from the view that the British took of the French.

The assumptions made by the two countries often set them against one another. The British were against alliances; the French sought to reinforce them. The British preferred to disregard ideology in the conduct of foreign policy; the French were enmeshed in it. The British thought the French were militarist and harsh in their policy towards Germany, the French thought the British were blind in their inability (or refusal) to see where German policy was heading. But at bottom each thought the other would be there in case of absolute need. The memory of 1914–18 was not yet dead. Unhappily, that memory cut two ways. Neither Britain nor France wanted to repeat the experience of the Great War. The British wanted no more talk of an Expeditionary Force, because in the past that had led to the Somme. The French wanted no more Verduns. The memories which drew them together also forced them apart.

CHAPTER 11

Storm Cone, 1935

1935 was a year of storm and stress in Anglo-French relations. The Anglo-German Naval Agreement of June 1935, and the Ethiopian crisis which simmered for much of the year before boiling over in the autumn, saw the two countries at loggerheads with one another. They did not come to an open breach, but their relations suffered profound damage.

THE ANGLO-GERMAN NAVAL AGREEMENT

The origins of the Anglo-German Naval Agreement, on the British side, lie in the development of British policy on armaments since 1932. In that year, the British Cabinet accepted in principle the abandonment of the so-called 'Ten Year Rule' – the working assumption that there would be no major war for ten years. For some time, abandoning the Ten Year Rule was as much a fiction as the Rule itself had been. While the Disarmament Conference still held hopes of success the government could not contemplate rearmament, and not until November 1933 did the Cabinet set guidelines for defence expenditure to replace the Ten Year assumption. British defence requirements were put in an order of priority: (1) British interests in the Far East; (2) commitments in Europe; and (3) the defence of India. The priority allocated to the Far East reflected the anxiety arising out of Japanese aggression in Manchuria and China, and is essential to an understanding of the events of 1935. If the prime enemy was Japan, then the Navy needed sufficient security in European waters to be able to send a fleet to the Far East. In 1934 and early 1935, the Germans were well aware of British anxieties about Japan, and exploited them in pressing for an Anglo-German naval agreement.

During 1934, three pressures were at work in the British discussions on defence requirements and expenditure. One was the desire to keep down the armaments bill, which meant that the government always looked for the cheapest way to rearm. The second was the ominous accumulation of evidence that German rearmament was proceeding at a rapid pace. The RAF knew the Germans were building military aircraft and training pilots. By November 1934 there were reports that the German Army was already approaching 300,000 men. In that month the Cabinet set up a committee to assess the progress of German rearmament; though at the end of its deliberations the committee only recommended helplessly that it would be useless to formulate a policy and dangerous to announce one. The third pressure was the long-standing determination to avoid any firm commitment to France, especially on land. In May 1934, Simon, the Foreign Secretary, told the Cabinet that everyone agreed that Germany could not be allowed to 'eat up' France, but he asked whether it would be necessary to send a land force to prevent this – could not the Royal Air Force do the job? (He was disappointed when the Chiefs of Staff said that it could not.) Early in January 1935, in discussions to prepare for a visit to London by French ministers, Simon himself had come to believe that France would have to be given some reassurance. He therefore wished to reaffirm Britain's commitment to the demilitarised zone in the Rhineland, and to permit staff conversations with the French. The Cabinet overruled him on both counts, holding that the demilitarised Rhineland was not a vital British interest, and that the staff talks before 1914 had dragged Britain into war and committed the BEF to the campaign on the western front. Even a limited proposal by Simon, to make a firm statement to the French that an attack on Belgium would be regarded as an attack on Britain, was resisted by Chamberlain on the ground that Britain could not protect Belgium without the help of France, and therefore a commitment to Belgium would amount to a commitment to France – which was to be avoided. Simon yielded the point.

These pressures pushed the British in different directions, reinforcing an already strong tendency to avoid difficult decisions. The best course they could think of was to accept that German rearmament was already a fact. This would mean abandoning the disarmament clauses of the Treaty of Versailles, which Simon admitted would be 'a bitter pill for the French to swallow, especially as they don't believe in any German promise.'[1] In return for this acceptance of the *fait accompli*, Simon hoped to secure the return of Germany to the League of Nations, and if possible achieve a general agreement on arms limitation. MacDonald took much the same line in Cabinet: they would have to make it plain to the French that 'it would not be enough to be bound to a kind of stilted logic. Facts must be faced.'[2] The British were thus prepared to face the fact of German rearmament, as they had done for some time; but they still hoped that this might be neutralised through a general armaments agreement. If that proved out of reach, then the next best solution would be a limited armaments agreement. The possibility of such an agreement was signalled by Hitler to Phipps, the British Ambassador in Berlin, on 27 November 1934. Hitler remarked that he did not contemplate building a fleet to compete with the Royal Navy, and would be content with 35 per cent of the British tonnage.

British policy was thus moving towards an acceptance of German rearmament, but hoping to gain something in return for that acceptance. But suddenly, in March 1935, within the space of eight days, Germany simply denounced the land and air disarmament clauses of the Treaty of Versailles. On 9 March the Germans announced that they already had a military Air Force, and on the 16th they proclaimed the introduction of conscription and the creation of an Army of 36 divisions.

The British tried to carry on as though nothing had happened. In February 1935 it had been arranged for Simon to visit Hitler in Berlin. After the German announcement about the Air Force, Simon said that he still wished to go ahead with this visit. After the announcement about conscription, the British government issued a purely formal protest, and again let Simon's visit stand. Simon, accompanied by Eden, duly went to Berlin on 25–26 March. During the conversations Hitler made the alarming claim that the German Air Force had already attained parity with the RAF. He also returned to the idea of a bilateral naval agreement between Germany and Britain, starting with a claim for parity between the German and French fleets (which would have meant a force more than half the size of the Royal Navy), and then reverting to the figure of 35 per cent. The idea of 35 per cent was thus made to look like a German concession. Hitler proposed that German representatives should visit London shortly to discuss a naval agreement on these lines, and Simon agreed.

1. David Dutton, *Simon: A political biography of Sir John Simon* (London, 1992), p. 188.

2. Nicholas Rostow, *Anglo-French Relations, 1934–36* (London, 1984), p. 49.

In these discussions, the British had acted alone in a matter which demanded consultation with France. At an Anglo-French conference in London in January 1935, the two governments had agreed on the principle of joint negotiations with Germany on armaments questions, and had rejected the idea of unilateral changes in the disarmament clauses of the Treaty of Versailles. Simply by going to Berlin, Simon had condoned the German denunciation of Versailles, in which France was an equal partner with Britain; and by accepting conversations about a naval agreement he had broken the pledge about joint negotiations. The French had every right to be affronted, but Laval's immediate reaction was muted and ambiguous. He insisted on consultations with Britain and Italy about German rearmament, which led to the holding of a three-power conference at Stresa in April. But he avoided any confrontation with the British, and urged French newspapers to tone down their criticisms of the British actions. In this, it seems that his main motive was that he too wished to improve relations with Germany, and so he sought to keep the temperature down.

The three-power conference at Stresa (11–14 April 1935) was inconclusive. The three governments (Britain, France and Italy) declared that they would oppose by all practical means the unilateral repudiation of treaties when such repudiation might endanger the peace of Europe. The fact that Germany had indeed just repudiated a treaty, with consequent danger to the peace of the continent, was passed over. During the meeting, MacDonald insisted that the object of British policy was to bring Germany back into the League, and to co-operate with France and Italy 'to make the League supreme as the moral authority of Europe . . .'[3]

This was a perfect example of the League mentality, unless it was merely an attempt at deception. In practice, the British set out, without reference to the League or to France and Italy, to reach a naval agreement with Germany. In doing so, they acted with almost indecent haste. On 21 May, in a much-heralded speech on foreign policy, Hitler publicly offered Britain a naval agreement with the German fleet at 35 per cent of the British. The British Ambassador in Berlin commented that as recently as March Hitler had been talking about naval equality with France and Italy, while his present proposal would mean a 15 per cent inferiority to those countries. Therefore, the Ambassador concluded, 'I think that not only we but the French and Italians should feel thankful for small mercies, and that we should

3. Ibid., p. 146.

not miss opportunities in the naval sphere, like we have done on land and in the air, owing to French short-sightedness.'[4] In London, Neville Chamberlain was 'intensely relieved' by Hitler's speech. Hankey, the Secretary to the Cabinet, advocated rapid action to get a deal. 'If the French are nasty', he wrote, 'we must put the strongest pressure on them . . . they cannot do without us. We are the soundest, the solidest and the most reliable people in Europe, as well as potentially the strongest – and the French know it.'[5]

No time was lost. The first meeting between British and German delegations took place in London on 4 June 1935. Ribbentrop, Ambassador in London and head of the German team, at once insisted that the British must accept the 35 per cent ratio as unalterable before any discussions began. The British accepted this on 6 June, though with the proviso that the proportion should apply to categories of warship as well as to total tonnage. An agreement was signed on 18 June, after only fourteen days of discussions – something utterly unprecedented in the whole history of prolonged and tortuous negotiations about naval armaments in the 1920s and 1930s. The treaty ratified the 35 per cent ratio, except for submarines, where the Germans were to have 45 per cent of the British tonnage, with the right to build up to 100 per cent when, in Germany's opinion, it was necessary to do so. The main reason for haste, as explained by the British delegation at the talks, was to grasp the German proposal while it was still on offer. To let it slip would only mean that the Germans would soon go over the 35 per cent mark, and the British would be left regretting that they had missed their chance – the error which they regularly attributed to the French. The delegation argued that the offer was so important that the British should not withhold acceptance 'merely on the ground that other Powers might feel some temporary annoyance at our action'.[6]

This last reference was primarily to the French, who had indeed much reason for annoyance. It is true that in February 1935 the British had given France indirect warning of their intentions; but when the talks themselves began, the British accepted a request by Ribbentrop that they should be confidential, with no communication to other governments except as agreed between the participants. The British

4. Phipps to Simon, 23 May 1935, *DBFP*, series 2, vol. XIII, No. 230.
5. Rostow, *Anglo-French Relations*, p. 167.
6. *DBPF*, series 2, vol. XIII, No. 305 and annexe. The importance of insisting that the figure of 35 per cent should apply to categories of warship as well as to the total tonnage was that it would exclude concentration of all building on one type, e.g. submarines, which would give Germany superiority in that particular category.

kept this agreement with a scrupulousness worthy of a better cause. While the talks were in progress, the information available to the French Naval Attaché dried up, and his reports to Paris were drawn entirely from the press – though in fact the articles in the *Daily Telegraph* by J. C. Bywater proved very close to the mark. Not until 18 June, after the agreement was signed, did the First Sea Lord, Admiral Chatfield, see the Naval Attaché to give him an account of the meetings. Chatfield was full of assurances. The figure of 35 per cent was better than leaving the Germans free to build as they wished. He had not lost sight of French interests during the talks, and indeed the interests of France and Britain were linked together – 'what was good for England was equally good for France', as he hopefully explained.[7]

Superficially and in the short run, the French reaction to these events was remarkably passive. They made no intervention while the talks were going on until 17 June, when it was effectively too late. In a note delivered on that date they pointed out that to concede Germany's naval demands would set a precedent for other claims, and for the British to do so unilaterally would be in breach of the agreements made in London in January and at Stresa in April. On 19 June Laval spoke to the Foreign Affairs Commission of the Chamber of Deputies, playing down the differences with Britain about the Naval Agreement, and giving the members a little homily on French and British ways of thought – the French were concerned with principles, as set out in the Treaty of Versailles, the British with facts as they stood at the present time. On 21 June Eden (recently appointed as Minister for League of Nations Affairs) went to Paris to see Laval and the Minister of Marine, Piétri. Taking his lead from Laval's remarks to the Commission, he accepted that the French had a strong case for complaint from a juridical point of view, but argued that practical considerations were more important. His reception was cool but not hostile. Laval criticised the British tactics, which he said had alienated French opinion, but he accepted the 35 per cent figure with little ado. He refused to send naval experts to London to discuss the details, on the ground that this would show too much complicity in what the British had done; but that was a minor matter.

It was all very low-key, and it seemed as though the British had carried through what they saw as a limited manoeuvre to protect their own naval position without serious damage to their relations with the French. The truth was very different. Behind a façade of restraint,

7. *Archives Marine*, Vincennes, 1 BB7, 34 (1935), Naval Attaché, *Compte rendu de renseignements*, No. 25, 18 June 1935.

Laval was furious, both on grounds of French interests and because he had been outplayed at his own game. The master of political manoeuvre found himself outmanoeuvred.[8] At the time he kept his anger to himself, but later in the year, during the Ethiopian crisis, and later still during the Second World War, he was ready to take his revenge. Admiral Darlan, the Chief of the French Naval Staff, was also offended that the British had acted alone, and the experience of 1935 weighed heavily with him in 1940, when he was afraid that Britain would again reach an agreement with Germany at the expense of France.[9]

It might in the long run have been better for Anglo-French relations if Laval had spoken his mind, as Clemenceau or Poincaré would surely have done; but that was not his way. As it was, the British seemed unaware of the consequences of their actions. They were taken by surprise when a wave of French resentment struck them later in the year, and they showed no understanding that their conduct over the Naval Agreement might inhibit them in taking a high moral tone over the Ethiopian crisis, which was lurking in the background in the early months of 1935.

DISCORD OVER ETHIOPIA

The Ethiopian crisis of 1935–36 was a tangled affair. The initiative lay with Italy. As long ago as 1896 the Ethiopians had defeated an Italian army at the battle of Adowa, and the idea of revenge for this humiliation had lingered in Italian minds. In the mid-1930s Mussolini was anxious to show that his Fascist state could succeed where the old Italy had failed. His plans took definite shape in 1932, and at the end of 1934 he laid down that the objective was to be the total conquest of Ethiopia. In December 1934 there was a clash between Italian and Ethiopian troops at Wal-Wal, near an ill-demarcated frontier, and from February 1935 onwards the Italians moved large forces through the Suez Canal and the Red Sea to Eritrea. These movements were necessarily conspicuous, and it was obvious that an Italian invasion of Ethiopia was imminent. It began on 3 October 1935.

Before 1914, these events might not have produced a severe international crisis. At that time it was common for European states to occupy parts of Africa, and under pre-1914 conventions, if Italy had secured the consent of Britain and France as the major powers

8. Fred Kupferman, *Laval* (Paris, 1987), p. 150.
9. Hervé Coutau-Bégarie et Claude Huan, *Darlan* (Paris, 1989), pp. 162–3.

concerned, there would have been no reason why the operation should not have gone forward as many other colonial wars had done. But since the creation of the League of Nations, new rules were supposed to apply. Ethiopia was a member of the League, with in principle the same standing and rights as any other member. Britain and France therefore faced a complicated problem. They were both colonial powers, and saw Italian ambitions in Ethiopia as another colonial question. They were European powers, concerned with the role of Italy in the European balance, especially as an ally against Germany. Britain was also a world power, anxious about the threat from Japan in the Far East and faced with the problem of stretching limited naval strength to meet too many commitments. But both Britain and France were also leading members of the League of Nations, and Britain in particular had a highly influential League-minded element in its public opinion. The two governments had to juggle with all these different aspects of the problem, and devise policies which would keep all the balls in the air at once. Preferably they both wanted to do so while remaining in harmony with one another – a sort of double juggling act. It is not altogether surprising that they failed.

To elucidate a complicated story, it is best to look first at how France and Britain saw the situation separately, and then turn to how they tried to deal with it together.

For the first half of 1935 the French regarded Ethiopia as merely a minor aspect of their policy towards Italy. Laval, then Foreign Minister, visited Rome on 4–8 January 1935, and signed a number of agreements with Mussolini, dealing with minor African matters. They also agreed to consult together if Germany attempted to bring about the *Anschluss* with Austria which was constantly threatened, or if Germany were to embark on open rearmament. Laval and Mussolini held one of their meetings without other witnesses, and it was an open question whether on this occasion Laval offered Mussolini a free hand in Ethiopia. Mussolini said later that he had. Laval insisted that he had referred only to economic affairs and action for peaceful purposes. It may be that there was simply a misunderstanding, perhaps arising from Mussolini's defective understanding of French. What is certain is that Laval did not regard Ethiopia as being of any great importance, and he did not see Italian ambitions there as an obstacle to good Franco-Italian relations.

After the Rome meetings, France and Italy moved towards a military agreement directed against Germany. On 27 June 1935 the Italian and French Chiefs of Staff, Badoglio and Gamelin, agreed on a set of arrangements for mutual assistance in the event of German aggression in either the Rhineland or Austria. While Gamelin was in Rome for the military talks, Mussolini told him that he intended to settle matters in Ethiopia, but would not allow this to weaken the Italian position on the Brenner Pass, between Italy and Austria. There is no sign that Gamelin demurred, and there was every appearance that Italy was offering France military support in Europe in exchange for a free hand against Ethiopia.

On grounds of European politics and strategy, this made good sense to the French government. Their main enemy was Germany, and Italian support was well worth having. (It should be emphasised that at the time Italian military strength, especially in the air, was rated highly.) In this context, the fate of Ethiopia was no more than a secondary matter. It is true that there were problems in terms of French public opinion, because the Left remained opposed to Mussolini and the Fascist regime; but as long as the issue was simply one of French security, it seemed that dissent on the Left could be contained. But when Italy actually invaded Ethiopia, and began to use aerial bombardment and poison gas against the population, there was a powerful reaction, not only on the Left. French opinion became sharply divided, and the former policy based on European calculations became hard to carry through.

The French also encountered increasing difficulties in their relations with Britain over the Ethiopian issue. In the first half of 1935 there had been no particular problem in combining French agreements with Italy with their existing links with Britain. But the actual Italian attack on Ethiopia changed the situation. As we shall shortly see, the British adopted at least an outward policy of opposition to the Italian invasion, threatening the French government with the danger of having to choose between Britain and Italy. If this choice were forced upon them, the French were in a cleft stick. To alienate Italy would mean forfeiting all the military advantages which they had just gained in the Gamelin–Badoglio agreements. There would, for example, be no prospect whatsoever that the British would make up for the large forces which the Italians had promised to send to France in the event of German aggression in the Rhineland. On the other hand, to break with Britain would undermine basic assumptions in French policy, and in the long term be a disaster. The only sensible course for the French was to try to avoid such a choice; and this sort of prevarication fitted in well with Laval's temperament and habits. To avoid choosing between Italy and Britain was the purpose of most of his actions in the autumn of 1935.

Britain too was in a state of uncertainty about the Ethiopian question. As an African power, established in Egypt, the Sudan and East Africa, Britain was bound to be concerned about Italian ambitions in Ethiopia, and particularly with possible Italian control of the Blue Nile. However, an examination of these problems concluded in June 1935 that, so long as the flow of the Blue Nile was safeguarded, there was no reason for Britain to intervene. As a European power, Britain had some reason to support Italy, on much the same grounds as the French. Those who continued to fear the German menace wished to secure the support of Mussolini against Hitler. Vansittart, the Permanent Under-Secretary at the Foreign Office, argued this case with particular force, maintaining that Italian expansion into Ethiopia was going to occur anyway, that the French were willing to accept it, and that Britain should do the same. The Cabinet accepted the gist of this argument, though only in part and with less ruthlessness than Vansittart would have wished. In June 1935 Eden, the Minister for League of Nations Affairs, was despatched to Rome to persuade Mussolini to settle for something less than he actually wanted in Ethiopia, and to secure it less forcibly than he intended. If this mission had succeeded, then British policy would have been on a course more or less parallel to that of France.

But British policy had to take account of other matters than interests in Africa or Europe. The League of Nations loomed large in British opinion, and the crisis itself developed at the same time as the declaration of the results of the so-called 'Peace Ballot' in June 1935, which emphasised the extent of public support for the League. Moreover, Baldwin had just taken over from MacDonald as Prime Minister, and wished to hold a general election in the autumn, and in those circumstances everyone knew that the government must express its whole-hearted support for the League. It is true that some ministers expected that such support would be no more than a pretence. Neville Chamberlain wrote that Britain and France should explore sanctions and find they would be futile; they would then inform the League of their conclusions. Samuel Hoare, the new Foreign Secretary, talked of 'playing out the League hand', so that it was the League itself, not Britain, which declared that sanctions against Italy would be impractical.[10]

The British government therefore embarked on two contradictory policies. One, based on power politics, sought to satisfy Italy by the sacrifice of parts of Ethiopia, and to secure an Italian alliance against

10.   R.A.C. Parker, *Chamberlain and Appeasement* (London, 1993), pp. 49–50.

Germany. This led eventually to the proposals for concessions to Italy agreed on by Hoare and Laval in December 1935 – the so-called Hoare–Laval Pact. The other, based on the need to satisfy public opinion, was one of support for the League of Nations and collective security. In large part, the second policy was adopted in the hope that it would only be a cover for the first, but in fact it developed a life of its own. Ultimately, it proved impossible for Britain to run the two policies at the same time; but for some months the attempt was made.

If the League policy was to be carried through, it raised the possibility of war with Italy. Could Britain risk such a war? This was primarily a naval question, and it received two quite different answers. As far as the C-in-C of the Mediterranean Fleet was concerned, he had no doubt that he could beat the Italians. The First Sea Lord, Admiral Chatfield, agreed; but he also had to look at the whole strategic situation across the world – Home waters, the Mediterranean, and the Far East. A war with Italy would make it impossible simultaneously to protect British interests in the Far East against Japan, and even a victorious battle might well involve losses which would take a long time to make good. The Admiralty therefore argued that Britain should not get into a war with Italy without being sure of French support, not in some vague diplomatic way but in precise and practical matters: the use of French bases at Toulon and Bizerta, and support by the French fleet and Air Force. Only this would make war with Italy an acceptable proposition in the global context.[11]

France and Britain thus each regarded the Ethiopian problem from its own point of view, but in practice neither could act in isolation. The French wanted at the very least to avoid a choice between Italy and Britain, and to avoid a break with the British. The British knew that a League policy, involving the danger of war with Italy, depended on French support. The two powers had to try to act in concert.

In the event, they adopted two lines of policy which they hoped would be complementary but which proved to be contradictory. The first was a policy of sanctions against Italy. On 11 September 1935 Hoare, the British Foreign Secretary, made a speech at Geneva, in ringing tones, to the effect that the League stood, and Britain stood with it, for collective resistance to all acts of unprovoked aggression. This was essentially a bluff, designed partly to put pressure on Mussolini to negotiate, and partly for domestic consumption in Britain. It was never meant to be fully carried out. Hoare and Laval had

---

11. Arthur J. Marder, *From the Dardanelles to Oran* (London, 1974), p. 88; and see the whole chapter, pp. 64–104.

already agreed between themselves that they would not use military sanctions, and that any economic sanctions introduced would be applied cautiously. In fact, the Italians went ahead with their invasion of Ethiopia, and the League introduced limited economic sanctions on 18 November. These were enough to cause considerable difficulties for the Italian economy (and no small damage to the countries which applied them), but not enough to halt the Italian operations. Both France and Britain opposed the addition of an oil embargo, which if tightly applied might have had severe effects – though no-one knew when, because the Italians had stocks of oil to draw on.

The policy of sanctions was thus no more than a half-measure. Even so, it involved the risk of conflict with Italy. To insure against that risk, and to bring psychological pressure to bear on the Italians, the British moved large naval forces to the Mediterranean in late September, and they asked for assurances of French support in the event of war. As we have seen, the Admiralty believed that support to be vital; but at first they did not get it. The first French reply was that British warships would not even be allowed to use the naval bases at Toulon and Bizerta. The British government then put heavy pressure on the French – Laval complained to Gamelin that the British were treating France as though she were Portugal. He complained, but he gave way. On 18 October he agreed that British warships could use French bases in case of need, and that the naval staffs should hold conversations. These talks began, but without conviction – the French representatives explained to their British counterparts that they were keeping the talks secret from their own Foreign Ministry! The British officers involved concluded that they could not entirely rely on French support being forthcoming. So even the half-hearted policy of sanctions brought the British and French into grave difficulties on a crucial point.

Meanwhile, the two countries were also pursuing their second line of policy, which in private they much preferred: to negotiate a settlement with Italy at the expense of Ethiopia. The British had begun this policy in June 1935, when Eden visited Rome and suggested large concessions by Ethiopia in return for an outlet to the sea at the expense of British Somaliland. At the time this got nowhere. In August, at meetings in Paris, Laval, Eden and an Italian representative discussed the idea of granting Italy a form of disguised protectorate over Ethiopia, theoretically under the auspices of the League; but Mussolini was not interested. The British and French did not give up, and pursued the idea of a protectorate during September at meetings in Geneva hotel rooms. On 1 November, at a meeting with Laval in Geneva, Hoare reverted to the idea of territorial concessions by Ethiopia; Laval indicated that he had no preference as between such concessions and an Italian protectorate.

These tortuous but persistent discussions came to a head on 8 December 1935, when Hoare visited Laval in Paris. This time, they agreed on a package which would offer Mussolini more than they had proposed before. Ethiopia should cede a large part of its territory to Italy outright, and reserve another part for exclusive Italian economic exploitation. The surviving rump of the country should receive as compensation for its losses a strip of British Somaliland giving access to the sea. These proposals were to be put to Mussolini, the Emperor of Ethiopia (Haile Selassie) and the Council of the League as the basis for a settlement. In essence, these ideas were not new, but on this occasion the secrecy which had remarkably been preserved at Geneva was broken in Paris. On 13 December two French newspapers published accurate reports of the Hoare–Laval proposals, with devastating effects, not so much in France as in Britain.

In mid-October 1935 the Conservatives had won a general election by a large majority, campaigning (among other things) on a strong pro-League platform. The Hoare–Laval plan, which amounted to a betrayal of the League and Ethiopia, and a reversal of the sanctions policy, provoked a sharp response. In part this was orchestrated by the League of Nations Union, but the reaction also came from Conservative stalwarts in the constituencies. One minister told the Cabinet on 18 December that he was receiving terrible letters from 'the best people' in his constituency, which he had represented for twenty-five years and knew well.[12] The scale of the movement of public opinion is difficult to establish, but its effects were powerful. Baldwin, who prided himself on his political antennae, made a sort of confession to the House of Commons on 19 December:

> I was not expecting that deeper feeling which was manifested by many of my Hon. Friends and friends in many parts of the country on what I may call the grounds of conscience and of honour. The moment I am confronted with that I know that something has happened that has appealed to the deepest feelings of our countrymen, that some note has been struck that brings back from them a response from the depths . . .[13]

Baldwin confessed, but it was Hoare who was compelled to take the blame and resign, while the Prime Minister and the Cabinet, who had in broad terms approved Hoare's mission, remained in office.

12. CAB 23/87, Confidential Annex, 18 December 1935.
13. *H.C. Deb.*, 5th series, vol. 307, cols. 2034–5.

In France, where consciences were less tender, Laval took responsibility for his own policy and survived a vote of confidence. But he had effectively lost the support of the Radical ministers in his government, who resigned their offices towards the end of January 1936 and brought down the government. The Hoare–Laval proposals, whose publication had caused all the furore, were allowed to drop. Thus the second line of Anglo-French policy came to a muddled and humiliating end.

The whole Ethiopian episode was a disaster for relations between France and Britain. The policy of sanctions demanded a co-operation between the two countries which chafed upon them both. Laval found the British demands for naval co-operation overbearing; the British found the French response to those demands evasive. The leaking of the Hoare–Laval proposals convinced the British that the French could not keep a secret. From the French point of view, the British proved thoroughly unreliable. They abandoned an agreement which had been worked out after long discussions, amid high-flown references to deep feelings, conscience and honour. To the French this was plain hypocrisy – always one of their favourite accusations against the British. In each country, harsh ideas about the other were encouraged and confirmed.

When all was over, nothing had been gained and much lost. Not even a part of Ethiopia was saved. In May 1936 the Italians occupied Addis Ababa, and Haile Selassie was driven into exile. The League was discredited by the failure of sanctions and Anglo-French double-dealing. The French lost their military agreements with Italy, and Gamelin asked forlornly whether the British would make up for the loss. His question was purely rhetorical, because he knew the answer already: there was no question of the British replacing the French forces which would now have to be deployed on the Italian frontier instead of the German. The British too now faced a hostile Italy and insecure communications through the Mediterranean, with dangerous consequences for their strategic situation across the globe. Their politicians and public opinion also lost the whole set of assumptions bound up with the League of Nations, though in practice it took some time for this to sink in. The two countries together now faced the challenge of a resurgent and menacing Germany with what remained of their unity – which was not much – in tatters.

SOME FRENCH VIEWS OF BRITAIN: DESPAIR OR DISLIKE?

The events of 1935 gave a sharp stimulus to Anglophobia in France, for reasons which can well be understood. But before examining the revival of these deep-seated antagonisms, we must note what was in many ways a more disquieting phenomenon in French opinion. In the early 1930s a number of writers profoundly sympathetic to Britain and convinced of the need for Franco-British friendship became gloomy about the prospects of their neighbours across the Channel.

André Siegfried had long been an affectionate and well-informed observer of Britain and the British. He was a Protestant, with an insight into the workings of the British mind, especially in the north of England and Scotland, which Catholics or atheists did not find easy. He had served with the British Army in the Great War, and admired the courage, tenacity and good humour of its soldiers. He combined the intellectual rigour of a French academic with the personal touch of deep friendships in Britain. This background gave particular weight to an acute analysis of Britain's position, written in 1930 and published in March 1931 as *La crise britannique au XXe siècle*. The book was in publishing terms an instant success, and reached a fourth edition by November that same year, when the author was able to point out to critics who thought he had been too pessimistic that the crisis which he had diagnosed beneath the surface had become obvious in the intervening months.

Siegfried's analysis had two main aspects, economic and psychological. The economic problem was that British predominance, founded in the nineteenth century, depended on conditions which had vanished in the twentieth. The pace of economic change and the rise of commercial rivals had produced a state, not so much of crisis, as of a chronic illness resulting in steady economic decline.

These observations later became staple fare in discussions of British economic decline. But it was Siegfried's psychological diagnosis that was the more striking. Siegfried found that the British were still buoyed up by an optimism amounting to complacency. The British people as a whole had not yet grasped that there was a problem: 'their optimism, made up of patriotism and torpor, is ineradicable'. They retained a strong sense of superiority over the 'continent'. The ordinary Englishman, Siegfried wrote, had a deeply condescending attitude towards his neighbours. He would not believe that Europe was modernising, that European hotels had baths and running water, or (more important) that competition to British products arose from technical progress. Competition, for the British, was always 'unfair'. Siegfried was convinced that the British were too lazy to think about their problems. 'The mental laziness of the English is extraordinary: they do not like to weary themselves with thought . . .' This was not just intellectual laziness. The British had immense physical courage, as they had shown in the war, but not the courage to settle down to work. The ruling classes set a bad example because it was not gentlemanly to work too hard or to do anything very well. Even British political stability, which Siegfried thought was still the envy of the world, contributed to the country's inertia.[14]

Siegfried reflected in prophetic strain on Britain's position as a world and a European power. Using the simplest economic facts, he explained Britain's dependence on imports (to feed her people and provide raw materials for industry), exports (to pay for her imports), and foreign exchange. Britain's essential interests were thus bound up with her sea communications, her ability to trade, and her control of international finance. Britain was therefore a world power, not from ambition, but out of necessity – 'condemned to having a world policy' was Siegfried's striking phrase.[15] This position was becoming increasingly difficult to sustain and the British were beginning reluctantly to recognise that the country must find a place in some international combination. 'So is she to turn towards the oceans, to try to share in the youth of the new Anglo-Saxon societies, or is she to return in the end to the old world, from which her culture sprang? It is such a current, such a pressing problem, that every alert Englishman today is constantly aware of it.'[16]

Siegfried was in no doubt about the attractions for the British of the 'Anglo-Saxon' option. The instinctive British reaction after the Great War had been to turn their backs on Europe and look to the English-speaking world. The Empire alone would not suffice. MacDonald, Baldwin and Lloyd George all thought that the Americans would have to be brought in. This would not be easy. The Americans did not like the British, and distrusted 'perfidious Albion' in much the same way as the French. Worse, if an Anglo-American partnership developed, the USA would certainly be the senior partner. At this point, Siegfried found the psychology of Anglo-American relations hard to grasp. In the past, the British had fought great wars to retain

14. André Siegfried, *La crise britannique au XXe siècle* (Paris, first published, 1931; the quotations are from the 1952 edition), pp. 19, 115; see generally pp. 113–26.

15. Ibid., p. 185.

16. Ibid., p. 194.

command of the sea, yet now they simply handed it over at the request of the Americans. This was partly out of necessity, but at a deeper level the British did not see the United States as a power like other powers, or the Americans as really foreigners. Siegfried reflected that it was almost as though Britain, sensing her age, was ready to let the youngster take over, feeling that the business would still after all be in the family. And yet, when the British thought about it, they still found the change painful.

As for Europe – that old world from which British culture had emerged – Siegfried had no doubt that the British did not feel themselves to be European. Their island was like a ship, anchored off the continent but always ready to put to sea. Yet they could not break free from the continent. Europe was simply too close for the British to separate themselves completely from it. So Siegfried concluded that Britain would refuse to make the choice between the Anglo-Saxon world across the oceans and Europe across the Channel. 'Faithful to her tradition, and also to her innate character, she will doubtless remain between the two groups, without giving herself completely to either of them.'[17] France would simply have to accept this and make the best of it, using Britain as a link between Europe and the rest of the world.

In the last resort, Siegfried strove to retain his faith in Britain. Behind everything, he wrote, there was still 'L'Angleterre tout court', whose heart was sound. 'The English people is, above all, a first-rate people.'[18] It was a vote of confidence, still oddly comforting to a British reader; but it was scarcely justified by the body of the book. Siegfried firmly believed that a strong and reliable Britain was vital to France, and he desperately wanted to believe that such a Britain still existed. Yet what his analysis actually showed was a Britain in deep crisis, without the will or the capacity to escape, and enmeshed in a world role which was becoming increasingly unsustainable. In the midst of their problems, the British were left hesitating between the old Europe and the Anglo-Saxon world, and the best that Siegfried could offer his compatriots was that Britain would be a link with the rest of the world. To be in search of an ally and find the political equivalent of a hyphen was far from encouraging.

Siegfried, with his Protestant upbringing and his understanding of northern England, continued to emphasise the significance of the religious inheritance in British politics. He was not alone. In 1933 the novelist Jules Romains (whose series of novels *Les Hommes de bonne volonté* enjoyed great success) wrote a remarkable commentary on the

17. Ibid., p. 210.
18. Ibid., Preface to the fourth edition.

English conscience. He found the key to what he called the perpetual idealism of the English people in:

> their natural tendency to be deeply moved by an exhortation or an objection made in the name of a moral ideal or moral law; all material interests are then abruptly set aside. It is, you might say, the legacy of the puritans and of Cromwell.

This sentiment, Romains believed, was present in no more than three million people, but if those three million felt strongly enough, then Britain and the Empire would follow.[19] André Maurois (who since the days of Colonel Bramble had become one of the most popular French interpreters of Britain and the British) wrote in similar vein in a book on *Les Anglais*, published in 1935. He quoted a remark by Disraeli (whose biography he had recently written), that no-one could govern Britain against the Nonconformist vote; and he commented; 'This remains true, and European diplomats must always bear this phrase in mind.'[20] If European statesmen and diplomats had indeed reflected on these matters, they might not have been so surprised by the outcry against the Hoare–Laval proposals in December 1935, which was in large part an expression of the Nonconformist conscience.

These observers, especially Siegfried and Maurois, were deeply sympathetic to the British, but even so they brought their French readers nought for their comfort. The British were in the grip of a profound crisis which they themselves scarcely understood. They still retained, out of necessity, the outlook of a world power, and looked for their salvation to the Anglo-Saxon countries across the oceans. They regarded Europe, though only a few miles away, as a distant and obscure land. To crown everything, an influential minority among this extraordinary people was likely at any moment to seize on a moral issue and push aside all material interests – including, very probably, the interests of France.

Since that was the best the Anglophiles could do, the outbursts of the Anglophobes are in some ways less surprising. The events of 1935 – the Anglo-German Naval Agreement and the Ethiopian crisis – provoked a revival of Anglophobia in a form more intense than at any time since the turn of the century. The Naval Agreement saw the British blatantly sweeping aside the Treaty of Versailles – part of the international law of Europe – in order to secure their own interests.

---

19.   Jules Romains, *Problèmes européennes* (Paris, 1933), pp. 113–14.
20.   André Maurois, *Les Anglais* (Paris, 1935), p. 47.

The Ethiopian crisis saw them in the role of champions of international law and the League of Nations, denouncing as immoral those who tried to secure their own interests. The contrast was glaring, and confirmed – if confirmation were needed – that the British were a nation of hypocrites. One barbed sentence sums up many comments: 'A people of hypocrites must of course form a hypocritical nation.'[21]

The French reaction was inevitable, but its ferocity was startling. Beginning in mid-September 1935, and persisting through October, there was a press campaign which the British Ambassador described as being 'of unrivalled bitterness'. At the heart of the storm were three articles by Henri Béraud in the weekly *Gringoire*, headed 'Faut-il réduire l'Angleterre en esclavage?' ('Must England be reduced to slavery?') The essence was in the first article, which rehearsed the whole tale of French hostility: Joan of Arc, Crillon, Jean Bart, Robespierre and Napoleon all knew that England was the enemy of France and of Europe, and the French people still thought the same. There were those who tried to say that Britain had rendered France a great service in the Great War, but Béraud dismissed this: 'the English fought with us. But it is by no means certain that they fought for us.' After that, the British had sabotaged the French victory, and intervened in French colonies through the intrigues of Lawrence of Arabia. Even if one were to forget all that, there would remain the events of the present year: the Anglo-German Naval Agreement (signed, as Béraud observed, on the anniversary of Waterloo) and the British attempt to push France into a war with Italy on behalf of British interests in Africa. 'When I see England upholding, with the Bible in one hand and the Covenant in the other, the cause of the weak or righteous principles, I cannot help thinking that her own interests are involved.' Béraud went through the whole catalogue of Anglophobia: foppish gentlemen ('fades puceaux d'Oxford'), the Intelligence Service, the cavalry of St George (from the device on the gold sovereigns, used for English bribes). His conclusion was brutal: 'I say that I hate this people ... I say and I repeat that England must be reduced to slavery, since in truth the nature of the Empire lies in oppressing and humiliating other peoples.' He quoted Napoleon on St Helena: 'You will perish like the proud Venetian Republic' and added as the final touch that only 'la concorde continentale' could save

21. M.-F. Guyard, *L'image de la Grande-Bretagne dans le roman français, 1914–1940* (Paris, 1954), p. 238. This was not Guyard's own view, but his summary of the views of others.

Europe and the world from the English – an interesting variation on the theme of European unity.[22]

The three articles were reprinted at once in pamphlet form. *Gringoire*'s owner recorded that some 20,000 letters were received, of which only 500 were critical. Béraud himself claimed that he was giving expression to a groundswell of French opinion which was denied an outlet in the mainstream French press, which under government guidance was playing down differences with Britain.[23] There was probably much truth in this. British policy over the Naval Agreement and Ethiopia was indeed hypocritical, and not even efficient in its pursuit of British interests. The British themselves, on later reflection, have found little to say for it. To the French at the time, it was intolerable, and Béraud said so. It is true that Alexander Werth described Béraud's articles as 'a Fascist mentality gone wild', but in fact they were more than that.[24] They caught a moment when the wilder strains of Anglophobia coincided with rational and well-grounded resentment against British policy.

In 1934, French political instability, the Stavisky scandal and the riots of 6 February had combined to bring the reputation of France to a low point in British eyes. In 1935 the reputation of Britain in France suffered a similar fate. The barometer of Anglo-French relations seemed set at 'Stormy'.

22. Henri Béraud, *Faut-il réduire l'Angleterre en esclavage?* (Paris, 1935). See the illuminating article by Martyn Cornick, '*Faut-il réduire l'Angleterre en esclavage?* A case study of French Anglophobia, October 1935', *Franco-British Studies*, No. 14, Autumn 1992, pp. 3–19.

23. Figures in Cornick, pp. 7–8; Béraud, *Faut-il réduire*, pp. 28–30, 44–5. The circulation of *Gringoire* reached 500,000 in 1935.

24. Alexander Werth, *The Twilight of France* (New York, 1942), p. 53.

CHAPTER 12

Appeasement and War, 1936–April 1940

'Things fall apart, the centre cannot hold.' Yeats's line, so often invoked to epitomise the 1930s in Europe, seemed to fit precisely the state of Anglo-French relations in the middle of that decade. Yet during the next four years the centre somehow held. Britain and France pursued policies which, though not identical, were at least compatible. The good recovered some of their conviction. Slowly and reluctantly the two peoples began to take the measure of the threat presented by Nazi Germany, and in September 1939 they went to war together for the second time in a quarter of a century. It was a remarkable transformation.

On 7 March 1936 German troops marched into the demilitarised zone in the Rhineland, established by the Treaty of Versailles in 1919 and confirmed by the Treaty of Locarno in 1925. These two treaties laid down that Germany was to station no military personnel in the Rhineland, and build no fortifications there. This was the last safeguard remaining to France from the 1919 settlement, and the unfortified frontier offered the only means by which the French could go to the help of their allies in eastern Europe. The German move was therefore an outright challenge to France, and less directly to Britain.

The German forces which actually entered the demilitarised zone were comparatively few in number – about 10,000 troops, who were joined by 22,700 armed police already in the area and at once incorporated into the Army. By the end of March 1936 the Germans had six infantry divisions, weak and only recently formed, in the Rhineland. Behind them lay the bulk of the German Army, made up of twenty-four infantry and three Panzer divisions, not yet fully trained or equipped since the re-introduction of conscription in 1935. The German Air Force could muster a large number of aircraft, but not many of them were modern. In general, the German forces were far from constituting that formidable military machine which was later to conquer most of Europe; but equally they were far from negligible. Their forward march into the Rhineland was accompanied by skilful diplomatic proposals. Hitler offered new non-aggression pacts with France and Belgium, the limitation of air forces, and new demilitarised zones on both sides of the Franco-German border. It was a masterly combination of diplomatic smoke-screen and military *fait accompli*.

On the precedents of the early 1920s, especially the French occupation of the Ruhr in 1923, these events might well have evoked very different responses from France and Britain – the French severe, the British emollient. But the circumstances of 1936 were very different from those of 1923, and the French and British reactions proved very similar.

The French faced a serious military problem. The German forces in the Rhineland and beyond were quite strong enough to demand a significant military response, not a mere 'police action' as was often later asserted. The French General Staff proceeded to exaggerate this perfectly real difficulty by producing grossly inflated estimates of German strength, adding to a reasonably accurate appreciation of the Army units in the Rhineland an extraordinary figure of 235,000 auxiliaries, supposedly organised into fifteen extra divisions. General Gamelin, the French Chief of Staff, claimed that the forces at his immediate disposal were only about half as strong as those of the Germans, and he therefore concluded that he could do nothing unless the government mobilised about half-a-million reservists.

Mobilisation on such a scale would have far-reaching economic, social and political consequences, and required a firm political will on the part of the government. In March 1936 the government of the day was headed by Albert Sarraut, a politician of no particular distinction, who was essentially acting as a caretaker before the legislative elections which were due at the end of April. Sarraut and his ministers were highly unlikely to order large-scale mobilisation, which was probably a prelude to war, without the certainty of widespread support. In fact, French public opinion in all its forms was almost unanimously opposed to strong action or any risk of war. The press, political parties of both Left and Right, the trade unions and the ex-servicemen's organisations all insisted that there must be no war. The socialists even denounced as provocative the limited defensive action (which was taken) of manning the Maginot Line. The French government thus had ample reasons, both military and political, for doing as little as possible. Almost as a substitute for action, they turned to Britain.

On 11 March the Foreign Minister, Flandin, went to London, where he speciously claimed that his government was preparing military action by land and a naval blockade by sea, and asked for British support. As he expected, the British offered no encouragement whatever. The Cabinet was afraid that the slightest sign of opposition would provoke Germany into a 'mad dog act'. Eden, the Foreign Secretary, was anxious to examine Hitler's proposals for new non-aggression pacts and the limitation of air forces. For the Labour opposition, Hugh Dalton had already declared in Parliament that his party would not support military or economic sanctions to expel German troops from the Rhineland. A senior staff officer, General Pownall, wrote privately that neither Britain nor France was in any position to use force, nor would they be justified in doing so. 'The kettle has been seething for years, now it has boiled over. The French are to blame for trying to keep the lid down . . . and we are to blame for condoning, even seconding, the French.'[1] The furthest the British government would go was to discuss Hitler's diplomatic proposals while agreeing to staff talks with the French; but even these staff talks, when they began in April, were restricted to exchanging information rather than preparing for action. Flandin returned to Paris convinced that Britain would do nothing to oppose the German occupation of the Rhineland.

There has been some tendency on the part of the French to claim that they were held back from decisive action by British reluctance. Georges Mandel, formerly Clemenceau's *chef de cabinet* and an advocate of a tough line, remarked at the time that France should behave like a grown-up and not cling to Britain's skirts.[2] After the war, the distinguished historian Maurice Baumont wrote that in this crisis 'She [France] no longer had her own foreign policy. She submissively followed in the wake of Great Britain . . .'[3] Such comments were wide of the mark. In March 1936 neither the French nor the British wished to take any decisive action, and the British government did no more than give the French one more reason for doing nothing. The two countries were united in passivity.

The consequences for France were grave and quickly felt. At the end of April 1936 General Gamelin told his government that if (he really meant when) the Germans fortified the Rhineland, the French Army would be unable to invade Germany. The military basis for the

1. Pownall diary, 8 March 1936, quoted in B.J. Bond, *British Military Policy between the Two World Wars* (Oxford, 1980), p. 227.
2. Hervé Alphand, *L'étonnement d'être* (Paris, 1977), p. 10.
3. Maurice Baumont, *The Origins of the Second War* (New Haven, 1978), p. 205.

French alliances in eastern Europe, notably with Czechoslovakia and Poland, would thus be undermined. Britain was not affected so directly, but could not escape the ultimate consequences of the German move.

SPANISH CIVIL WAR

The French legislative elections of April–May 1936 resulted in a victory for the Popular Front of Socialists, Radicals and Communists. At the beginning of June Léon Blum took office as the first Socialist Premier of France. There were strikes, occupations of factories, street demonstrations, and a general atmosphere of Left-wing euphoria and Right-wing alarm. In London, Baldwin's National government, mainly Conservative in outlook, observed these events with some dismay. This was rapidly tempered by experience. Eden formed a high opinion of Blum, and by early 1937 even Neville Chamberlain thought him straightforward and sincere. Even so, the two governments differed widely on political principles and in their approach to the ideological issues which divided Europe at that time.

A principal focus of this ideological excitement was the Spanish Civil War, which broke out in July 1936 and lasted nearly three years. The war was a complicated struggle, with deep roots in Spanish history, but for propaganda purposes it was easily simplified into a conflict between democracy and Fascism or between Christian civilisation and communism. Such images were reinforced as outside powers intervened in the war: Fascist Italy and Nazi Germany on the Nationalist side, the Soviet Union on the Republican. The Spanish war and foreign intervention clearly raised the danger of a rift between Blum's Popular Front government, which instinctively sympathised with its counterpart in Spain, and the predominantly Conservative administration in London, which tended to favour the Nationalists. However, events turned out otherwise.

It was Blum who had to make the first decision. On 20 July the Spanish government appealed to him personally for the sale of French aircraft, arms and ammunition. Acting alone, Blum agreed and asked for details of what was needed. He then rapidly found that his Cabinet was divided on the issue, which threatened to break up the government. Even worse, Blum soon came to fear that intervention in Spain might precipitate civil war in France itself. There followed a period of acute uncertainty. In three weeks between 20 July and 9

August the French government changed its mind three times. The sale of aircraft to which Blum originally agreed was countermanded, restored, and finally called off again. In the midst of this vacillation, the French produced on 1 August a proposal for an international policy of non-intervention, which might help them out of their difficulties. Britain agreed on 4 August, followed by Germany, Italy and the Soviet Union; so that when, on 15 August, the French and British formally proposed a general non-intervention agreement, they were sure of acceptance. A Non-Intervention Committee to supervise the agreement began its meetings in London in September.

The French government, for its own internal purposes, thus took the lead in the policy of non-intervention, and was quickly encouraged by the British. As early as 24 July Eden urged prudence upon Blum with regard to sending arms to Spain, and the British were glad to provide a meeting-place and a chairman for the Non-Intervention Committee. The two governments, which might well have been divided by the Civil War, thus found themselves on the same path. The British motives were different from those of the French, arising mainly not from internal politics but from considerations of foreign policy. The British wanted to contain the Spanish war and prevent it from spreading to the rest of Europe. They wanted to be sure that whoever won the war would be at least benevolently neutral towards Britain – that is to say they did not wish to fall out with the winner, which from an early date seemed likely to be the Nationalists. Perhaps most important, they were set on improving relations with Italy and Germany, and had no intention of allowing Spain to stand in the way. For all these reasons the British government adopted the policy of non-intervention, and persisted in it even when it was clearly being ignored by Italy, Germany and the Soviet Union. Even a leaky dam, Baldwin argued, was better than no dam at all.

To the supporters of the Spanish Republic in France and Britain, non-intervention was an ignoble policy, based at best on pretence and at worst on fear. There was much agitation against it by the Left in both countries, and those who were determined to defy it went to Spain to serve as volunteers. But the governments held to their policy, and it seems that most of their peoples were relieved to stand aside.

In detail and on occasion, French and British actions diverged somewhat. French non-intervention leaned towards the Republic. The Pyrenean border was sometimes opened to allow armaments to pass, and the government turned a blind eye to the activities of the International Brigades at their transit camp near Perpignan. British non-intervention leaned the other way, and the British chairman of the Non-Intervention Committee took a very lenient line on the large-scale Italian and German assistance to the Nationalists. But these divergences caused no serious difficulties between the two governments. They also worked well together when, for once, they decided to take a strong line against Italy. In August 1937 so-called 'pirate' submarines, generally known to be Italian, made a number of attacks on merchant ships bound for Republican ports. In September, Britain and France called a conference at Nyon to deal with this outbreak. Italy and Germany declined to attend, and in their absence the conference agreed that British and French warships should attack any unidentified submarines found in the western Mediterranean. The 'pirate' attacks ceased. The moral effect of this show of strength was later diminished, because the British and French allowed Italian warships to join in the 'anti-pirate' patrols, which was an absurd pretence. Even so, Britain and France had managed to act together, and to some effect.

ANNEXATION OF AUSTRIA

Over the Rhineland and Spain, France and Britain were agreed on their policies, even if this amounted to little more than a sort of union in inactivity. In monetary policy, on the other hand, they took joint action. In September 1936 Blum's government was finally forced to devalue the franc, a course which its predecessors had struggled against for some five years. But there would be little point in a French devaluation without the co-operation of Britain and the United States, because if the British and Americans were also to devalue, the fundamental relations between the franc, the pound and the dollar would merely be restored. So the French devaluation was dependent for its effects on a stabilisation agreement between the three powers, and it was actually announced in a statement issued by the three governments together, not just by the French. Similar arrangements had to be made when there were further devaluations in July 1937 and May 1938. Elisabeth du Réau writes delicately of a 'symbiosis' between France and the Anglo-Saxon powers in these events.[4] At the time, the French felt all too sharply that they were dependent on the British and Americans in monetary matters, which was a constant, if

4. Elisabeth du Réau, *Daladier* (Paris, 1993), p. 238.

usually unmentioned, element in Anglo-French relations at the end of the 1930s.

Exchange rates were important, but only in the background. What held everyone's eyes was the rise of Germany, and the advance of German power in central and eastern Europe. It was no secret in 1937 that Hitler aimed at *Anschluss* (union) with Austria, and would then turn against Czechoslovakia. There was every sign that the British government was willing to accept, or even promote, this German advance. In November 1937, Lord Halifax (Lord President of the Council, and soon to become Foreign Secretary) visited Hitler and suggested that there were changes in the European order which might come about with time. He specifically mentioned Austria, Czechoslovakia and Danzig, and explained that Britain's concern was that change should come about by peaceful evolution – not that it should be prevented. This was in line with the general policy of the Prime Minister, Neville Chamberlain, who had succeeded Baldwin in May 1937. Chamberlain was determined to try for a negotiated settlement with Germany which would somehow meet German demands without serious damage to British interests. This was the basis of his policy of 'appeasement'; and with immense self-confidence he was sure that he could pull it off.

In principle and on paper, such a policy seemed likely to run counter to that of France. The French had treaties of alliance with Czechoslovakia and Poland, and in late 1936 and 1937 they had been trying to revive their influence in central and eastern Europe. It was not clear what this would amount to in practice, and when French determination was put to the test over Austria it failed miserably. On 11 March 1938 the Germans imposed a Nazi government on Austria; on the 12th the German Army entered the country, ostensibly by invitation; and on the 13th Hitler proclaimed its annexation to Germany. In three days a sovereign state, for whose independence France (and also Britain) had repeatedly declared support, had been removed from the map. All that the French and British did in response was to deliver separate protests in Berlin.

But despite this fiasco the French still showed signs of resolution. On 11 March, the crucial day in Austria, France was actually without a government. Chautemps's administration had just fallen, and Léon Blum was in the process of forming a new one, which took office on 13 March. Blum's Foreign Minister was Paul-Boncour, who at once began at least to go through the motions of preparing an active policy in eastern Europe. He called a meeting of the Committee for National Defence, and brought the French representatives in the Soviet Union,

Poland, Czechoslovakia and Rumania back to Paris for a conference. He wanted to visit London to discuss the situations in Czechoslovakia and Spain. The British were alarmed by this flurry of activity. Phipps, the Ambassador in Paris, urged the Foreign Office to put Paul-Boncour off from his visit to London, and Halifax took this advice. In the Foreign Office, Orme Sargent actually told Phipps that anything that could be done to weaken the new French government and bring about its fall would be in British interests. Since the British normally lamented the instability of French ministries, this was extraordinary. But in so far as it represented antagonism to Paul-Boncour, it was not a flash in the pan. When Blum's government actually fell on 10 April, after a very brief life, and Daladier set about forming a new one, Phipps heard that Paul-Boncour might stay on as Foreign Minister. He at once intervened with Daladier to oppose this. Daladier's biographer, Elisabeth du Réau, believes that Phipps's opposition had some effect, though there were also other influences at work against Paul-Boncour. At any rate Phipps was relieved – 'We were nearly cursed by having Paul-Boncour again at the Quai d'Orsay', he wrote to Halifax on 11 April.[5]

Paul-Boncour's absence did not remove all British anxieties about French policy. Halifax's policy remained what it had been in mid-March: 'to keep both France and Germany guessing as to what our attitude in any particular crisis would be'.[6] Germany must never be sure that Britain *would not* intervene in a crisis in central Europe, while France must never be sure that she *would*. Both would therefore be restrained.

It was an illuminating situation. That the British Ambassador should intervene in French Cabinet-making, without being restrained or reproved from London, speaks volumes about British presumptions with regard to Anglo-French relations at the time. That Halifax should see his role as being to restrain France and Germany by keeping them both guessing as to British intentions showed that the British still saw themselves as being above the Franco-German struggle.

There was a curious last twist to the Paul-Boncour story. The Foreign Ministry in Daladier's government went to Georges Bonnet,

5. A.P. Adamthwaite, *France and the Coming of the Second World War, 1936–1939* (London, 1977), p. 105. Alexander Werth, working as a journalist in Paris, knew of the British intervention against Paul-Boncour at the time, so we may assume that others were equally well informed – see A. Werth, *Twilight of France* (New York, 1942), p. 162. It is surprising that no-one blew the gaff.

6. Andrew Roberts, *The Holy Fox. A biography of Lord Halifax* (London, 1991), p. 93.

whom a Foreign Office official was to describe by the end of the year as 'a public danger to his own country and ours'.[7] The British might have been better off with the devil they knew.

THE CZECHOSLOVAKIAN CRISIS AND MUNICH

After Austria had been absorbed into Germany in March 1938, a crisis over Czechoslovakia was certain. Czechoslovakia had come into being as a new state in 1919. It comprised half-a-dozen different nationalities, including rather over three million German-speakers, mainly living along the frontiers with Germany and the former Austria, and usually referred to as Sudeten Germans. Among these German-speakers had arisen a Nazi Party, imitating its original across the border and led by Konrad Henlein. The Sudeten Nazis demanded large measures of local self-government for their areas. The Czech government rejected these demands, which would be bound to lead to the break-up of the state. There seemed no way out of this impasse, which was transferred to the international plane by the intervention of Germany. The Sudeten Nazi Party was financed and largely controlled from Berlin, and Hitler used it as an instrument of his own policy, which was directed ultimately at the destruction of Czechoslovakia, perhaps by political pressure but if necessary by force. Military planning for a German invasion of Czechoslovakia went ahead from December 1937 onwards.

The likely French and British involvement in this problem was alarmingly apparent. If Germany attacked Czechoslovakia, France would be drawn in by her alliance with the Czechs, renewed as recently as 1935; and it was almost inevitable that Britain, however reluctantly, would have to support France. British Members of Parliament were appalled at the prospect of having to defend 'a country which we can neither get at nor spell'; but the logic seemed inexorable.[8] Moreover, the Soviet Union also had a treaty with Czechoslovakia, so the scenario for a general European war seemed ominously complete.

In these circumstances, the British set themselves to find a way out of the problem without war. Their policy was to put pressure on the Czech government to make concessions to the Sudeten Germans. So the British urged the Czechs to yield to Sudeten German demands,

---

7. Adamthwaite p. 105.
8. John Barnes and David Nicholson, eds, *The Empire at Bay. The Leo Amery Diaries, 1929–1945* (London, 1988), p. 499.

and at the same time discouraged the French from fulfilling their treaty obligations to Czechoslovakia. About this Chamberlain was quite brutal, remarking in Cabinet that 'however upset the French Government might be, he did not see what other alternative was open to them than to acquiesce. It was a disagreeable business which had to be done as pleasantly as possible.'[9] Behind these policies lay the fundamental assumption that an agreement with Germany, first on Czechoslovakia and later on other issues, was attainable. As Halifax wrote on 19 March 1938, he did not believe that Hitler's racial ambitions would develop into an 'international power lust', nor that after making advances in central Europe, Germany 'will in over-whelming might proceed to destroy France and ourselves'.[10] That, alas, proved to be precisely Hitler's course of action; but at the time the British dismissed the idea, and they wanted the French to dismiss it too.

In fact, the French position was much less clear-cut than their treaty obligations implied. The French high command ruled out any prospect of an immediate assault on the newly built German fortifications in the west, which meant that the best they could hope to do was to rescue Czechoslovakia at a final peace treaty and not by prompt military action. Daladier's Cabinet was deeply divided. One group, led by Paul Reynaud and Georges Mandel, advocated a strong line of support for the Czechs, to the point of war if necessary; though in their optimistic moments they hoped that Hitler was bluffing, and a strong stand would not lead to war but to a bloodless political victory. Against this, another group, headed by the Foreign Minister Georges Bonnet, maintained that Hitler was not bluffing. If opposed over Czechoslovakia, he would fight, and in the ensuing war not only the Czechs but the French would be defeated. They therefore proposed, rather like the British, to press the Czechs into making concessions which would avoid war. Daladier hovered between the two schools. Sometimes he argued forcibly that the crisis was not really about Czechoslovakia but about German domination of Europe, which would have to be opposed; but then he would suddenly retreat and accept a policy of concessions. In these circumstances, French policy was variable and uncertain, and open to influence from London, which was usually exerted in the direction advocated by Bonnet.

On 28–29 April 1938 Daladier and Bonnet visited London to

9. Chamberlain quoted by R.A.C. Parker, 'The Anglo-French Conversations April and September 1938', in *Les relations franco-allemandes, 1933–1939* (Paris, 1976), p. 373.

10. Halifax, in G.L. Weinberg, *The Foreign Policy of Hitler's Germany. Starting World War II* (Chicago, 1980), p. 348.

confer with the British. At the beginning of the conference Daladier expounded his sternest views. He argued that Henlein was not really seeking concessions but the disruption of Czechoslovakia, and that German policy was one of continuous expansion. After Czecho-slovakia, the target would be Rumania; and if France and Britain submitted to violence then further violence would follow. Only firmness would bring peace. This diagnosis, which now appears remarkably accurate, was described by Cadogan, the permanent head of the Foreign Office, as 'Very beautiful, but awful rubbish.'[11] If Daladier had stuck to his views, the conference would have broken up in disagreement; but in fact after the lunch break he gave way almost all along the line. He agreed that Britain and France together should urge the Czechs to meet the demands of the Sudeten Germans, while the British alone should approach Berlin to find out exactly what the Germans wanted. The only British concession was to agree to open staff conversations.

It remains unclear whether Daladier was sincere in his early exposition, and gave way only under British pressure, or whether he hoped all the time that the British would force him into a policy which he really wished to follow but shrank from putting forward as his own. Either way, the result was the same. After an apparently severe difference of opinion, the two governments were agreed on a policy of putting pressure on the Czechs to reach a negotiated solution of the Sudeten problem favourable to Henlein and to Hitler.

From May to September 1938 the British and French pursued this policy. On 18 May Halifax told the British Cabinet that Bonnet wanted the British to bring as much pressure as possible to bear in Prague, 'to save France from the cruel dilemma of dishonouring her agreements or becoming involved in war'.[12] Between 19 and 21 May there were rumours of an imminent German attack on Czecho-slovakia. The crisis proved false, but the alarm it occasioned was real, and the British and French redoubled their diplomatic efforts. On 20 July Bonnet told the Czech ambassador in Paris bluntly that France would not go to war over the Sudeten question. She would declare her support in public, to help the Czechs to negotiate, but on no account should they expect anything more. At almost exactly the same time, the British government forced upon the Czechs the appointment of a so-called 'independent' mediator, Lord Runciman (a former

11. David Dilks, ed., *The Diaries of Sir Alexander Cadogan, 1938–1945* (London, 1971), p. 73.
12. *DBFP*, Series 3, vol. I, No. 219, n. 2.

British Cabinet minister), whose actual task was to persuade the Czechs to make concessions. Revealingly, this move by Britain was simply announced to the French, without consultation. Halifax told Daladier and Bonnet the news in the course of a visit to Paris by the King and Queen on 19–21 July.

During August tensions increased, with well-authenticated reports of German military preparations. Early in September Henlein broke off his negotiations with the Czech government about autonomy, and it seemed likely that the Nazi Party rally at Nuremberg, which Hitler addressed on 12 September, would bring the crisis to a head. On 13 September Daladier proposed to Chamberlain a three-power conference between France, Britain and Germany to save the peace. But for some days Chamberlain had been maturing a plan of his own to fly to meet Hitler alone. Chamberlain put Daladier's suggestion aside, and then simply instructed the British Ambassador in Paris to tell the French Premier early in the morning of 14 September that he was flying to see Hitler that very day. Daladier did not look pleased, understandably enough, and remarked that he would have preferred a meeting *à trois*, as he had originally proposed. France was left on the side-lines, while Chamberlain acted alone.

At Berchtesgaden on 14 September, Chamberlain swiftly agreed in principle to drop the policy of concessions to the Sudeten Germans within Czechoslovakia, accepting instead the complete transfer of the Sudeten areas to Germany. Chamberlain returned to England, where the Cabinet accepted the principle of the transfer of territory. Then Daladier and Bonnet came to London on 18 September. By this time, British policy was decided, and the French ministers were effectively being required to follow suit. When the meeting began, Chamberlain opened by explaining that after the Sudetenland Hitler had no more territorial claims in Europe. The racial unity of the German people was his sole aim, which would then be accomplished. Daladier at first demurred. It was difficult, he said, to advise a friend to have one of his legs – perhaps even both – cut off. In private conversation with the French delegation he revealed his distress and mental agony. France, he said, had engagements to the Czechs and was not keeping them, and he was not proud of what he was doing. What a negotiation, he lamented, with a knife at one's throat.[13] Did he mean that the British and French were holding a knife at the Czechs' throat, or that the British were holding a knife at his own? The latter seems more likely. At any rate, despite his misgivings he yielded, and accepted the cession

13. Du Réau, *Daladier*, p. 258.

of the Sudetenland to Germany. He secured in return a reluctant British agreement to an international guarantee of the remains of Czechoslovakia after the transfer. The French Cabinet accepted these terms on 19 September, and the Czechs followed, after much anguish, on the 21st.

Chamberlain was thus able to return to Germany (this time to Godesberg) on 22 September, bearing what Hitler had said he wanted. But Hitler now had new demands: Polish and Hungarian claims for Czech territory must also be met, and Germany must occupy the Sudetenland (as defined by himself) by 1 October. Chamberlain, set on his policy, was again in favour of accepting the new German demands. But this time Halifax, realising that appeasement was turning into surrender, opposed him, prompted by Cadogan, the Permanent Under-Secretary at the Foreign Office, who had now decided that 'I'd rather be beat than dishonoured.'[14] The Cabinet, to Chamberlain's dismay, decided to reject Hitler's new terms. Thus when Daladier and Bonnet came to London yet again, on 25 September, the situation was very different from that on their previous visit. Then Chamberlain had simply wanted them to accept a British decision. He now wanted the French to give him ammunition so that he could go back to his own Cabinet and get ministers to change their minds. He tried to extract from the French a statement that they were in no position to fight, and therefore the German demands would have to be accepted. Simon, by profession a barrister, was cast in the role of prosecuting counsel to trap the French into damaging admissions about their own weaknesses. But this time the French stood firm. Daladier insisted that each country would have to do its duty. He agreed to a suggestion by Chamberlain for a last appeal to Hitler, to be made by Sir Horace Wilson, the Prime Minister's principal civil service confidant. But if that failed, Daladier declared that France would go to war, and he received what amounted to a British undertaking that they would follow. For the first time in the Anglo-French conferences of 1938, Daladier stood his ground and Chamberlain failed to get what he wanted.

On 26–28 September war seemed imminent. Opinion in France was gravely divided. Anti-war petitions attracted much support and preyed heavily on Daladier's mind, but on the other hand mobilisation got under way and the country reluctantly steeled itself for the ordeal. In Britain the fleet was mobilised and men dug trenches in the London parks, showing a greater fear of air-raids than knowledge of

14. Roberts, *Holy Fox*, pp. 116–17; *Cadogan Diaries*, p. 104.

how to cope with them. At that point Hitler suddenly decided not to press on with his real objective, the destruction of Czechoslovakia, but to settle temporarily for his ostensible aim of annexing the Sudetenland. On 28 September he agreed to a four-power conference (Germany, Italy, France and Britain), which met at Munich on the 29th.

The British and French made no attempt at joint preparation for this meeting, and there was no co-operation between Chamberlain and Daladier while it was in progress. Chamberlain was briskly determined to get on with the business, which was to agree on the methods and timing of the transfer of the Sudeten German territories to Germany, with a promise of further Czech losses to Hungary and Poland to come. Daladier was taciturn and withdrawn, taking little part in the proceedings. By all accounts they hardly spoke to one another. Finally, when the conference was over, at about one-o'clock in the morning of 30 September, Chamberlain, without even telling Daladier what he was going to do, asked Hitler for a private meeting, at which they signed a statement, produced by Chamberlain, affirming the desire of their two peoples not to go to war again and their determination to remove sources of difference and so contribute to the peace of Europe. This was the piece of paper which Chamberlain waved triumphantly when he landed at Heston airport. For the French, it was another occasion when the British stole a march on them, even when they were going down the same road.

It was a wretched end to an unhappy story. It is true that for most of the Czechoslovakian crisis Britain and France followed essentially the same policy. But they did not do so in close co-operation, or in equal partnership. The British took important initiatives – on the Runciman mission, on Chamberlain's flight to meet Hitler alone, on the Chamberlain–Hitler meeting and joint declaration – without the slightest consultation with the French. When there was consultation, in the course of three Anglo-French conferences, the British attitude was frequently condescending and sometimes harsh. Even the agreement on policy rested on uncertain foundations. Chamberlain knew what he wanted and pressed ahead with great determination, but Daladier was torn in mind and heart, plagued by the fear that he was wrong to betray the Czechs and that in the long run he had done no more than sign their death-warrant.

In fact, Anglo-French policy proved a short-term success, in that peace was saved for a time, but a long-term failure. Czechoslovakia survived for a mere six months. The quest for a permanent European settlement came to nothing. In later years the Munich agreement came to be regarded in both Britain and France as a symbol of surrender and shame, remembered with pain and as an object-lesson of what to avoid in the future. So it came about that when Britain and France, after many years of dissent and dispute, finally achieved a common policy on a major issue, they found that this policy went sour and its success turned to ashes.

BRIEF SUNSHINE: THE ROYAL VISIT, 1938

In the midst of the long-drawn-out Czechoslovakian crisis there took place a formal state visit to France by King George VI and Queen Elizabeth. It had been a sign of the difficulties in the relations between the two countries that such ceremonies had lapsed, and this visit was a deliberate attempt to assert a renewed friendship. The original initiative appears to have come from the British side, but it was eagerly taken up by the French government, which spent large sums of money on preparations and did everything possible to ensure its success. For four days (19–22 July 1938) the two countries were on their best behaviour towards one another. The French press, even including the often fiercely anti-British *Gringoire* and the communist *L'Humanité*, showed a remarkable unanimity in its welcome to the King and Queen, going further than the government guidance which was obviously applied. The weather was fine, the crowds large and enthusiastic, and the internal divisions of France were for a moment put aside. The British press, for its part, was delighted by the warmth of the welcome.[15] Alexander Werth, not a natural monarchist, described the enthusiasm as 'enormous – and spontaneous'.[16]

The two countries were obviously determined to see the best in one another. What did they find? The strongest theme of the visit was comradeship in the Great War. The King inaugurated the great Australian war memorial at Viller-Bretonneux, and over the four days several speeches paid solemn tribute to the dead and invoked the spirit of unity in battle. That was in the past. For the present, the *leitmotif* was that the two countries wanted peace. The King, in his speech at the Elyseé, struck the notes of appeasement and reconciliation in international affairs. Throughout the programme there ran an appeal to a common culture and common values. There was here a contrast,

15. Richard Dubreuil, 'La visite des souverains britanniques', in René Rémond et Janine Bourdin, eds, *La France et les Français en 1938–1939* (Paris, 1978), pp. 77–94.
16. Werth, *Twilight of France*, p. 186.

ever-present but left unspoken, with the new barbarism of Nazi Germany. There was a pervading sense that France and Britain were almost the last outposts of democracy and liberal civilisation in Europe.

The dominant themes of the Great War and shared values pointed towards a continuing partnership. This mood was caught, theatrically and yet with sincerity, in an 'Ode à l'Angleterre', read on the radio by an actress from the Comédie Française:

O restes de ceux-là qui passèrent la Manche,
Débarquant comme on vole au secours d'un ami,
Soldats anglais couchés dessous une croix blanche
Héros de la Bassée et vainqueurs de Vimy,
Voici que, rapprochés comme ils l'étaient naguère
Dans les mornes travaux et les deuils de la guerre,
Nos pays dans la paix vont la main dans la main,
Marchant du même pas sur le même chemin.[17]

Oh spirits of those who once crossed the waves,
Who sped in your ships to a needy friend's aid,
You silent white lines of fresh English graves
Where the heroes of Vimy, la Bassée are laid.

Our nations, as close now as in days of yore
During wearisome labours and sorrows of war,
Hand in hand are advancing in peace to this day
And marching together down our common way.

It is too easy to dismiss these verses, and the glow generated by the royal visit, as mere shallow sentiment. It is unhappily true that a mere six months after the visit Daladier told the American Ambassador, Bullitt, that the King was a moron and the Queen excessively ambitious; for good measure he added that Chamberlain was a desiccated stick and Eden a young idiot. He was perhaps a bit liverish that day, but the contrast with the compliments exchanged during the visit is still painful. Yet it is too easy to look back with cynicism. The sentiments expressed during the royal visit represented an important aspect of reality. France and Britain were indeed the last bastions of liberty in Europe. The values which they shared were fundamentally more important than their quarrels. The two countries frequently regarded one another with a jaundiced eye, but when they looked at Nazi Germany they knew they were on the same side. There is much in the royal visit to France in July 1938 that is worth pondering.

17. Dubreuil, p. 87.

UNWILLINGLY TO WAR

After Munich, officials in the British Foreign Office found much to think about. Germany was now without question the predominant power in central Europe, and was likely to extend its influence eastwards. In the Foreign Office view there was little to be done about that. On the other hand, British security was closely bound up with western Europe and the Mediterranean, where France held a crucial position. France in fact was vital to British safety; and yet officials judged her undependable or even dangerous. Cadogan thought that Britain must keep close to France, but not allow 'this very uncertain guide' to dictate British policy.[18] Orme Sargent recognised that Britain's defence relied on France, but lamented that pacifism was so powerful there, and that French policy was controlled by 'a Prime Minister incapable of taking a decision, and . . . a Foreign Minister who is completely untrustworthy'.[19] It was an odd mixture. Britain was dependent on France, yet the foreign policy experts found France undependable.

France too took stock after Munich. The situation appeared disastrous. A Belgian diplomat remarked to Jean Chauvel: 'It's quite extraordinary . . . a great country which has abdicated.'[20] The Polish Ambassador in Paris wrote that France was 'too feeble to break with her international engagements, and too feeble firmly to stand by them'.[21] These were grim diagnoses. The French government felt bound to keep up with the British in running after the Germans to secure a Franco-German declaration like that signed by Chamberlain and Hitler. They invited Ribbentrop to Paris on 6–7 December 1938, and the meetings produced a vague text referring to good relations and consultations between the two countries. Ribbentrop later claimed that behind the scenes Bonnet had accepted German predominance in eastern Europe. Bonnet denied it, but that was at any rate the appearance. Yet this apparent collapse was accompanied by signs of a stiffening resolve. In eastern Europe an economic mission visited Rumania, Yugoslavia and Bulgaria in November to strengthen French

18. Memorandum by Cadogan, 14 October 1938, quoted in Donald Lammers, 'From Whitehall after Munich: the Foreign Office and the future course of British policy', *Historical Journal*, XVI, No. 4, 1973, p. 837.

19. PRO, FO 371/21592, C14138/13/17, memorandum by Sargent, 18 November 1938.

20. Jean Chauvel, *Commentaire*, vol. I (Paris, 1971), p. 37.

21. L.B. Namier, *Diplomatic Prelude* (London, 1950), p. 73.

economic influence there. When at the end of November the Italian Chamber of Deputies mounted an anti-French demonstration, with cries of 'Tunis, Corsica, Nice', Daladier responded firmly that France would hold all her territories, and later made an ostentatious tour of the threatened areas by warship.

On one point the French were absolutely clear. For a strong policy they depended on British support, of a material kind. General Vuillemin, the Chief of the Air Staff, declared in a memorandum of 25 October 1938 that help from the RAF was the only quick way to remedy French weakness in the air. On land, a French staff officer (General Petitbon) told the British military attaché that France looked to Britain for 'un effort du sang'. What the French wanted was that the British should introduce conscription, and Bonnet inspired an article in *Le Temps* to that effect – carefully explaining to the British ambassador that he had inspired it. France could not engage in another great war unless the British put a large army into the field.

The British were by no means happy about all this. Chamberlain and Halifax, before visiting Paris on 23–25 November, agreed before setting off that the RAF's job was to defend Britain, and they could offer no air defence for Paris. On land, there could be no question of adding to the two divisions which had been offered during the Czechoslovakian crisis. In Paris, they held firmly to this line. Daladier pleaded that at least the two divisions should be sent in eight days rather than three weeks, but got nowhere. This British attitude was consistent with long-established policy. British strategy rested on the concept of 'limited liability' on the continent of Europe. Just before he became Prime Minister, on 5 May 1937, Chamberlain had told the Cabinet that: 'He did not believe that we could, or ought, or, in the event, would be allowed by the country, to enter a Continental war with the intention of fighting on the same lines as in the last.'[22] That ominous French phrase, 'un effort du sang', was the last thing the British wanted to hear.

Yet after the Paris visit in November 1938 Halifax could see that 'limited liability' was no longer enough. Unless the French secured assurances of further British support, they might lapse into defeatism and not fight even in self-defence. He had seen the danger signal, that without a large British army France could not necessarily be relied upon as the first line of defence for Britain. Early in 1939 this problem grew more pressing. The British picked up alarming reports of imminent German moves in eastern Europe, and – more dangerously

---

22. P.J. Dennis, *Decision by Default: Peacetime Conscription and British Defence, 1919–1939* (London, 1972), p. 98.

– possible attacks on the Netherlands or Switzerland. On 1 February the Cabinet agreed that if either of these countries were attacked Britain would have to go to war. On 6 February Chamberlain declared in the House of Commons that '... any threat to the vital interests of France from whatever quarter it may come must evoke the immediate co-operation of Great Britain'.[23] This was a remarkably firm statement of support for France, but how could it be made good? On 1 February the Cabinet had agreed to begin detailed staff talks with the French, and these got under way at the end of March and were steadily pursued. On 20 February the Chiefs of Staff presented the Cabinet with a review of Britain's strategic position, concluding that it was hard to see how the security of the British Isles could be maintained if France were forced to surrender in war. Therefore, even self-defence 'may have to include a share in the land defence of French territory'.[24] The Cabinet accepted this view, and agreed that in the event of a European war Britain should create a large, continental-style army. A figure of thirty-two divisions was, somewhat arbitrarily, agreed upon.

In principle, this was the end of the doctrine of 'limited liability'. It held out the promise of resolving a long-standing problem in Anglo–French relations. But it was only a promise. The British had not decided to set about creating a large army at once, but only in the event of war – which might prove rather late. They had not decided to introduce conscription, which was against tradition and would raise all manner of difficulties with the Labour Party and the trade unions, which believed that military conscription would be merely a prelude to industrial conscription. Only in April 1939 did the government announce the introduction of conscription, and the legislation was passed in May. In peacetime, this was a remarkable gesture, but its practical effects were extremely limited. Full-time military service was to be for only six months, and a large proportion of the recruits (80,000 out of 200,000 each year) were to form anti-aircraft units for home defence. The first contingent was not to be called up until August. British policy on a strong army was rather like St Augustine's prayer for chastity – Lord, make us strong, but not yet.

The French knew they needed British military support, and after the defeat of 1940 they were to feel (with much justification) that it had been too little and too late. The British finally recognised that even the logic of self-defence demanded a large army to fight in

23. *H.C. Deb*, 5th series, vol. 343, col. 623.
24. Michael Howard, *The Continental Commitment: The Dilemma of British Defence Policy in the Era of two World Wars* (London, 1972), p. 129.

France, but the weight of tradition and memories of the Great War pulled the opposite way and inhibited them from acting on that recognition. Even in the face of necessity, there was a gap for the British between logic and emotion, and this caused an even wider gap between French expectations and British actions.

For most of 1938 Britain and France had both pursued a policy of appeasement, though not always in perfect step with one another. During the winter of 1938–39 they both hesitated as to their future policy. The event which ended that hesitation was the Prague *coup* on 14–15 March 1939. In two days Germany wiped the remains of the former Czechoslovakia off the map. German troops marched into Prague and installed a German governor there. Hitler's claim that he sought only to unite German-speaking peoples in the *Reich* was exposed as a lie.

In Britain there was a brief moment of indecision. On 15 March Chamberlain spoke of not being deflected from his course. Then on the 17th, in his native Birmingham, he asked whether the German move was the last attack on a small state or the first step towards dominating the world by force. If it were the latter, Britain would resist such a challenge. Chamberlain was personally affronted that Hitler had deceived him at Munich, and he was under political pressure from Halifax and the Conservative Party in the country. In any case, he had never regarded appeasement as meaning 'peace at any price', but peace compatible with British security – which did not allow for German domination of Europe. In the country as a whole, Prague created a new consensus. Even liberals found a good word to say for the balance of power – Norman Angell wrote in his autobiography that 'power politics were the politics of not being overpowered'.[25] It was not simply a matter of power politics, because the new threat was from Nazism, which was already being found repulsive even though its full appalling significance was far from being understood.

In France, Daladier was not personally shocked in the same way as Chamberlain. He had long predicted what would happen. But Prague was a turning-point for French opinion. On the Left, Léon Blum had already moved in the autumn of 1938 to a policy of national defence, carrying most of the Socialist Party with him. After the occupation of Prague he urged Daladier to reaffirm French obligations to Poland and to open military conversations with the Soviet Union. On the Right, a spokesman for Colonel de la Rocque's Parti Social Français (the

25. Michael Howard, *War and the Liberal Conscience* (London, 1981), p. 108.

successor to the Croix de Feu) declared that Hitler's word could no longer be trusted. Even Doriot, the leader of the only serious French Fascist party, the Parti Populaire Français, asked at what point France must consider that Germany's rise was incompatible with her own existence.[26]

In both countries the common reaction was that Hitler could not be trusted and that Germany would have to be stopped. Such feelings were simple, instinctive, and deeply felt. There was a reaction, perhaps belated but none the less profound, against the rise of Germany, against the methods of the Nazi regime, and against Hitler himself. This last point was by no means the least. The issue of peace and war became increasingly personalised. This did not mean, in either country, that war was considered inevitable. There were still hopes that Hitler was bluffing, that a firm stand could bring him to a halt without war, and that negotiation might yet find a basis for European peace. Such hopes were very natural; but there was a growing certainty that, if the worst came to the worst, Britain and France would have to fight.

At first, it was Britain which took the lead in improvising a new policy. On 31 March 1939 Chamberlain announced in the House of Commons a guarantee of Polish independence. French support had been requested on the 27th, but even so the actual wording of the guarantee, which was largely Chamberlain's own work, was made public without the French having time to comment on it. France already had an alliance with Poland, and was in that way not adopting any new commitment. But the new guarantee accepted that Poland was to be the judge of whether its independence was threatened, and thus the French were hustled into a position where their troops might be asked to 'die for Danzig', as Marcel Déat was to put it in a famous newspaper article on 4 May.

The British government hoped that the guarantee to Poland would deter Germany from further aggression. If the deterrent worked, the guarantee would not have to be carried out. The trouble was that, after a series of surrenders, the guarantee in itself carried little conviction. It needed support – a more convincing deterrent. To many observers, it appeared that a firm military alliance between France, Britain and the Soviet Union offered the best chance of confronting Hitler with a combination against which he dared not go to war. In the pursuit of such an alliance it was France which took the initiative. Bonnet, the leading appeaser of 1938, was now ardent for a new treaty with the Soviets. In April 1939 France proposed an

26. J.-L. Crémieux-Brilhac, *Les Français de l'an 40* (Paris, 1990), vol. I, pp. 26–7.

agreement by which they and the USSR would go to the defence of Poland and Rumania. The Soviets demurred, insisting on a three-power pact which would include Great Britain. The French then pressed on eagerly with the negotiations, while the British moved slowly and reluctantly, raising one objection after another. There was a long dispute as to whether a military agreement should follow or coincide with the signing of a political treaty. At the end of July the British finally agreed that the two should go together. It was characteristic of the attitudes of the two countries that the French nominated their delegation for military talks on 24 July, and the British not until ten days later. The British then insisted that the two delegations should travel to Moscow by the slow route by sea and rail. The French delegates were instructed to conclude a military convention as quickly as possible, and were given the powers to do so; the British had to ask for full powers from their government after they arrived in Moscow. When the talks began, the principal Soviet representatives put the crucial question as to whether Poland would allow Soviet troops to enter Polish territory in advance of a German attack. It was the French who tried desperately but fruitlessly to persuade the Poles to agree, and finally tried the forlorn device of saying that they themselves agreed. Voroshilov, the Soviet representative, insisted on asking whether the Poles too had agreed, and the French had to admit that they had not.

None the less, the French had tried from start to finish to make the negotiations succeed, and could say in the end that failure was not their fault. The failure when it came was spectacular. The Soviet Union concluded, not a three-power alliance *against* Germany, but a pact *with* Germany which opened the way for the German attack on Poland which began on 1 September 1939. The British and French were left with their guarantee to Poland, which they had hoped not to have to carry out. In the final crisis, they hesitated. Poland fought alone for two days before Britain and France declared war.

What were they waiting for? For the French there were two considerations. They wanted to gain time to carry out their mobilisation, and to complete the evacuation of civilians from near the border with Germany. Second, Mussolini produced a proposal for a Munich-style conference, which Bonnet was desperately anxious to take up. In London, it seems that for a few hours on 2 September Chamberlain and Halifax also wanted to give Mussolini's proposal a chance, though only on condition that the Germans must first withdraw from Poland. Mostly, the British were waiting for the French. Finally, it was the anger of the House of Commons in the evening of 2 September, and a revolt in Chamberlain's own Cabinet (led by the unlikely figure of Sir John Simon, previously an advocate of appeasement) that brought Chamberlain to the sticking point. It was then the British who brought the French to the point of sending an ultimatum. When the two countries finally declared war, they did so at different times, the British at 11 a.m. on 3 September, the French at 5 p.m.

These events left the impression, to some degree correct, that Britain had pushed France into war – a point which was to rankle in 1940. Certainly the attitude of the two parliaments was very different. The House of Commons showed greater resolution than the government, and when war began the House remained in almost permanent session to supervise and galvanise the war effort. The French Chamber and Senate met on 2 September and voted war credits while avoiding the word 'war', and did not meet again until 30 November.

It is not surprising that there were hesitations in both countries, after such a long and deep revulsion against war. Yet the two governments, and for the most part their peoples, realised that they had no real choice. They accepted war without enthusiasm but with a reluctant determination. In France, mobilisation went forward quietly but resolutely. There were no flowers at the Paris railway stations, as there had been in 1914, but there was no panic, no protest, and a minimal rate of refusal to answer the call-up. The petitions against war which had loomed so large in September 1938 were not repeated. Jean-Louis Crémieux-Brilhac, in his detailed study of French opinion, found a people with a strong sense of fatality – they knew in their bones that a world was coming to an end – but resolved to see their task through. 'Il faut en finir' was the common phrase.[27] In Britain the picture was much the same. The British people accepted the war quietly (those who could remember 1914 noted the absence of crowds in London), but with few doubts as to its necessity. A Gallup poll taken in the last week of September asked: 'Should we continue to fight until Hitlerism goes?', and evoked the answers: Yes – 89 per cent, No – 7 per cent, Don't Know – 4 per cent. The question was vague, and showed the importance of Hitler's personality; but the figures remain remarkable.[28]

These were important similarities, but behind them lay a deep difference between the two countries. In France there was a profound

27. Ibid., pp. 55–65.
28. PRO, INF 1/261. BIPO Set 62. This poll was taken for the Ministry of Information, and its results were not published.

pessimism. France had lost so many dead, and so many children unconceived, during the Great War that she was, in Crémieux-Brilhac's phrase, biologically exhausted. She could endure no more victories, never mind defeats. The British, on the other hand, remained at bottom hopeful. They believed they would win, and that somehow they would attain a better world when the war was over. This belief doubtless showed a strange lack of realism, but it was no small advantage when embarking on a long struggle – and it was to prove remarkably durable.

THE PHONEY WAR

Britain and France declared war on 3 September 1939, but (except at sea) they did not wage it. They did nothing to help Poland during the five weeks' campaign in which the Polish armies were crushed, first by a German attack from the west and then by a Soviet invasion from the east. The two countries were in close agreement on their long-term strategy. The French envisaged a long period of defence, in which the Maginot Line would protect their territory and the German economy would be undermined by blockade. Meanwhile Britain and the Dominions would mobilise their forces, and eventually – perhaps in the third year of war – Germany could be overcome by an Allied offensive. This programme fitted in well with British conceptions. They envisaged a long period for the building up of an army and for the intervention of the Dominions. They put great faith in the blockade, and in their more optimistic moments they even hoped that Germany could be defeated by economic warfare alone, with a land assault only as the last push to a tottering edifice.

The French and British were also in broad agreement on their war aims. They had gone to war because Hitler had proved that he could not be trusted. They were determined to fight until they had achieved firm guarantees of security for the future, which meant above all that Hitler must be got rid of. Beyond this it was difficult to go, and they were shy of trying to work out any detailed plan of war aims. They diverged somewhat in attitudes to Germany, in that the British tended to stress the Nazi menace, while the French thought of a German danger which this time happened to have taken a Nazi form. They could agree that Poland should be restored as an independent state, but did not speculate as to where its boundaries should be. They were uncertain as to how Czechoslovakia should be re-established, or whether

Austria should be treated as part of Germany or as the first of Hitler's victims. Despite such problems, there was a strong basis of agreement on fundamentals, and neither government showed any sign of wavering in the face of Hitler's 'peace offer' after his victory over Poland.

The French and British quickly reactivated the machinery of co-operation which they had set up with so much difficulty during the previous war. A Supreme War Council was at once established, meeting frequently. Unity of military command was assumed, and the commander of the new BEF, Lord Gort, was placed under the command of the French C-in-C, General Gamelin, though with a right of appeal to his government if the safety of his Army was endangered. With only four British divisions in France at the start, building up to ten by May 1940, Gort's position was in any case bound to be subordinate. The French, with 90 divisions under arms and the prestige of their Army still high, naturally resumed the major role in the alliance which had passed to Britain during the 1930s.

Economic co-operation was also resumed. A financial agreement signed in December 1939 fixed the rate of exchange between the two currencies at 176.5 francs to the pound, and provided for the holding of that rate until six months after the conclusion of a peace treaty. Certain joint expenses incurred by the two governments were to be shared in the ratio of three-fifths by Britain and two-fifths by France, so that the British in part made up for the paucity of their military contribution by shouldering a greater share of the economic burden. At the same time an Anglo-French Purchasing Board, to co-ordinate orders in the United States, was set up on the same lines as in the previous war, and Jean Monnet returned to his old duties to provide personal as well as institutional continuity.

After twenty years of disputes over policy and clashes of personality, these were considerable achievements. The two governments tried to cap the edifice of co-operation by publishing a joint declaration on 28 March 1940, undertaking not to negotiate an armistice or a peace treaty except by mutual agreement; not to discuss peace terms before agreeing on the conditions necessary for their long-term security; and to maintain their community of action after peace was concluded. The case being envisaged, of course, was a victorious peace, not the defeat which actually occurred in 1940. By the declaration, the French sought to tie Britain into some means of security against Germany after the war was won. The British for their part realised that they must offer France the psychological reassurance of making the two countries effectively a single unit in post-war Europe, a counter-weight to the eighty million Germans.

This line of thinking led to much discussion of schemes for union between Britain and France. The two governments undertook a campaign of propaganda for this idea, which fell on fruitful ground. During the phoney war, the idea of European federation was much in vogue as a solution for the ills of the continent, and Anglo-French union fitted snugly into such concepts. It was taken up with an eagerness which, though owing much to a propaganda lead, went beyond government inspiration. On 30 March 1940 Churchill produced in a broadcast the striking phrase that Britain and France were 'joined together in indissoluble union so that their full purposes may be accomplished'.[29] *The Times*, in a sonorous first leader on 22 April, declared that the two countries were moving towards 'ever closer union. Here if anywhere is the firm foundation for "the Parliament of Man, the Federation of the World." ' By a curious echo, the words 'ever closer union' were to find a place in the language of European integration in the post-war years, and ultimately in the Treaty of Rome in 1957.

All this later came to assume an air of painful unreality in the light of the disasters of May and June 1940. Even at the time there were difficulties within the alliance. The machinery of the Supreme War Council whirred round in a void, because there were no great strategic decisions to be taken. At least in part because politicians and planners had little serious work to do, they produced a number of dubious schemes which divided the Allies at the discussion stage and would have been downright dangerous if carried out. The French were keen to construct a Balkan bloc, to divert German energies from the west and impede German oil supplies from Rumania; but the British applied the brakes. The British for their part put forward schemes to lay mines in Norwegian waters, to cut off the traffic in iron ore from Sweden to Germany, which in winter had to pass down the coast of Norway. In December 1939 the Soviet Union attacked Finland, and a scheme was developed to combine assistance to the Finns with an attack on German iron ore supplies. An Anglo-French expeditionary force was assembled in Scotland early in 1940 to respond to an appeal for help from the Finns; and the idea was that this force, while *en route* for Finland across northern Norway and Sweden, should make a diversion to blow up the Swedish iron ore mines. Doubtless fortunately, the Finnish government never made the expected appeal, and the expeditionary force was dispersed without attempting this strange operation. But politically Daladier's government committed

29. Martin Gilbert, *Finest Hour. Winston S. Churchill, 1939–1941* (London, 1983), p. 201.

itself strongly to the Finnish cause, and the British, though more cautious, followed suit. The Finnish defeat in March 1940 was widely construed as a reverse for the Allies, and it was followed by the fall of Daladier's government on 20 March.

At much the same time, in the early months of 1940, the Allies also discussed an extraordinary scheme to bomb the Soviet oil-wells at Baku, on the ground that Soviet oil supplies were vital to the German war effort. The RAF actually flew two photographic reconnaissance missions over Baku in March, though the Chiefs of Staff were properly cautious about the operation, and kept it under review largely to please the French, who were apparently keen on it. Even though nothing further happened, this scheme revealed a disturbing frame of mind among the Anglo-French planners. There was something radically wrong with the strategic direction of the alliance when it produced ideas which were so far removed from strategic and political reality.

There was another disturbing element in the grave disparity between the British and French forces in the field. The BEF in France began with only four divisions, while the French mustered 90. French and British propagandists were acutely aware of the German slogan that Britain was ready to fight to the last Frenchman, and did their best to combat it by advertising the British presence in France while saying little about its scale. Newsreel films showed British Tommies helping French farmers. Parades were held and decorations exchanged. British divisions were detached from the BEF to do a turn in the Maginot Line and be seen by their French neighbours. (There was a difficulty even in this, because the French troops found them vastly overpaid – later to be a British complaint against the Americans.) In general, these propaganda exercises carried little conviction. Behind the scenes, at the beginning of October 1939, Daladier complained bitterly to General Armengaud: 'The English, behind the Channel . . . have the possibility of conserving their energies so as to last out, to wait for the Americans, perhaps the Russians. But as for us, we risk becoming, after the Czechs, after the Poles, the prey of the Reich.' The French, he said, had three million men in the line, the British a mere 100–150,000. He talked of sending Armengaud to London to tell the British that they must make a greater effort in the air, or France would have to make peace.[30] Nothing came of this outburst, but it is significant to find Daladier, a convinced advocate of the British alliance, speaking in such terms. It was a line of thought which many found it easy to follow after the defeat of 1940.

---

30. Crémieux-Brilhac, vol. I, pp. 139–40.

As in the previous war, the French thought the British were not pulling their weight. The British for their part harboured doubts about French determination and political stability. Phipps reported during the autumn of 1939 on the persistence of a defeatist group in parliament, with Laval and Flandin at its centre, and he thought that there were defeatists even in Daladier's Cabinet. When Daladier fell, his successor, Paul Reynaud, achieved a majority of only one vote over his opponents and those who abstained when his government was presented to the Chamber of Deputies. The new British Ambassador, Sir Ronald Campbell, could not prophesy a long life for the new administration; and he passed on some disobliging remarks about Reynaud himself – clever but superficial, with the nickname of Mickey Mouse. More seriously, Reynaud's personal and political feud with Daladier persisted, and yet Reynaud had to keep his predecessor on as Minister of Defence, a key post. The new Premier and his Minister of Defence disagreed on most things and communicated with one another only by means of notes; which augured ill for the efficiency of the government as well as its cohesion.

The phoney war period brought out some of the best and the worst in Anglo-French relations. The two countries went to war reluctantly but with determination, in a cause which combined their national interests and security with the defence of their common civilisation against the barbarism of Nazi Germany – solid and honourable causes. They devised methods of co-operation which built on the experience of the previous war and revealed visions of the future which others would later pursue. At the same time the Allies suffered from a desperate streak of unreality in their thinking, and from a pervasive feeling that the other partner was not wholly reliable. In that feeling there was a dangerous element of truth. The British were painfully slow in building up an army and organising their economy for war. French governments were weak and ill-adapted to the conduct of war; and there was a significant number of politicians who had not wanted the war in the first place and did not believe it could be won. This made a shaky foundation for an alliance. As long as the war remained phoney, it sufficed, but the terrible ordeals which followed in May and June 1940 brought far greater strains to bear than this foundation could support.

CHAPTER 13

Their Finest Hour – L'Heure Tragique, 1940

The second volume of Winston Churchill's memoirs of the Second World War is entitled *Their Finest Hour*. The French translation bears the title *L'heure tragique*. Behind that stark contrast lies the story of what remains the most intense, dramatic and tragic episode in the long history of relations between France and Britain.

Churchill's advent to power marked in itself a transformation in British relations with France. Churchill, in contrast to his predecessor Neville Chamberlain, held France and its people in deep affection. He was a regular visitor to the country, moving easily among his French friends and using their language confidently if sometimes erratically. He was familiar with French history, and had a strong sense of the enduring greatness of France. Not least, he had an instinctive faith in the French Army which had been deeply ingrained during the 1914–18 war, and which was so strong as to mislead him at the opening of the crisis of 1940. Churchill was often moved by instinct and swayed by emotion, and the lead which he gave to British policy and opinion towards France in 1940 was very different from that which any other politician of that day would have imparted.

If any man could have secured unity between the two countries, it was Churchill. But in the event his appointment as Prime Minister on 10 May 1940 coincided with the opening of the German offensive in the west which brought immediate disaster for the Allied armies. On 13 May German armoured forces crossed the Meuse at Sedan, and moved at astonishing speed towards the Channel, reaching the sea at the mouth of the Somme on the 21st. To the north of this corridor driven by the Panzers there was cut off a large French force, the great majority of the BEF, and the Belgian Army. The Dutch Army had already surrendered, though Queen Wilhelmina and her government had not. They went to London, and there continued the war, setting an example of resistance in exile which it was open to others to follow.

These rapid German victories opened dangerous fissures in the Franco-British alliance. At first, the British did not grasp what was happening in France. At 7.30 in the morning of 15 May the French Premier, Paul Reynaud, rang up Churchill and said to him, in English: 'We are beaten; we have lost the battle.'[1] Churchill did not believe him, and was confident that (following the pattern of 1918) the German advance would slow down in a few days and give the Allies a chance to recover. However, he decided to fly to Paris, where he arrived at the British Embassy in the afternoon of 16 May, 'full of fire and fury, saying the French were lily-livered and must fight. After conference with P.R. [Paul Reynaud] he took [a] graver view. . . .'[2] Churchill had every reason for gravity. The meeting of the Supreme War Council, held at the Quai d'Orsay, lacked its usual order, and the participants sometimes got up and walked about. Outside the windows they could see smoke rising as officials of the Foreign Ministry tried to burn their archives. One official, Jean Chauvel, had been woken by telephone at 5 a.m. that morning and summoned to the Quai, to be told that the Germans might be in Paris that very evening. He started to burn papers in the grate, but set fire to the chimney; the fire brigade arrived to put it out. Some of his colleagues tried to use petrol, but still half-burned papers floated up in the breeze and came down in the streets. When they paused for coffee, one official remarked that they would be the laughing-stock of Europe.[3] But Churchill, looking out on the scene, felt no wish to laugh.

In the conference room, General Gamelin, the French Commander-in-Chief, gave a brief description of the military situation. When he finished, Churchill asked, in French: 'Où est la masse de manoeuvre?' (Where is the strategic reserve?) Gamelin shrugged helplessly and said there was none. Churchill was dumbfounded. Worse still, Roland de Margerie (the senior official who was keeping a record of the meeting) took Churchill aside and told him that on the previous evening Reynaud had been talking about fighting on the Loire or the Garonne, or even retreating to North Africa. Defeat was in the air.

1. Winston S. Churchill, *The Second World War*, vol. II, *Their Finest Hour* (London, 1949), pp. 36–9.

2. John Harvey, ed., *The Diplomatic Diaries of Oliver Harvey, 1937–1940* (London, 1970), p. 359.

3. Jean Chauvel, *Commentaire*, vol. I (Paris, 1971), pp. 95–6.

Churchill returned to London on 17 May, and met the War Cabinet at 10 a.m. The minutes record him as expressing the hope that, if the French could get four or five days' respite from air attack, they would be able to rally; but the impression left on his hearers was very different. Cadogan noted in his diary: 'W.S.C. gave an account of his trip. French evidently cracking, and situation awful.'[4] Churchill's actions were even more revealing. He asked Chamberlain to form a committee to examine the consequences of a French defeat. This committee reported the very next day on the possibility of being compelled 'to continue our resistance single-handed in this country . . .'[5] The essence of its recommendations was that Britain should continue the war alone until the United States came to her aid, adopting the most drastic methods of civil administration. At the same time, the Chiefs of Staff were set to work on the military aspects of the same question, and on 19 May they considered a draft report on 'British strategy in a certain eventuality' – the euphemism used to avoid a straightforward reference to a French collapse. Thus, within ten days of the opening of the German offensive, the machinery of British government, operating at high speed, was preparing for the fall of France.

So far this was only a possibility. The campaign in France might yet be saved, by turning the tide of battle in the air. To this end, the French asked repeatedly for British help. On 14 May there were ten RAF fighter squadrons operating from bases in France, with several others flying from England. That day, Reynaud appealed for ten more. On the morning of 16 May, the War Cabinet agreed to send the equivalent of four extra squadrons; and later that day, during his visit to Paris, Churchill recommended the despatch of another six. In London, however, the Air Staff insisted that fighters must be saved for home defence, and the War Cabinet would only agree to allow six squadrons to operate over France from bases in England. In the event, the Germans advanced so quickly during the next few days that the RAF simply had to get out of north-eastern France as best they could. But the question of fighter squadrons continued to plague Franco-British relations, and made a lasting mark upon them.

The British thus embarked on a double line of policy: to prepare for the defeat of France and make ready to fight on alone; and at the same time to help the French to stave off defeat. In principle these lines were complementary to one another, but in practice they were

4. David Dilks, ed., *The Diaries of Sir Alexander Cadogan, 1938–1945* (London, 1971), p. 285.
5. CAB 63/13, WM(40)128th Conclusions, Confidential Annex.

hard to reconcile. To prepare openly for a French collapse would be fatal to French morale and to British relations with France; yet to try to prevent defeat by pouring in all possible help would squander resources which would be needed to keep up the struggle alone.

The days following Churchill's visit to Paris on 16 May saw a rapid worsening of the military situation. On 19 May Gamelin proposed (without actually ordering) a counter-offensive from both north and south of the German corridor to the sea. That same day Reynaud dismissed Gamelin and appointed in his place General Weygand, who had been Foch's chief of staff in the previous war. Though 73 years old, he still had a reputation for energy and decisiveness. At the same time, Reynaud tried to strengthen his government by appointing Marshal Pétain, the greatest surviving hero of the 1914-18 war, as Vice-Premier. Weygand made a difficult and chaotic visit to the armies cut off in Flanders, and on 22 May gave a firm order for a combined offensive from north and south.

This offensive failed to materialise. In the south, the French had too few reserves to achieve anything serious. In the north, a small British force under General Franklyn, along with a French division, had already made a successful local attack south of Arras, which for a time alarmed the Germans. But by the evening of 23 May Franklyn's advance had been checked and his force was in danger of being surrounded. He therefore secured from Gort an order to retreat. This comparatively minor episode had extensive consequences. When Weygand heard of the British retreat, during the morning of 24 May, he was furious. He had only just issued his formal order for an offensive, and he claimed that the orders for the retreat must have come from London. It was impossible, he told Reynaud, to command an army which was controlled from another capital. In fact there had been no orders from London, where neither Churchill nor the Chief of Staff (General Ironside) understood what was happening round Arras. Franklyn's withdrawal was simply caused by local circumstances, and occurred at a time when many units, British and French alike, were in retreat. But the affair rankled in Weygand's mind, and formed part of a general impression that the British had let the French down during the battle of Flanders.

The battle in general continued to go badly. As early as 19 May Gort had warned his government in London that he might have to retreat to Dunkirk and evacuate the BEF by sea. General Ironside replied at once that this could not be permitted; but in fact on 20 May the Admiralty began to make contingency plans for an evacuation. On 25 May Gort came to the conclusion that his force was in mortal danger, and on his own responsibility he abandoned any idea of an attack southwards and began to withdraw the BEF towards Dunkirk. In doing so, he undoubtedly saved his army, but at the cost of grievous damage to relations between Britain and France. The sort of crisis which had threatened the Allies in September 1914 and May 1918, but had then been averted, now came about. The British and French armies in Flanders began to act separately, and a breach opened between them.

The political signs were also ominous. On 25 May the French *Comité de Guerre* met in Paris – an unusual gathering of the principal ministers and the three commanders-in-chief, with the President of the Republic in the chair. The panic of 16 May had subsided as the anticipated German dash for Paris did not materialise, but Weygand's summary of the military situation was still sombre. He believed that the forces cut off in Flanders would be lost, and he predicted that by mid-June the French Army would muster only fifty-nine effective divisions, plus another ten in the Maginot Line, to face about 130–150 German divisions. The numerical odds were about three to one. The only plan he could propose was to hold a line along the rivers Somme and Aisne to the last; if that failed, the army could only fight for its honour, without hope of military success.

There followed a long and rambling discussion, in which it became clear that all the senior figures in the French administration, civil and military alike, accepted the likelihood of defeat. President Lebrun raised the question of what to do in the event of a German peace offer. He knew that France had an agreement with Britain forbidding a separate peace, but he thought that if the Germans offered advantageous terms the French should examine them carefully. Pétain argued that the two countries' duties to one another should be proportionate to their contribution to the battle: the French had 80 divisions in the field, the British only 10. Campinchi, the Minister of Marine, though stressing the necessity of loyalty to the British, none the less remarked that it was the present government which had given its word, and a successor would be less constrained over making a separate peace. At one point, almost as a side-issue, Reynaud introduced the question of asking Britain to make sacrifices to prevent Italy from entering the war on Germany's side.

At the end of the meeting, Reynaud said he would go to London the next day and explain that France would soon be faced with odds of three to one. He emphasised that the British could insist that France was bound by her signature not to make a separate peace. Weygand said that Reynaud must explain that the French Army might be completely destroyed, and added that he must have enough forces intact to maintain order in the country. The meeting was confused and its conclusions obscure; but it was plain that the French government accepted the imminence of defeat, and ministers were already wondering how to escape from the no-separate-peace agreement.[6]

Thus as early as 17 May the British government concluded that France was on the verge of defeat, and had begun to prepare for that eventuality. By 25 May the French government too accepted the imminence of defeat, though without as yet drawing any clear-cut resolutions in consequence. Within fifteen days of the opening of the German assault the alliance was in deep difficulty.

As agreed at the *Comité de Guerre*, Reynaud visited London on 26 May. Before he arrived, Churchill told the Cabinet that he might well be coming to say that France could not carry on the fight. Reynaud did not say this in so many words, but he left no doubt as to what was in his mind. Cadogan noted in his diary: 'Cabinet at 2. W.S.C. gave us account of his conversation with Reynaud at lunch. R. doesn't *say* that France will capitulate, but all his conversation goes to show that he sees no alternative . . .'[7] What Reynaud did raise openly was the possibility of trying to keep Italy out of the war by making a joint Franco-British approach to Mussolini, offering territorial concessions to buy him off. Reynaud also suggested approaching Mussolini to find a basis for a general European settlement, which meant in practice opening the possibility of peace with Germany.

For a very few days it seemed just possible that France and Britain might both take this path of negotiation and a compromise peace – if one was available. In a series of tense and difficult meetings on 26, 27 and 28 May the British War Cabinet discussed the linked questions of an approach to Italy and a wider negotiation with Germany. Halifax, the Foreign Secretary, pressed the case for ascertaining the German terms and seeing whether they would endanger British independence or not. Churchill at one point went so far as to say that, while he would not join the French if they asked for terms, 'if he were told what the terms offered were, he would be prepared to consider them'. But in the main, Churchill held strongly that it would be dangerous to embark on the slippery slope of negotiation. Even Halifax was not prepared to consider terms which threatened British independence. At the end of three days, the War Cabinet rejected the idea of an approach to Mussolini to keep Italy out of the war, and simply

---

6. The corrected record of this meeting of the *Comité de Guerre* is in MAE, Papiers 1940, Baudouin 16, ff. 4–9.

7. Dilks, *Cadogan Diaries*, 26 May 1940, p. 290.

dropped the idea of a wider peace negotiation. On 27 May, in the midst of these discussions, the War Cabinet accepted the Chiefs of Staff report on British strategy in the event of the fall of France, concluding that Britain could hold out as long as air superiority was maintained.[8]

The British War Cabinet thus discussed and rejected the idea of a negotiated peace, and decided instead that it would be possible to continue the war alone. This was a crucial decision in British history; and it was also of momentous significance in relations between Britain and France. If France chose to negotiate or was compelled to surrender, she would do so alone. Britain was determined to fight on, if necessary alone. From that fundamental difference far-reaching consequences were to follow.

DUNKIRK

While the *Comité de Guerre* and the War Cabinet wrestled with these problems of high policy, the battle in Flanders continued. On 26 May the British government confirmed Gort's decision of the 25th to fall back on Dunkirk and try to evacuate the BEF by sea. Churchill told Reynaud of this during the Premier's visit to London on the 26th, and asked that similar orders should be given to the French forces in the north-east. For whatever reason, this request had no effect. Weygand issued no orders for withdrawal until 29 May, continuing instead to send instructions to attack southwards in pursuit of his earlier plan. For a few days the two armies were at complete cross-purposes. The British headed for the sea, while the French were still trying to move south, or at least to hold their ground. On 27 and 28 May liaison between the French and British headquarters in the north-east broke down completely, and members of the French liaison mission searched in vain even for the location of the British command posts.

By midnight on 30/31 May, the British evacuation had been under way for four full days, and nearly 135,000 British troops had been taken off in addition to 28,000 who had left earlier. Not a single French soldier had so far accompanied them. On 31 May Churchill went to Paris for a meeting of the Supreme War Council, and announced that the evacuation was going unexpectedly well, giving a figure of 165,000 rescued so far. Weygand asked sharply how many

8. For these War Cabinet discussions, see Bell, *A Certain Eventuality*, pp. 38–50.

French this included, and complained that his troops were being left behind. Stirred by deep emotion, as he often was in his affection for France and the French Army, Churchill declared that in future the evacuation must proceed on equal terms – 'Bras dessus, bras dessous', he said, emphasising his point by breaking into French. At one stage he even claimed that the British would form the rearguard during the evacuation. Before the end of the meeting, this was reduced to an undertaking that the British would remain behind as long as possible; but Churchill's impulsive offer to provide the rearguard was remembered by the Frenchmen present, even though it was not formalised in the conclusions of the meeting.

Astonishingly, Churchill's undertaking about equality in the evacuation was fulfilled. On the Admiralty's figures, the numbers taken off between 29 May and the last departures in the early hours of 4 June were 139,732 British and 139,097 French. By midnight on 2/3 June nearly all the British troops had escaped, but still the overwhelmingly British rescue ships continued their hazardous crossings to bring off about 41,000 French troops in the last 26 hours of the operation.[9] This was a remarkable and selfless action. One French writer called it a miracle – not a word the French care to use about Dunkirk; and he added that it might have cemented the friendship of the two countries.[10] In fact it did nothing of the kind. The evacuation, though successful, took place among a great deal of muddle and friction between the two armies, with some violent clashes which lost nothing in the telling afterwards. One of the last British divisions to leave insisted that there were to be no embarkations by the French in its zone until all its own troops had gone; and action was taken accordingly. A British historian has summed the matter up. 'If Churchill had had his way the rearguard would have been entirely British. Gort had expected the final honour and sacrifice to be shared; in the event the rearguard was entirely French.'[11] The British, for perfectly understandable reasons and to the ultimate benefit of their country, showed a single-minded determination to get away. Many of the French did not get away at all. Somewhere between 30,000 and 40,000 French troops covered the last retreat and were left behind to surrender.

These events, and even the name 'Dunkirk', have left utterly different impressions in the two countries. For the British, Dunkirk was a deliverance. The word 'miracle' was freely used at the time.

9. Brian Bond, *Britain, France and Belgium, 1939–1940* (2nd edn, London, 1990), p. 115; Bell, *A Certain Eventuality*, p. 17.
10. Gilbert Martineau, *L'Entente Cordiale* (Grenoble, 1984), p. 205.
11. Bond, *Britain, France and Belgium*, p. 114.

Moreover, it was a tremendous national achievement, heightened by the role played by the 'little ships' manned by volunteer civilians, which received much publicity; though most of the work was in fact done by the Royal Navy. On 4 June *The Times* published a leading article, declaring that 'No British army is encircled if a way to the sea is open or can be forced.' The memory was long-lasting and it was to be many years before the British, in times of trouble, ceased to invoke the 'spirit of Dunkirk'.

The reaction in France was very different. In May 1940 Pétain and Weygand recalled the time in May 1918 when the British had almost split off from the French to head for the ports. This time they had done so. For *The Times* leader-writer, and doubtless for his readers, to head for the sea was historic good sense, with an air of glory besides. For many in France it was the coward's way out. Admiral Darlan, the C-in-C of the French Navy, wrote to his wife: 'The British lion seems to grow wings when it's a matter of getting back to the sea.'[12] After the armistice, and under the Vichy regime, such views grew into a wider belief in British betrayal at Dunkirk as an explanation of French defeat. At another level, there were tens of thousands of French soldiers who had been left behind and did not forget. From whatever point of view, the facts remained that the British had first decided unilaterally on evacuation, and had then left the French to provide the rearguard and the prisoners. For the French, Dunkirk was no sort of a miracle. It was a disaster on the road to further disasters.

ARMISTICE AND SEPARATION

The evacuation from Dunkirk ended during the night of 4/5 June. Dawn on the 5th saw the beginning of the next phase of the German offensive, starting on the Somme and extending along the River Aisne on 9 June. By this stage, the Germans possessed overwhelming numerical superiority, as well as all the confidence born of victory. Yet at this very time, for a few days the spirit of the French Army suddenly recovered. As Jean-Louis Crémieux-Brilhac has vividly shown, morale was high. The German combination of tanks and dive-bombers which had previously played havoc was now faced with determination and some success. It was a remarkable recovery, too

---

12. John C. Cairns, 'Great Britain and the Fall of France: A Study in Allied Disunity', *Journal of Modern History*, vol. 27, No. 4, December 1955, p. 374. This article remains a key analysis of the whole problem.

often omitted from accounts of the campaign; and it was achieved almost without help from the British. This last stand came from within the French Army.[13]

It was too late, and the odds were too heavy. By 9 June the Germans were across the Somme and heading for Rouen. On the 10th they crossed the Aisne. The French government left Paris on 10 June, and the Germans entered the city on the 14th. The German columns fanned out across the country, meeting only sporadic resistance. Co-ordinated defence came to an end.

At the same time, the French government fled in disorder. Ministers and senior civil servants left Paris for the Loire valley, whose châteaux provided dignified but inefficient refuges for ministries. On 14 June, moving as much by historical memory as by conscious decision, the core of the government followed the examples of 1870 and 1914 and went to Bordeaux. During this migration, the administrative machinery of France fell to pieces. On 14 June the Secretary-General of the Foreign Ministry, Charles-Roux, gathered together such officials as he could find and told them that the *chefs de service* were going to Bordeaux. Everyone else was to receive two months' pay and could go where they liked. The previous day, the Minister of Commerce had told his staff much the same: draw three months' salary, and go off into the blue. Hervé Alphand, who was present, commented in his diary: 'France no longer has an administration.'[14] This was an experience which the British did not share. In June 1940 the War Cabinet met regularly, and the machinery of which it was the centre continued to work, though under heavy pressure. Later on, under German air attack, London continued to function as a capital city, and the innumerable tasks of wartime administration were carried out without interruption. The experiences of the two countries could scarcely have been more different.

The French military collapse and the disintegration of the French state brought to a head the crisis in relations between France and Britain which had been latent since the first success of the German offensive in mid-May 1940. The British now had to confront the actuality of the defeat of France, while the French were faced with the stark question of whether to ask for an armistice.

The British government, watching from a distance the collapse of French resistance, continued to follow, with increasing difficulty and

13. J.-L. Crémieux-Brilhac, *Les Français de l'an 40* (Paris, 1990), vol. II, pp. 635–48. This passage puts the battle in a completely new light.

14. Chauvel, *Commentaire*, vol I, p. 116; Hervé Alphand, *L'étonnement d'être: Journal 1939–1973* (Paris, 1977), p. 45.

desperation, the double line which they had adopted in mid-May: to prepare for a French defeat, and at the same time to strive to keep France, somehow or other, in the fight. The two lines, never easy to reconcile with one another, were to end in confusion.

The long-term preparations for a French defeat, set in motion by Churchill on 17 May and given shape in the Chiefs of Staff paper on 'British strategy in a certain eventuality', depended in the long run on securing the intervention of the United States in the war. It was on that prospect that Churchill set his sights, with crucial long-term consequences for British relations with France. In the short run, the British had to concentrate on what might be saved from the wreck of defeat in France. Lists were drawn up of French assets which might be used for British purposes: gold reserves, merchant ships, armaments and machine tools. A few men with special knowledge thought anxiously about the fate of French atomic scientists and their stocks of heavy water, which might prove crucial in the making of an atomic bomb. Others were much concerned about intelligence secrets, and especially French work on deciphering the German 'Enigma' codes. Above all there loomed the fate of the powerful French fleet, which in German hands could prove fatal to the safety of Britain. The importance of all these matters was clear; though in the chaos of mid-June the British found themselves frustratingly unable to do anything about most of them.

The best way to save something from the wreck was to keep France in the war, and to this end the British directed such efforts as they could muster. The only means which they could use without stint was exhortation, at which Churchill was a past master. On 11–12 June Churchill went to meet Reynaud at the château du Muguet in the Loire valley. In the discussions he deployed all the argument, oratory and vision at his command. He invoked memories of spring 1918, when Ludendorff's offensive had seemed to carry all before it, and yet had finally been checked. He urged that Paris should be defended, swallowing up German forces in the rubble of its buildings. Constantly he repeated that defeat in France would not mean the end of the war. Britain would fight on, and would ultimately win a war of continents. It was a tremendous performance, but his audience was not impressed. About the parallel with 1918, Pétain observed that he had then been able to send 40 divisions to help the British. Where now were Britain's 40 divisions to help the French? To defend Paris street by street would merely reduce the city to ruins without affecting the outcome of the campaign. It may be that Reynaud, who wanted to fight on, was stimulated for a time by the fire of Churchill's rhetoric, but for the most part it seems that the Prime Minister's efforts were counter-productive, confirming the impression already held by Pétain and Weygand that he merely wished France to sacrifice herself for the sake of Britain.

Exhortation was not enough. What the French asked for with unremitting insistence was material help. The British War Cabinet discussed this question repeatedly between 2 and 5 June. Chamberlain and Halifax opposed sending any more forces, air or ground, in order to concentrate on home defence. Attlee wanted to keep the fighters, but thought that a couple of divisions would be a symbol of British intention and put heart into the French. Churchill was the strongest advocate of sending help, and in a fierce struggle against his Cabinet colleagues and the reluctant Chiefs of Staff, he got a part of what he wanted. As early as 2 June General Brooke was instructed to return to France as commander of what was grandly called a 'new BEF', made up of a British division, the 1st Canadian division and the troops still in France. In the air, the RAF had 144 fighters operating over France on 6 June, mainly flying from England but some using landing-grounds in France. The French pressed hard for ten fighter squadrons to be sent to France; on 8 June the War Cabinet reluctantly agreed to send two. This was the last time. Even Churchill concluded that it would be too dangerous for home defence to send any more fighters to France.

This question came to a head at the Supreme War Council at the château du Muguet on 11 June in a sharp exchange between Weygand and Churchill. Weygand told the Prime Minister: 'Here is the decisive point. Now is the decisive moment. It is therefore wrong to keep *any* squadrons back in England.' Churchill replied: 'This is not the decisive point and this is not the decisive moment. That moment will come when Hitler hurls his Luftwaffe against Great Britain. If we can keep command of the air, and if we can keep the seas open, as we certainly shall keep them open, we will win it all back for you.'[15] This was the crux, and Churchill was adamant. The French regarded the British contribution to the final battle after 5 June as tiny; and indeed it was. Yet from the British point of view it was surprising that anything was sent at all. In the event, the two divisions of the 'new BEF' got to France, did little, and were lucky to get out again, losing most of their equipment, which could ill be spared. From a military point of view, they should not have been sent at all and politically their effect was negligible.

These British attempts to keep France in the war by exhortation and by limited material help were the best that they could muster, but

15. Churchill, *Second World War*, vol. II, p. 137.

they did not match the scale of the crisis which confronted the French government. On 9 June it was clear that the line of resistance along the rivers Somme and Aisne had been broken. On 12 June Weygand formally told the French Cabinet, meeting at the château de Cangé, near Tours, that only the end of hostilities could save the French armies from collapse, and that the government should seek an armistice.

The French government now faced a grievous choice. On the one hand it could acknowledge defeat, and ask for an armistice, to be followed by a peace settlement. On the other it could accept defeat in the battle of France, but carry on the war, probably from French North Africa. This would follow the example set recently by Queen Wilhelmina of the Netherlands and her government, now continuing the war from London.

The advocates of an armistice carried great weight. Pétain bore the prestige of a Marshal of France, the victor of Verdun and the champion of the ordinary French soldier. Weygand too had a high reputation from the previous war. Both were convinced that to lose the battle of France was to lose the war – anything else was mere illusion. Moreover, both believed that Britain would rapidly make peace, following France or even getting in first if the opportunity offered. There seems to be no firm evidence that Weygand actually said that 'England will have her neck wrung like a chicken'; and Churchill, who used the phrase in a famous speech ('Some chicken! Some neck!') did not attribute it to Weygand, but only to unspecified French generals. But in any case there is ample evidence that Weygand believed that British resistance would not long outlast that of France. Finally, both Pétain and Weygand were determined not to leave the soil of France, which would be the equivalent of desertion. Instead, they would stay to protect the French people from the victor. This stance attracted the support of an increasing number of ministers as the days went by – though not a clear majority even by 16 June.

Reynaud and his supporters took the opposite view, claiming that the war would not be lost with the battle of France, but could be sustained from overseas by the French fleet and Empire, in co-operation with the British. Reynaud, convinced by Churchill's repeated declarations, did not believe that the British would surrender. Moreover, he refused to accept that there could be any reasonable peace with Nazi Germany. Pétain thought that Hitler was no more than 'a plebeian Kaiser Wilhelm II'.[16] Reynaud knew that he

16. Crémieux-Brilhac, *Les Français*, vol. I, p. 577.

represented a new barbarism – 'Hitler is Gengis-Kahn', he exclaimed.[17] There could be no compromise with such an enemy. On these fundamental issues Reynaud proved in the long run to be right. But in the short run he had neither the personality nor the political backing to prevail. He liked to compare himself with Clemenceau, but lacked Clemenceau's rock-like purpose and strength of character. He knew that his Cabinet was profoundly divided, and therefore he summoned it only rarely. He was conscious too of his lack of support in parliament, demonstrated at the very moment of his installation as Premier. Among the French people, he could not match Pétain's immense prestige – on which, indeed, he had counted when he appointed the Marshal as a minister. Therefore, though Reynaud held the more realistic view of Hitler, he was not strong enough to impose it upon others.

This dispute, for and against asking the Germans for an armistice, went on with growing intensity from 12 to 16 June. On the evening of the 12th, when Weygand raised the question with the Cabinet, Reynaud insisted that the British must be consulted. Dautry, the Armaments Minister, who opposed an armistice, suggested that when Churchill came over to France he should be invited to meet the whole French Cabinet, and this was agreed. Reynaud therefore telephoned Churchill and asked him to come to Tours the next day.

On 13 June there took place what proved to be the last meeting of the Supreme War Council. Reynaud reported that Weygand had requested the government to ask for an armistice. Speaking carefully in hypothetical terms, he asked Churchill: supposing a French government were to say that it must come to terms with Germany, would Britain agree to France making a separate peace? Churchill refused to give his consent, though he surrounded his refusal with other remarks about not wasting time on reproaches and on the need to appeal to Roosevelt for American help, and then to await an answer before reaching a decision. As soon as the meeting was over, Paul Baudouin (recently appointed by Reynaud as Under-Secretary at the Foreign Ministry) put into circulation a report that Churchill had said that he would 'understand' if France made an armistice. Whether it arose from deliberate misrepresentation or mere wishful thinking, this report was widely believed and became the root of much controversy. Any misunderstanding might have been cleared up if Reynaud had invited Churchill to meet the French Cabinet, as had been agreed; but he did not. Instead, the Prime Minister left at once for England.

17. Paul Reynaud, *La France a sauvé l'Europe* (Paris, 1947), vol. II, pp. 313–16.

On 14 June the French government made its way to Bordeaux, where on the 15th Reynaud and Weygand had a fierce confrontation. Reynaud said that France should follow the same course as the Dutch: the Army in France should capitulate, while the government with other forces continued the war from North Africa. Weygand flatly rejected this proposal, claiming that it would be shameful for the Army and for himself, and that it was the government's responsibility to ask for an armistice. At the Cabinet meeting which followed, the Vice-Premier, Chautemps, put forward a compromise proposal. The French people, he argued, would only understand a decision to carry on the war from overseas if they could see plainly that German terms were unacceptable. He therefore proposed to ask Britain for permission to seek terms. These could then be shown to be impossible, and the government could go to North Africa with the assurance of popular support. Chautemps's suggestion postponed the basic decision as to whether to ask for an armistice or not, and temporarily offered a course which everyone could accept. The Cabinet quickly agreed to it, and that evening (15 June) Reynaud telegraphed to ask for British permission to seek armistice terms, though adding the assurance that he was sure that they would prove unacceptable. The surrender of the fleet was specifically ruled out.

On 16 June the British War Cabinet made two completely different replies to this request. The first concentrated on the fate of the fleet, and agreed to a French enquiry to ascertain terms, 'provided, but only provided, that the French Fleet is sailed forthwith for British ports pending negotiations'. The British government declared that it was resolved to continue the war, and excluded itself from any part in such an enquiry.[18] The British did not take their stand on the no-separate-armistice agreement, on the ground that a flat refusal would lead to Reynaud's resignation and replacement by someone less reliable. On the other hand, they did not accept as sufficient Reynaud's assurance that the fleet would not be surrendered, but wanted the physical security of its despatch to British ports. Two telegrams were despatched to this effect.

The second response was the extraordinary offer of union between Britain and France which was adopted by the War Cabinet at a further meeting during the afternoon of 16 June. This proposal occupies a particular place in the history of Franco-British relations. It is rightly described as dramatic, though no-one knows whether it should be classified as high drama, *grand guignol* or the theatre of the absurd. It

18. CAB 65/13, WM(40)168th Conclusions, Confidential Annex.

was the handiwork of a small group, French and British, including Jean Monnet, Corbin (the French Ambassador), Leo Amery (Secretary of State for India), Vansittart, and Desmond Morton, a close associate of Churchill's. This group had worked on the idea of a union of the two countries during 15 June, and on the 16th they were joined by de Gaulle, on a visit to London; so that we have the surprising spectacle of this ardent patriot lending his support to a proposal to merge the identity of France with that of Britain.

The actual document adopted by the British War Cabinet during the afternoon of 16 June declared that France and Britain 'shall no longer be two nations, but one Franco-British Union'. There were to be joint organs for defence, financial and economic policies. The two peoples would share common citizenship. There was to be a single War Cabinet, controlling all the forces of the two countries, and governing 'from wherever it best can'. The two Parliaments were to be formally associated. France was to keep all her forces in the field, and the Union would concentrate all its energy against the enemy, 'no matter where the battle may be'. The proposed declaration ended with a flourish: 'And thus we shall conquer.'[19]

The meeting of the War Cabinet which accepted this proposal was confused and hasty. The document's implications were obscure, and it was apparently not even made clear whether the proposed Union was intended to be permanent or only a wartime measure. (Halifax later told Hankey that the offer was only for the duration of the war, but there is no sign of this in the text.) For the War Cabinet, the key to the document lay in its final section: France was to keep fighting, and the Union would concentrate its energy against the enemy. The proposal therefore did not represent the conversion of those two great patriots Churchill and de Gaulle to some federal ideal, but their determination to keep fighting and win – 'And thus we shall conquer.' The analogy of drama is completely appropriate. The declaration was essentially a piece of theatre, designed to give a psychological boost to Reynaud and his Cabinet, to avoid an armistice and keep France in the war.

For a moment it seemed to have a chance of success. De Gaulle telephoned the text to Reynaud, who responded in terms which were themselves theatrical. 'I will die defending these proposals', he told Campbell and Spears.[20] But of course he did not. When he read out

19. The draft of the Declaration of Union put to the War Cabinet, and the version finally adopted are printed in Bell, *A Certain Eventuality*, pp. 303–5.
20. E.L. Spears, *Assignment to Catastrophe*, vol. II, *The Fall of France, June 1940* (London, 1954), p. 293.

the document to his colleagues in the French Cabinet, it was simply brushed aside. One minister said that the British were trying to turn France into a Dominion. The Cabinet turned at once to the only question that mattered: whether to ask for an armistice. By the end of the meeting, in the evening of 16 June, Reynaud was exhausted, and felt that the pressure in favour of an armistice was too great to be resisted any longer. He presented his resignation to the President of the Republic, who at once asked Pétain to form a government. He did so within an hour.

The British actions on 16 June thus ended in irretrievable confusion. Their first position had been clear; they agreed to a French enquiry as to armistice terms, provided that the fleet was sent first to British ports. But then this was dropped in favour of the offer of union. A telegram was sent to Bordeaux instructing the ambassador to 'suspend action' on the earlier messages about the fleet; and at Bordeaux the word 'suspend' was changed to 'cancel', which made matters worse. The offer of union then fell completely flat, and its only practical effect was that Reynaud did not read to the French Cabinet, or even give the sense of, the British telegrams about the fleet. Thus the original clear-cut British position was lost and replaced by something which proved to be no more than a spectacular irrelevance.

In Bordeaux, there was no doubt that Pétain had been appointed as Premier to ask for an armistice, and he formed a ministry which was overwhelmingly in favour of that course. With no further ado about consulting the British government, the new Foreign Minister, Baudouin, met the Spanish Ambassador at 12.30 a.m. on 17 June, and asked him to transmit to Germany a request for terms for an armistice and for peace, a phrase which made clear that it was not simply a cessation of hostilities that was sought, but a full peace settlement. At 1 a.m. Baudouin simply told the British Ambassador what he had done. At 12.30 p.m. on the 17th Pétain spoke on the radio to the French people: 'I tell you today that we must end the fighting.' For the press this was changed to: 'We must try to end the fighting', but the original version represented the truth.

There was an agonising delay before Hitler received the French armistice delegation on 21 June at Rethondes, where the armistice had been signed on 11 November 1918. The German terms were severe but not catastrophic for France. They demanded the occupation of some two-thirds of the country, including Paris and all the Channel and Atlantic coasts. The French Army was to be reduced to 100,000 men. The fleet was to be disarmed under German or Italian supervision at the peace-time stations of the warships concerned. (This was a clause of particular importance to the British, who were desperately anxious about the fate of the fleet.) The French proposed a few amendments, which were swept aside; and the armistice was signed on 22 June. An armistice with Italy, on similar lines though with only a very small Italian zone of occupation, followed on 24 June. Both armistices came into force at 12.35 a.m. on 25 June. France was no longer a combatant in the war.

Until the actual signature of the German armistice, the British government continued to hope that Pétain's government might yet change its mind and go to Algiers to continue the war. It was not until the evening of 22 June that the British concluded that the issue was settled. On the 23rd Churchill made a broadcast expressing his 'grief and amazement' that the French government had agreed to terms which would be unacceptable to any government possessing 'freedom, independence and constitutional authority'. On the 24th he told the Cabinet that relations with France 'might well approach very closely to those of two nations at war with each other'.[21] Within the next few days this was to prove all too true.

The French armistice of June 1940 marked the culmination of the breach between the two countries which Churchill had foreseen as early as 16–17 May, though he had striven with all his immense energy and force of personality to prevent it. The policy of the French government was to cease fighting immediately, and then to adjust to the consequences of German victory. The main reaction of the French people appears to have been one of relief, accompanied by an immense passivity after the convulsions of the six-week conflict. Jean Chauvel wrote that with the armistice the French people entered a state of 'compulsory neutrality' which was universally welcome.[22] In Britain, on the other hand, Churchill's government was dedicated to carrying on the war. As Churchill had explained when presenting his ministry to the House of Commons on 13 May, his sole policy was to wage war. At the end of June 1940 this purpose was supported by the vast majority of the British people. On this fundamental issue there was therefore no longer any point of contact between the two governments and the two peoples.

Geographically and physically also the two countries were completely separated from one another. The narrow seas of the Channel might almost have divided two planets – they were certainly harder to cross than the Atlantic. Just as important (perhaps in the long

---

21. Bell, *A Certain Eventuality*, pp. 102–4.
22. Chauvel, *Commentaire*, vol. I, p. 131.

run even more so), the two countries passed through utterly different national experiences. France suffered a shattering defeat which left a deep wound. A French soldier and historian has summed it up:

> The disaster of 1940 made a profound impression on our national consciousness. Never throughout our long history had our army been so swiftly and decisively defeated, our territory so comprehensively invaded, our economic potential taken over so absolutely by the enemy, our independence so completely destroyed.[23]

This defeat was no distant matter, settled upon the battle-field. It penetrated directly and personally to nearly everyone in France. There were some 1,800,000 prisoners of war in German camps, taking a mass of Frenchmen in the prime of life from their families and their work. There were vast numbers of refugees, about six millions in all. An eye-witness captured the scene in one small town:

> . . . in twenty-four hours the unhappy town has emptied like a burst water bottle. What a panic! I am sure that three-quarters of the population has left already. A few grocers, a few foodshops are still open, and two or three cafés. All the rest is shut up. No more cinema, no more newspapers – I find the metal gates closed at the swimming pool.[24]

As the refugees fled, the German Army moved in, settling across two-thirds of France, with a base and billets in every town.

The British experienced none of this. The great majority of the BEF came safely home. The only British territory to be occupied was the Channel Islands. The enduring sounds of 1940 were Churchill's speeches and the air-raid sirens, and the strongest images, often evoked in later years, were the Spitfires and their pilots in the Battle of Britain. The final memory was of survival and victory, so that men really did say of the British people, as Churchill predicted that they would, 'this was their finest hour'. In all this the fall of France, a shock and a disaster at the time, was quickly pushed aside. It was, after all, only the prelude to victory.

From these profoundly different experiences there developed a breach between the two peoples which lasted for many years.

23. General Charles de Cossé-Brissac, Preface to Pierre Le Goyet et Jean Foussereau, *La corde au cou: Calais, mai 1940* (Paris, 1975), p. 5.
24. Jean Vidalenc, *L'Éxode de mai–juin 1940* (Paris, 1957), pp. 129, 139, 359.

Conclusion

The French armistices of June 1940 marked a fundamental parting of the ways between Britain and France. France as a country, and the French people as a whole, dropped out of the war. Only a defiant handful rallied round General de Gaulle to continue the fight. The British, government and people alike, fought on with intense determination, and looked across the Atlantic to the United States for immediate help and ultimate salvation. For Britain, an American alliance now had to replace that with France as the means of fighting the war and eventually securing peace. The political consequences of that change were profound, and were still not fully worked out more than fifty years later.

But the relationship between Britain and France involved more than politics or strategy, and the separation of 1940 was also psychological – for some, it was like a cut in living tissue. On the evening of 17 June, after Pétain had announced that he was asking for an armistice, Churchill made a very brief broadcast. 'The news from France is very bad', he began, 'and I grieve for the gallant French people who have fallen into this terrible misfortune. Nothing will alter our feelings towards them, or our faith that the genius of France will rise again.' Britain, he continued, would fight on 'until the curse of Hit   s lifted from the brows of men. We are sure that in the end all will be well.'[1]

Churchill was sincere in his grief. Nothing did alter his feelings towards the French people or his faith in the genius of France. Some four months later he was to make a moving broadcast to the French

1. Winston S. Churchill, *Second World War*, vol. II, *Their Finest Hour* (London, 1949), p. 191. The whole broadcast, by a man sometimes accused of being verbose, contained some 120 words in all.

people, in French, in which he repeated the prayer on the old *louis d'or*, 'Dieu protège la France', with all the force of heart-felt emotion.[2] In this he echoed the deep sentiments of a small but ardent company of British Francophiles, who in June 1940 suffered a sense of loss so acute as to amount almost to bereavement. A leader-writer for *The Economist* felt that 'We lose part of ourselves when France's liberties are trampled underfoot.' He regretted that France had been compelled to bear the brunt of the fighting with so little help from the British, and promised that 'There can and must be no recrimination.'[3] Raymond Mortimer, novelist and literary critic, felt as though half of England had fallen into the sea. R.B. McCallum, historian and political writer, sensed that 'In the hour of France's disaster all that she represented in European civilization stood out with a wonderful clarity.'[4] Denis Brogan, from the depth of his affection for France, wrote bitterly that Pétain's government had decided 'to try the daring and despicable experiment of saving all but honour'. But he still believed that the true France remained – 'the eternal France, to which we will extend our friendship until the day of her resurrection'. That day would surely come. 'The France of all civilized men is not dead or even captive. . . .' Her voices still bid her:

> . . . Sors de la poussière,
> Quitte les vêtements de ta captivité,
> Et reprends ta splendeur première.[5]

> . . . Rise from the dust,
> Cast off thy captive's garb,
> And assume once more thine inborn splendour.

It was a remarkable testimony to a profound sense of kinship, which was shared by others, though not always with Brogan's intensity of feeling and language.

Popular feeling appears to have been less deeply stirred, and less sympathetic. The press mainly took the line that Pétain's government was a puppet of the Germans, and directed little criticism towards the French people. Opinion in the country as a whole seems largely to have followed this lead; though the reports about public opinion

---

2. Ibid., p. 451.
3. *The Economist*, 22 June 1940.
4. R.B. McCallum, *England and France, 1940–1943* (London, 1944), p. 59.
5. D.W. Brogan, 'Il y avait la France', and 'France: 1940', reprinted in *French Personalities and Problems* (London, 1946), pp. 133, 135, 155.

relayed to the Ministry of Information also recorded frequent remarks to the effect that 'At last we have no more allies', or 'We're better off without the French', or 'We should have looked after ourselves all along'.[6] In any case, public attention rapidly moved elsewhere. All eyes were soon fixed on the Battle of Britain, on the threat of invasion, and on aerial bombardment. A bomb in one's own street was far more immediate and important than anything happening across the Channel. The sense of loss felt by Denis Brogan and those like him was intense and persistent; but most of the British people saw France merely as a place where German bombers came from and where the German Army was massing to cross the narrow seas. Those seas themselves resumed all their old importance. Never since the days of Nelson had the British been more conscious of living on an island, or happier with that dispensation of Providence. The consequences of that instinctive reaction, which was far more than a frame of mind, were to be profound and long-lived.

Moreover, the sudden and utter defeat of France brought to the fore an impression of that country which had been lurking in British minds during the 1930s and now secured an almost permanent lodgement: that France had been rotted from within before the blow fell from without. This was the predominant explanation of the French defeat, frequently expounded in the press and on the radio, and lent the weight of Churchill's authority in a broadcast on 14 July. The picture was comforting to the British, who were confident in their own minds that they did not suffer from the same kind of internal division and decay. This impression of endemic French weakness, produced by political instability, social dissension, and lack of national purpose, became almost indelible in Britain for many years to come. Coupled with the victorious British stand in 1940, it was to have its effects on British relations with France long after the war was over.

Across the Channel, the French people were dazed by the speed and shock of their defeat. Their overwhelming first reaction to the armistice was relief that the fighting was over, and a desire to attain some sort of normality and stability after such a tremendous upheaval. It was part of Pétain's appeal at that time that he offered a promise of stability, the reassurance of a father-figure, and an escape from the war. Such reactions cut the French people off psychologically from the British, just as the German occupation of the Channel coast cut them off physically.

In the first days after the armistice, Pétain set out to offer the

6. P.M.H Bell, *A Certain Eventuality: Britain and the Fall of France* (Farnborough, 1974), p. 127.

French people some explanations for their defeat. He assured them that the Army had fought with a courage worthy of its traditions, but had been overwhelmed by great numbers and superior armaments. He condemned the Third Republic for fostering a spirit of pleasure-seeking and decadence, for which the country must now pay the price. He developed also the theme that Britain had let France down, and even betrayed her – the cry of 'nous sommes trahis' arose easily and naturally in the circumstances of 1940. Pétain repeated in public the criticisms which he had earlier made in private: the British had retreated at Arras when they should have attacked; they had deserted the French at Dunkirk; they had refused to commit their fighter aircraft to the battle in France. In sum, the British had looked after themselves and left France to bear the brunt of the fighting. After all, France had mobilised some three million men, while Britain sent only about three hundred thousand to France. These criticisms contained quite enough substance to carry conviction, especially in the immediate aftermath of defeat. Thus with one part of their minds the French preferred to forget about Britain, and turned inwards upon their own affairs; while with another they blamed the British for their defeat. Later there developed an obscure resentment that Britain had stood when France fell; but that was another story.

These reactions on both sides of the Channel marked the breakdown of the cohesion between the two countries which, despite many difficulties, had persisted for nearly forty years since the making of the *Entente*. France and Britain had combined against Germany; but now the German victory of 1940 produced opposite responses from Britain and France. Britain continued the war, with the ultimate aim of overthrowing German dominance in Europe. France withdrew from the fight, and set out to find some way of living under that same German dominance. Since the beginning of the century, the two countries and the two peoples had developed a sense of respect, even sometimes admiration, for one another. In June 1940 those British Francophiles whose affection ran true and deep retained their admiration, but it had become a matter of faith, relying on the evidence of things not seen. French faith in Britain was for the most part numbed, though it still lived in a few and was shortly to revive in many. For the most part, and for a time, the two countries turned in upon themselves, seeking salvation in completely different ways. They had gone from *entente* to a profound estrangement. It remained to be seen how permanent that estrangement would prove to be.

Bibliographical Essay

G. K. Chesterton once observed, introducing his book on *The Victorian Age in Literature*, that 'It is rather reassuring than otherwise to realise that I am now doing something that nobody could do properly.' To attempt a reader's guide to the literature relating to the subject of this book merits a similar comment, and it is better to be comforted by Chesterton's observation than daunted by the size of the task. The following bibliographical essay is no more than an indication of books which I have found particularly illuminating, and to which the reader may turn for further information and reflection.

The place of publication is London for books in English and Paris for those in French, unless otherwise stated.

GENERAL

The reader in search of an introduction to the manifold contacts between France and Britain cannot do better than start with Richard Faber's *French and English* (1975) – erudite, witty and sympathetic to both peoples. Robert Gibson, *Best of Enemies: Anglo-French Relations since the Norman Conquest* (1995) is entertaining and enlightening. Douglas Johnson, François Bédarida and François Crouzet, eds, *Britain and France: Ten centuries* (Folkestone, 1980), a collection of essays by historians from both countries, is full of interest. François Crouzet, deeply versed in British history, distilled much wisdom into an article, 'Problèmes de la communication franco-britannique aux XIXe et XXe siècles', *Revue Historique*, 515, juillet-septembre 1975. Neville Waites, ed., *Troubled Neighbours. Franco-British Relations in the Twentieth Century*

France and Britain 1900–1940: Entente and Estrangement

(1971) is a valuable symposium, mainly concentrating on diplomacy and war. Georges Roissard, *De l'Entente Cordiale à l'Europe* (Grenoble, 1973) puts Franco-British relations in the best possible light, and includes some striking illustrations; Gilbert Martineau, *L'Entente Cordiale* (Grenoble, 1984), which begins in the 1830s, is also amicable in tone.

France and Britain as nation states have been partly shaped by long contacts and conflicts with one another, and some account of their general histories is necessary for an understanding of their relations. G. M. Trevelyan's *History of England* (1926, frequently reprinted and revised) was immensely influential over many years; Paul Johnson's *The Offshore Islanders: A History of the English People* (1972; revised edn 1992) emphasises the effects of conflict with France. Linda Colley, *Britons: Forging the Nation, 1707–1837* (1992) argues that the long wars with France were a crucial element in forming the British nation. Jules Michelet, *Tableau de la France*, part of vol. II of his *Histoire de France* (1833; revised edn 1861; also published separately) made much the same point in relation to French national identity. Fernand Braudel, *L'identité de la France* (2 vols, 1986–87), translated as *The Identity of France* (1988–89) presents a much more subtle view of French nationhood, but is still conscious of the influence of relations with 'the other'.

Relations between Britain and France were much influenced by changes in the power and world positions of the two countries. Brief surveys of these matters may be found in Bernard Porter, *Britain, Europe and the World* (1983); David Reynolds, *Britannia Overruled: British Policy and World Power in the Twentieth Century* (1991); and Roland Marx, *La Grande-Bretagne et le monde au XXe siècle* (1986). For France, see M. Tacel, *La France et le monde au XXe siècle* (1989); Jean Doise et Maurice Vaïsse, *Diplomatie et outil militaire, 1871–1969* (1987). Michael Howard, *The Continental Commitment: The Dilemma of British Defence Policy in the Era of two World Wars* (1972) is essential reading on a subject which plagued British relations with France for many years. D. C. Watt, *Succeeding John Bull: America in Britain's Place, 1900–1970* (1984) discusses the American dimension which had far-reaching effects on British relations with France. René Lauret reflects on relations between France and Germany in *Notre Voisin l'Allemand* (1960), translated as *France and Germany* (1965). Raymond Poidevin et Jacques Bariéty, *Les relations franco-allemandes, 1815–1975* (1977) provides an invaluable historical perspective.

Colonial relations form a large subject, to which good introductions may be found in P. Gifford and W. R. Louis, eds, *France and Britain in*

Africa (1971), and Ann Williams, *Britain and France in the Middle East and North Africa* (1968).

VIEWS ACROSS THE CHANNEL

The period examined in this book was fertile in studies of France and Britain by observers from across the Channel. In 1898 J. E. C. Bodley published a massive study, simply entitled *France* (2 vols; revised edn one vol., 1899), combining history and politics with reflections on national characteristics. Sir Thomas Barclay's *Thirty Years of Anglo-French Reminiscences* (1914) is light-weight by comparison, but has illuminating moments. Kipling published a remarkable poem on France in 1913, and an interesting collection of occasional pieces, *Souvenirs of France* (1933). D. W. (Sir Denis) Brogan was deeply learned in French history and culture: his *Development of Modern France, 1870–1939* (1940) was very influential and remains well worth reading; *French Personalities and Problems* (1946) offers a selection of articles published between 1935 and 1945. (Did anyone else reflect on how reading Alexandre Dumas *père* could help one understand de Gaulle and Pétain in 1940?) In the 1930s Alexander Werth, correspondent in Paris for *The Manchester Guardian* and the *New Statesman*, published a series of vivid accounts of French politics: *France in Ferment* (1934); *The Destiny of France* (1937); *France and Munich* (1939); and *The Last Days of Paris* (1940). D. W. Brogan edited an abbreviation of the last three volumes as *The Twilight of France* (New York, 1942). A discussion of British views of France, full of insight and humour, is provided by John C. Cairns, 'A Nation of Shopkeepers in search of a suitable France, 1919–1940', *American Historical Review*, vol. 79, No. 3, June 1974. The life and work of a sympathetic observer of French politics and culture may be studied in James Lees-Milne, *Harold Nicolson* (2 vols, 1980–81).

Two valuable and often entertaining French surveys of British views are: Paul Gerbod, *Voyages au pays des mangeurs de grenouilles: La France vue par les Britanniques du XVIIIe siècle à nos jours* (1991); and Sylvaine Marandon, *L'image de la France dans l'Angleterre victorienne* (1967).

Among French observers of Britain, Jacques Bardoux's vast output may be approached through his massive *Essai d'une psychologie de l'Angleterre contemporaine* (2 vols, 1906–7); *L'Angleterre radicale* (1913); and *Lloyd George et la France* (1923). In 1936 he gave the Zaharoff Lecture at Oxford, *Angleterre et France: leurs politiques étrangères* (Oxford,

1937). Félix Bonafé, *Jacques Bardoux* (1977) offers a sympathetic portrait of the man and his writings. André Maurois (pseudonym of Emile Herzog) was for many years the most familiar interpreter of Britain in France. *Les silences du colonel Bramble* (1918, often reprinted) was the novel, based on his experience as a liaison officer with the British Army, which made him famous; it was equally popular in translation as *The Silence of Colonel Bramble* (1919, with several reprints). See also his *Histoire d'Angleterre* (1937), translated as *A History of England* (1937); *Les Anglais* (1935); and his *Memoirs, 1885–1967* (1970). Louis Cazamian, an eminent student of English literature, turned his gaze on national character in *Ce qu'il faut connaître de l'âme anglaise* (1927). André Siegfried's *La crise britannique au XXe siècle* (1931, often reprinted) was the work of a learned and sympathetic observer; it was translated as *England's Crisis* (1931). Paul Morand, diplomat, writer and *poseur*, wrote a perceptive *Londres* (1933), a work of deeper interest than a simple description of the city. He also produced a fulsome *Salut à l'Angleterre, 19–22 juillet 1938* (1938), on the occasion of the visit to France by King George VI and Queen Elizabeth. Some acid and brilliant articles by Jacques Bainville are collected in *L'Angleterre et l'Empire Britannique* (1938). Pierre Bourdan (pseudonym of Pierre Maillaud), who spent much of the Second World War in London, looked back with critical sympathy on the 1930s in *Perplexités et grandeur de l'Angleterre* (1945).

In a class of his own stands Elie Halévy, whose *Histoire du peuple anglais au XIXe siècle* (5 vols, 1912–32), translated as *A History of the English People in the Nineteenth Century* (1924–34), did much to explain their own history, and their own country, to the British.

Among surveys of French views of the British, Andris Barblan, *L'image de l'Anglais en France pendant les quérelles coloniales, 1882–1904* (Berne, 1974) is interesting on its period. Marius-François Guyard, *L'image de la Grande-Bretagne dans le roman français, 1914–1940* (1954) is both fascinating and essential reading. A scholarly discussion of a near-obsession may be found in Maurice Larès, *T. E. Lawrence, la France et les Français* (1980); the author summarises his findings in 'T. E. Lawrence and France: Friends or Foes?', in Stephen A. Tabaschnik, ed., *The T. E. Lawrence Puzzle* (Athens, Georgia, 1984).

There ran in France, even during the years of the *Entente*, a current of hatred for England which broke surface from time to time. See Henri Béraud, *Faut-il réduire l'Angleterre en esclavage?* (1935; reprinted, July 1940). Large sections of this pamphlet were reproduced, with approving comments, in André Avice, *Mésentente cordiale: La politique séculaire de l'Angleterre* (1964), which itself acts both as an example of and a guide to the streak of Anglophobia. Martyn Cornick provides an acute introduction to the whole subject in 'The Myth of "Perfidious Albion" and French National Identity', in David Dutton, ed., *Statecraft and Diplomacy in the Twentieth Century: Essays presented to P. M. H. Bell* (Liverpool, 1995), pp. 7–33.

The project for a Channel Tunnel often revealed much about the views held in each country about the other, especially British views of France. See Bernard Sasso et Lyne Cohen-Solal, *Le Tunnel sous la Manche: Chronique d'une passion franco-anglaise* (Lyon, 1987); and Keith Wilson, *Channel Tunnel Visions, 1850–1945: Dreams and Nightmares* (1995).

BEFORE THE GREAT WAR, *c.* 1900–1914

The foreign policies of France and Britain are analysed in John Keiger, *France and the Origins of the First World War* (1983), and Zara S. Steiner, *Britain and the Origins of the First World War* (1977); to which should be added the stimulating reflections of Keith Wilson in *The Policy of the Entente: Essays on the Determinants of British Policy, 1904–1914* (1985). The classic work on the making of the agreement of 1904 is P. J. V. Rolo, *Entente Cordiale: The Origins and Negotiation of the Anglo-French Agreements of 8 April 1904* (1969) – still essential reading. On the ministers who negotiated the *entente*, Lord Newton's *Lord Lansdowne* (1929) has not been replaced; Christopher Andrew, *Théophile Delcassé and the Making of the Entente Cordiale* (1968) is indispensable. For the role of Edward VII, see Gordon Brook-Shepherd, *Uncle of Europe: The Social and Diplomatic Life of Edward VII* (1975). For later developments, see Keith Robbins, *Sir Edward Grey: A biography of Lord Grey of Falloden* (1971), and the excellent collection of essays in F. H. Hinsley, ed., *British Foreign Policy under Sir Edward Grey* (1977). E. M. Carroll, *French Public Opinion and Foreign Affairs* (1930) is still useful. On the diplomats who were then so important, see Henri Cambon, ed., *Paul Cambon: Correspondance 1870–1924* (3 vols, 1940–46); also Keith Eubank, *Paul Cambon, Master Diplomatist* (Norman, Oklahoma, 1960). Keith Hamilton, *Bertie of Thame, Edwardian Ambassador* (1990) discusses the role of the long-serving British Ambassador in Paris. Harold Nicolson's life of his father, *Sir Arthur Nicolson, Bart., First Lord Carnock: A Study in the Old Diplomacy* (1930) is a marvellous picture of a vanished world.

On particular episodes, see D. Bates, *The Fashoda Incident of 1898*

(1984); and Jean-Claude Allain, *Agadir 1911* (1976). On military matters, Samuel R. Williamson, *The Politics of Grand Strategy: Britain and France prepare for war, 1904–1914* (Cambridge, Mass., 1969) is immensely thorough and the key book; but should be supplemented on the British side by John Gooch, *The Plans of War: The General Staff and British Military Strategy, c.1900–1916* (1974); and on the French side by Douglas Porch, *The March to the Marne: The French Army 1871–1914* (1981). On naval matters, see A. J. Marder, *From the Dreadnought to Scapa Flow*, vol. I, *The Road to War* (1961), and Paul Halpern, *The Mediterranean Naval Situation, 1908–14* (1971). A curious work of fiction deserves notice: Capitaine Danrit (pseudonym for Driant), *La guerre fatale: France–Angleterre* (1901–2), a novel of nearly 1,200 pages, by the end of which the French Army has captured London; though not typical of French opinion, it enjoyed a wide circulation in serial form.

THE GREAT WAR, 1914–1919

The Great War has produced an overwhelming literature, even in the area of relations between France and Britain. Paul-Marie de la Gorce, ed., *La Première Guerre Mondiale* (2 vols, 1991) is a French account of the war by a number of specialist contributors; J. M. Bourne, *Britain and the Great War, 1914–1918* (1989) is succinct, scholarly and moving. David Stevenson, *The First World War and International Politics* (1988) is masterly. The same writer's *French War Aims against Germany, 1914–1918* (1982) and V. H. Rothwell, *British War Aims and Peace Diplomacy, 1914–1918* (1971) provide excellent surveys based on careful research. Georges-Henri Soutou, *L'or et le sang: les buts de guerre économiques de la Première Guerre Mondiale* (1989) is a massive and original work.

Among the political figures of the war, Clemenceau has been fortunate in his biographers: see David R. Watson, *Georges Clemenceau: A Political Biography* (1974) for a first-rate life in English; in French, J.-B. Duroselle, *Clemenceau* (1988) and Pierre Guiral, *Clemenceau en son temps* (1994). Clemenceau's memoirs, *Grandeur et misères d'une victoire* (1930), still repay study. On Lloyd George, John Grigg, *Lloyd George: From Peace to War 1912–1916* (1985) only takes us part-way through the war; Peter Rowland, *Lloyd George* (1975) is a useful one-volume treatment. Lloyd George's own *War Memoirs* (revised edn in 2 vols, 1938) are fierce and sometimes unreliable, but well worth reading.

On some generals, see Pierre Varillon, *Joffre* (1956); Jean Autin, *Foch, ou le triomphe de la volonté* (1987); Guy Pedroncini, *Pétain: Le soldat et la gloire, 1856–1918* (1989); R. Holmes, *The Little Field Marshal: Sir John French* (1981); John Terraine, *Douglas Haig: The Educated Soldier* (1963, re-issued 1990).

Maurice Hankey, *The Supreme Command, 1914–1918* (2 vols, 1961) is written with all the restraint of a former Secretary to the Cabinet and yet is still enlightening; it should be supplemented by Stephen Roskill, *Hankey: Man of Secrets*, vol. I (1970). Together, these books tell us much about Franco-British relations at the summit. Among the liaison officers, Edward Louis Spears's books have become classics: *Liaison 1914: A Narrative of the Great Retreat* (1930); *Prelude to Victory* (1939). General Huguet, *L'intervention militaire britannique en 1914* (1928) is illuminating but leaves a bitter taste; Emile Herbillon, *Souvenirs d'un officier de liaison pendant la guerre mondiale* (2 vols, 1930) is more matter-of-fact, and more sympathetic to the British.

Some of the profound effects of the war are analysed in J. M. Winter, *The Great War and the British People* (1986); Jean-Jacques Becker, *1914: Comment les Français sont entrés dans la guerre* (1971); and the same author's *Les Français dans la Grande Guerre* (1980), translated as *The Great War and the French People* (Leamington Spa, 1985). Between them, these books have transformed our understanding of the war as experienced by the two peoples. Albert Chatelle et G. Tilson, *Calais pendant la guerre* (1927) tells us much about the French town where the British made themselves very much at home. Richard Cobb's *French and Germans, Germans and French. A personal interpretation of France under two occupations, 1914–1918, 1940–1944* (1983) gives a striking evocation of the German-occupied departments of north-eastern France.

The war of the 'ordinary' French soldier is described in Stéphane Audouin-Rouzeau, *14–18: Les combattants des tranchées* (1986); the ex-servicemen and their organisations are exhaustively studied in Antoine Prost, *Les anciens combattants et la société française, 1914–1939* (3 vols, 1978). Ian F. W. Beckett and Keith Simpson, eds, *A Nation in Arms: A social study of the British Army in the First World War* (Manchester, 1985) opens up a big subject to good effect. On the 'ordinary' British soldier, see (among a number of recent books) Denis Winter, *Death's Men: Soldiers of the Great War* (1978), and Malcolm Brown, *Tommy Goes to War* (1978).

The imaginative literature of the Great War forms a study in itself. Frank Field, *British and French Writers of the First World War* (1991) is subtle and wide in its sympathies, and seems to be the only book to cast its net on both sides of the Channel. John Cruickshank, *Variations on a Catastrophe: Some French Responses to the Great War* (1982) is also excellent. Paul Fussell's *The Great War and Modern Memory* (1975) is very illuminating.

Peace-making has also produced a vast literature. We now have an admirable and succinct analysis by Alan Sharp, *The Versailles Settlement: Peacemaking in Paris, 1919* (1991). For France, Pierre Miquel's *La Paix de Versailles et l'opinion publique française* (1972) is a remarkable survey; and J. C. King, *Foch versus Clemenceau: France and German Dismemberment, 1918–1919* (1960) is a good short book on a big subject. On the British side, M. Dockrill and J. D. Goold, eds, *Peace without Promise: Britain and the Peace Conferences 1919–1923* (1981) is brief, balanced and wide-ranging; Antony Lentin, *Guilt at Versailles: Lloyd George and the Pre-History of Appeasement* (1985) is penetrating and original. Marc Trachtenberg, *Reparations in World Politics: France and European Economic Diplomacy, 1916–1923* (New York, 1980) re-opened an old controversy and redressed the balance in favour of the French; see also the treatment in Bruce Kent, *The Spoils of War: The politics, economics and diplomacy of reparations, 1918–1932* (1989). Marion Kent, ed., *The Great Powers and the End of the Ottoman Empire* (1984) examines different aspects of a complicated subject. Older books are still required reading: J. M. Keynes, *The Economic Consequences of the Peace* (1920); Etienne Mantoux, *The Carthaginian Peace, or The Economic Consequences of Mr Keynes* (1946); Harold Nicolson, *Peacemaking 1919* (1933); W. M. Jordan, *Great Britain, France and the German Problem* (1943).

BETWEEN THE WARS, 1919–1939

Most of the books mentioned under 'peace-making' above are also relevant to the period between the two world wars. Students of French foreign policy in the 1920s must start with Jacques Bariéty's massive work on *Les relations franco-allemandes après la Première Guerre Mondiale, 1920–1925* (1977), which transformed our understanding of the subject. Stephen A. Schuker, *The End of French Predominance in Europe* (Chapel Hill, N. Carolina) is equally illuminating from its different point of view. Georges Suarez, *Une nuit chez Cromwell* (1930), a remarkably vivid account of Herriot's visit to Chequers in 1924, has been largely confirmed by Bariéty. On Franco-British relations in the 1930s, Nicholas Rostow, *Anglo-French Relations, 1934–36* (1984) deals well with a crucial period; Comité d'Histoire de la 2e Guerre

Mondiale, *Les relations franco-britanniques de 1935 à 1939* (1975) publishes papers given at two conferences of historians from the two countries. J.-B. Duroselle's *La décadence, 1932–1939* (1979), a volume in the series on the history of French foreign policy published by the *Imprimerie Nationale*, is indispensable. Anthony Adamthwaite's *France and the Coming of the Second World War* (1977) deals thoroughly and thoughtfully with the period 1936–39. On the British side, W. N. Medlicott's *British Foreign Policy since Versailles, 1919–1963* (1968) remains a valuable introduction.

Studies of British statesmen who were much involved with France include David Dutton's excellent *Austen Chamberlain: Gentleman in Politics* (1985); the same author's *Simon: A Political Biography of Sir John Simon* (1992) also has some material on France. On Eden, a genuine Francophile among British statesmen, see David Carlton, *Anthony Eden: A Biography* (1981), which tends to be hostile; and Robert Rhodes James, *Anthony Eden* (1986). R. A. C. Parker, *Chamberlain and Appeasement* (1993) and Andrew Roberts, *The Holy Fox: A Biography of Lord Halifax* (1991) contain much about relations with the French. On British diplomats, see Norman Rose, *Vansittart: Study of a Diplomat* (1978); David Dilks, ed., *The Diaries of Sir Alexander Cadogan, 1938–1945* (1971); and John Harvey, ed., *The Diplomatic Diaries of Oliver Harvey, 1937–1940* (1970).

On the French side, Geoffrey Warner, *Pierre Laval and the Eclipse of France* (1968) remains impressive; Fred Kupferman, *Laval* (1987) has additional information and a different perspective. Elisabeth du Réau, *Daladier* (1993) offers a scholarly and sympathetic interpretation; René Rémond et Janine Bourdan, eds, *Daladier, chef du gouvernement* (1977) includes papers by several historians on aspects of Daladier's premiership, 1938–40. Diplomatic memoirs include Charles de Beaupoil de Saint-Aulaire, *Confessions d'un vieux diplomate* (1953), by the Ambassador in London in the mid-1920s; Jean Chauvel, *Commentaire*, vol. I, *De Vienne à Alger, 1938–1944* (1971) gives a vivid impression of the state of French diplomacy at the end of the 1930s.

On military affairs, the essential starting-point on the British side is Brian Bond, *British Military Policy between the two World Wars* (1980). P. J. Dennis, *Decision by Default: Peacetime Conscription and British Defence, 1919–1939* (1972) provides an interesting discussion of a subject which touched Franco-British relations in many ways, not only military ones. Martin Alexander, *The Republic in Danger: General Maurice Gamelin and the Politics of French Defence, 1933–1940* (1992) provides a detailed review of French defence policy, including relations with the British. On the navies, see Stephen Roskill, *Naval Policy between the Wars* (2 vols, 1968, 1976); and on the French side the careful and sympathetic study of *Darlan* by Hervé Coutau-Bégarie et Claude Huan (1989). On the air forces, see Patrick Fridenson et Jean Lecuir, *La France et la Grande-Bretagne face aux problèmes aériens, 1935–mai 1940* (Vincennes, 1976).

THE PHONEY WAR AND THE DEFEAT OF FRANCE, 1939–JUNE 1940

On the phoney war, Comité d'Histoire de la 2e Guerre Mondiale, *Français et Britanniques dans la Drôle de Guerre* (1979) comprises papers by historians from both countries. François Kersaudy, *1940: La guerre du fer* (1987), translated as *Norway 1940* (1990) casts its net more widely than the Norwegian campaign itself. François Bédarida, ed., *La stratégie secrète de la drôle de guerre: le Conseil Suprême Interallié, septembre 1939–avril 1940* (1979) publishes the French records of the Supreme War Council, with a valuable commentary. J.-B. Duroselle, *L'abîme, 1939–1945* (1982) begins by tracing French foreign policy during the phoney war and the defeat.

On the defeat of France, Jean-Louis Crémieux-Brilhac, *Les Français de l'an 40*, vol. I, *La guerre, oui ou non?*, vol. II, *Ouvriers et soldats* (1990) is a profound, detailed and original work. Eleanor M. Gates, *The End of the Affair: The Collapse of the Anglo-French Alliance, 1939–1940* (Berkely, California, 1981), provides a full and fair-minded account of relations between the two countries in the summer of 1940. P. M. H. Bell, *A Certain Eventuality: Britain and the Fall of France* (Farnborough, 1974) examines British reactions to the French defeat. John C. Cairns, 'Great Britain and the Fall of France', *Journal of Modern History*, vol. 27, No. 4, December 1955 remains illuminating. Max Beloff, *The Intellectual in Politics* (1970) includes an essay on 'The Anglo-French Union Project of June 1940'.

The events of 1940 have produced a remarkable crop of memoirs. On the British side, Winston S. Churchill, *The Second World War*, vol. II, *Their Finest Hour* (1949) remains vivid and indispensable. E. L. Spears, *Assignment to Catastrophe*, vol. I, *Prelude to Dunkirk*, vol. II, *The Fall of France* (1954) is astonishing in its immediacy; through it runs the thread of Spears's disillusion with France. Paul Reynaud wrote his account of events twice, in *La France a sauvé l'Europe* (2 vols, 1947), and in *Au coeur de la mêlée* (1951); the latter was abridged and translated as *In the Thick of the Fight* (1955). Charles de Gaulle,

Mémoires de Guerre, vol. I *L'Appel, 1940–1942*, has epic qualities; it was translated as *The Call to Honour* (1955). François Charles-Roux, *Cinq Mois tragiques aux Affaires Etrangères* (1949) is sober and detailed. Paul Baudouin, *Neuf Mois au Gouvernement* (1948), cast in diary form, puts the point of view of an advocate of the armistice and Pétain's first Foreign Minister. Both these books stand up well to an examination of the recently opened French documents.

Martin Gilbert, *Winston S. Churchill, 1939–1941*, is an immensely detailed volume of biography; François Kersaudy, *Churchill and de Gaulle* (1981) catches the opening drama between these two great men.

Walter Lord, *The Miracle of Dunkirk* (New York, 1982); Jacques Mordal (pseudonym of Hervé Cras), *La bataille de Dunkerque* (1948); and Albert Chatelle, *Dunkerque, ville ardente, mai–juin 1940* (1950) offer different perspectives on the Dunkirk evacuation; many other books have been written. Finally, Jean Vidalenc, *L'exode de mai–juin 1940* (1957) is a vivid account, with telling quotations from participants' stories, of an experience which the British escaped in 1940: the flight of millions of refugees. More than any other single book, its contents signal the difference between the fates of the two countries and the two peoples at that time.

Index

Action Française, 9, 181
    journal, 164
Adowa, Battle (1896), 190
Agadir crisis (1911), 43–7, 49
Africa, Anglo-French colonial
    rivalry, 9, 14, 23, 27–8
Agincourt, battle (1415), 6
Albert, King of the Belgians, 58
Albert, Prince, 8
Alexander, King of Yugoslavia, 182
Algeciras conference (1906), 36, 38,
    40, 43
Allied Economic Conference, June
    1916, 87
Alphand, Hervé, 241
Alsace-Lorraine, 11, 14, 54, 60,
    83–6, 89–90, 114, 120
Amery, Leo, 16–17, 57, 247
Amiens, 45, 61, 76
Anatolia, 88, 129
Anciens combattants, 109–10, 181
Angell, Norman, 223
Anglo-American guarantee to
    France, 1919, 120–1
Anglo-French Purchasing Board
    (1939–40), 228
Anglo-German naval rivalry, before
    1914, 25–6, 41–2
Anglo-German Naval Agreement
    (1935), 184–90, 201–3
Anglo-Japanese Alliance (1902), 26

Anglophobia in France, 11, 165,
    198, 201–3
Anglo-Russian Agreement (1907), 15
'Anglo-Saxons', French views, 2,
    116–17, 119, 126, 199–200
Antwerp, 47, 61
Appeasement, 1919, 119
    in 1930s, 177–9, 204–27
Armengaud, General Jules, 230
Armistice (1918), 114–15
    Franco-German (1940), 244–9,
    251, 253–4
Armistice Day, 109
Arras,
    in First World War, 94, 100
    battle (1940), 235, 254
Asquith, H.H., 44, 46, 53, 58, 60,
    65–6, 69, 84–5
Atomic scientists, French, 242
Attlee, Clement, 176–7, 243
Australia, 13, 64, 176, 218
Austria, *Anschluss*, 191–2, 209–10, 228
Autin, Jean, 154

Badoglio, Marshal Pietro, 191–2
Bainville, Jacques, 9, 95, 164–5
Baku, oil-wells, 230
Baldwin, Stanley, 142, 149, 176,
    178–80, 193, 196, 199, 207–8
Balfour, A.J., 35, 38, 52, 54, 66,
    118, 160–1

Balfour Declaration (1917), 88
Barbusse, Henri, 108
Barclay, Sir Thomas, 22
Bardoux, Jacques, 16–20, 27, 31, 162–4
Bariéty, Jacques, 140
Barnett, Correlli, 177
Barthou, Louis, 174, 179, 181–2
Battle of Britain (1940), 253
Baudouin, Paul, 245, 248
Baumont, Maurice, 206
Beaverbrook, Lord, 176
Belgium,
    neutrality, 1914, 47, 49, 55, 58–9, 84
    British aims in Frist World War, 83–4, 89
    in 1930s, 185
    in 1940, 232
Bell, Gertrude, 128
Benjamin, René, 108
Benoît, Pierre, 128
Béraud, Henri, 128, 165, 202–3
Bizerta, 194–5
Bloch, Marc, 96
Blum, Léon, 207, 211, 223
Bodley, J.E.C., 21–2
Boer War, 4, 10–11, 13–15, 18, 23, 25–7
Bolshevik Revolution (1917), 73, 118, 154
Bonnet, Georges, 211, 213–16, 220–1, 224–5
Bordeaux, French government in (1940), 241, 246, 248
Bossuet, Bishop, 11
Bourgeois, Léon, 119
Bourne, John, 68, 108–9
Brailsford, H.N., 161
Briand, Aristide, 66, 132, 135–6, 138, 145, 149–52, 165–6, 182
Briand Plan (1929–30), 166, 168
Britain,
    attitudes to France before 1914, 19–22
        during First World War, 107, 110–12

1920s, 160–4
1930s, 178–80, 218–20
1940, 251–3
attitudes to Germany, 41–2, 118, 133–4, 146, 175, 177–8, 219, 227
foreign trade, 19, 134, 164, 169, 198–9
Labour Party, 144–5, 164–5, 176, 222
Liberal Party, 38, 55, 165
British Expeditionary Force (BEF), 1914–18, 45–7, 49, 61–3, 66–7, 72, 77, 93; 1939–40, 221–2, 230, 243, 250
British-French-Russian Agreement (Sept. 1914), 83
British Legion, 109–10
Brogan, Sir Denis, 5, 154, 252–3
Brooke, General Sir Alan, 243
Browning, Robert, 51
Brüning, Heinrich, 173
Buchan, John, 107, 176
Bullitt, William C., 219
Burma, 9
Burns, John, 58
Bywater, J.C., 189

Cadogan, Sir Alexander, 214, 216, 220, 234, 237
Caillaux, Joseph, 43, 45, 89
Calais, British presence (1915–20), 98–9
Calais conference (Feb. 1917), 71
Camaret Bay, 9
Cambon, Jules, 42, 162, 165
Cambon, Paul, 18–20, 23, 25, 27–31, 34, 36, 38–40, 48, 50, 56–7, 162, 165
Campbell, Sir Ronald, 231, 247
Campbell-Bannerman, Sir Henry, 38, 40, 52–3
Campinchi, César, 236
Canada, 13, 64, 176, 243
Canning, George, 163
Casablanca, 43

Casey, Richard, 3
Casualties, 1914–18,
  French, 62, 64, 67, 92–4
  British, 69, 92–4
Catroux, General Georges, 3, 128
Cazamian, Louis, 16
Cecil, Lord Robert, 119
Central Asia, 14, 32
Chad, Lake, 28
Chamberlain, Austen, 149–51, 164–5
Chamberlain, Joseph, 25–7
Chamberlain, Neville, 176, 178,
  188, 193, 207, 219, 221, 232
  policy of appeasement, 210, 213,
    215–17, 220
  declares support for France, Feb.
    1939, 222
  in 1939, 223–6
  in 1940, 234, 243
Chanak crisis (Sept. 1922), 130–1
Channel Tunnel, 25, 51–3, 155–60
Channel Islands, 250
Charles, Emperor of
  Austria-Hungary, 89
Charles-Roux, François, 241
Chatfield, Admiral Lord, 189, 194
Chautemps, Camille, 210, 246
Chauvel, Jean, 132, 220, 233, 249
Chequers conference (June 1924)
  ('une nuit chez Cromwell'), 145–8
Churchill, Winston S., 45, 48, 60,
  101, 103, 127–8, 150, 158, 173
  in 1940, 229, 232–5, 237–8,
    242–5, 247, 249–50
  affection for France, 232, 239,
    251–2
Clarke, Sir George, 51
Clemenceau, Georges,
  First World War, 64, 73–4, 76–7,
    86, 90, 107, 109
  Paris Peace Conference (1919),
    114–20, 122–7, 131
  mentioned, 10, 148, 156, 179,
    190, 206, 245
Clémentel, Etienne, 80–1, 86
Clive, Lord, 6

Cobb, Richard, 100
Cobden, Richard, 8, 18
Comité de Guerre (25 May 1940),
  236–7
Committee of Imperial Defence,
  45–6, 51, 53, 151, 161–2, 179
Commonwealth, see Dominions
Conscription,
  in Britain, 54, 69, 125, 221–2
  in France, 60, 69, 125
Coolidge, President Calvin, 142
Cooper, Duff, 176
Corbin, Charles, 247
Crécy, battle (1346), 6
Crémieux-Brilhac, Jean-Louis,
  226–7, 240
Crimean War (1854–56), 8
Croix de Feu, 181, 224
Cromer, Lord, 31
Crowe, Sir Eyre, 53–4, 146
Curzon, Lord, 130, 149, 156, 159
Czechoslovakia, 182, 207, 210–11
  crisis, 1938, 212–18, 221
  destroyed, 223, 227

Daladier, Edouard, 211, 213–17,
  219, 221, 223, 229–31
Dalton, Hugh, 179, 206
Danzig, 210, 224
Dardanelles (1915), 65
Darlan, Admiral François, 190, 240
Dautry, Raoul, 245
Dawes Plan, 144, 146–8, 152
Déat, Marcel, 224
Declarations of war, by France and
  Britain, 1939, 225–6
Delcassé, Théophile, 9, 18, 23–5,
  27–8, 31–6, 54, 84
Depression, 1929–30s, 167–72
  British response, 168–70
  French response, 168
Derby, Lord, 161–2
Disarmament Conference
  (1932–34), 172–5, 184
Dominions/Commonwealth, 67,
  93, 116, 123, 134, 155, 169, 227

importance in British opinion, 1930s 175–6
Dorgelès, Roland, 108
Doriot, Jacques, 224
Doumayrou, Captain, 66
Dover, Straits, 48, 158
Dreadnought, HMS, 41
Dreyfus Affair, 12
Dunkirk evacuation, 1940, 4, 235–6, 238–40, 254
Duroselle, Jean-Baptiste, 172, 178
Dutton, David, 151

'Easterners' in First World War, 64–5, 69
Economist, The, 252
Eden, Anthony, 174–5, 178–9, 181, 186, 189, 193, 195, 206–8, 219
Edward VII, King, 2, 8, 22, 27–8, 36, 42
Egypt, 23–4, 28–9, 31–2, 193
Eisenhower, General Dwight D., 76
Elizabeth, Queen, 218
Entente Cordiale, 1, 7–8, 40, 42, 50, 53–4, 58
  Agreement of April 1904, terms, 23, 29–32
Ethiopia, 177
  crisis, 1935–36, 190–7
  French policy, 191–2, 201
  British policy, 193–4, 203
Etienne, Eugène, 24
Eugénie, Empress, 8
European Coal and Steel Community (ECSC) (1950), 42, 124, 152
European federation, discussed, 1939–40, 229
Ewart, General Sir Spencer, 51, 53
Exchange rates,
  sterling-franc-mark, 79, 133, 143, 152, 168–9, 171
  sterling-franc-dollar, 1936, 209–10
  sterling-franc, Dec. 1939, 228

Faber, Richard, 5, 11

Fabre-Luce, Alfred, 128
Fallières, President Armand, 50, 54
Fashoda crisis (1898), 3, 4, 9–11, 14–15, 23–4, 27, 159
Feisal, King, 88, 126–7
Fell, Sir Arthur, 52, 157
Figaro, Le., 3
Finland, 229
Fisher, Admiral Lord, 34
Fisher, Sir Warren, 177–8
Flandin, Pierre-Etienne, 206, 231
Foch, Marshal Ferdinand, 18, 47, 63, 69, 73–7, 115, 120–1, 154, 156, 162
France,
  Air Force, British fears of, 161–2
  attitudes to Britain, before 1914, 15–19
    during First World War, 94–100, 106–7
    1920s, 128, 154, 162–6
    1930s, 183, 198–203, 218–19
    1940, 253–4
  attitudes to Germany, 14, 117–18, 154, 181–2, 218–19, 227, 254
  Communist Party, 171, 181
  culture, 20, 22, 154–5
  economic co-operation with Germany, foreshadowing ECSC and EEC, 42, 124, 137
  foreign trade, 13–14, 152, 170–1
  frivolity, alleged, 21–2
  Right-wing groups, 1930s, 171, 180–1, 223–4
  Socialist Party, 42, 85, 89, 207
Franchet d'Esperey, Marshal Louis, 101
Franco-British conferences, First World War, 65–7
Franco-British economic co-operation,
  First World War, 78–82
  1939–40, 228
Franco-British unified command,
  First World War, 71, 75–7, 82
  Second World War, 228

Franco-German Committee (between the wars), 152
Franco-Prussian War (1870–1), 9, 11, 14, 92
Franco-Russian Alliance (1894), 12, 14, 24, 38, 42, 55, 57, 95
Franco-Soviet Treaty (1935), 182, 223
Franconi, Gabriel-Tristan, 108
Franklin-Bouillon, Henri, 129, 131
Franklyn, General H.E., 235
Franz Ferdinand, Archduke, 55
French, Field Marshal Sir John, 53, 61–3, 99, 102, 104–5
French Congo, 43–5
French Fleet, 1940, 242, 246, 248–9
French language, *francophonie*, 2, 63, 117

Gallup poll (Sept. 1939), 226
Gambetta, Léon, 22
Gambia, 29
Gamelin, General Maurice, 191–2, 195, 197, 205–6, 228, 233, 235
Gamond, Thomé de, 51
Gaulle, General Charles de, 3, 127, 148, 247, 251
Geddes, Auckland, 160
Genoa conference (April 1922), 139
George V, King, 50, 99
George VI, King, 218–19
Germany, German policy,
  before 1914, 25, 33–7, 40–4
  First World War, 75, 90
  1920s, 137–42, 152–3
  1930s: rearmament, 173–4, 185–9
    Rhineland, 1936, 204–5
    Anschluss, 1938, 210
  Czechoslovakia, 212–17, 223
  Poland, 225
  1940, 232–3, 240–1, 248–9
Gibraltar, 24, 45
Gladstone, W.E., 9, 51
Godesberg meeting (22 Sept. 1938), 216
Gold Bloc, France leads, 168–9, 170–1

Gort, Field Marshal Lord, 228, 235, 238–9
Gough, General Sir Hubert, 76
Green, J.R., 21
Grey, Sir Edward, 38–40, 43–6, 48, 54, 56–8, 60, 66
Grey-Cambon letters (Nov. 1912), 48–9, 56
Grierson, General Sir James, 46
Gringoire, 202–3, 218
Guizot, François, 7

Haig, Field Marshal Sir Douglas, 60, 63, 68–77, 100, 103
Haile Selassie, Emperor, 196–7
Haldane, Richard, 46, 60
Halévy, Elie, 16
Halifax, Lord, 176, 178, 210–11, 213–16, 221, 223, 225, 237, 243, 247
Hankey, Sir Maurice, 66, 73–4, 157, 159, 188, 247
Hardinge, Lord, 130, 159, 161
Henlein, Konrad, 212, 214–15
Henty, G.A., 6
Herbillon, General, 72
Herriot, Edouard, 145–8, 172, 174
Hitler, Adolf, 153, 173, 175, 177–9, 181, 186–7, 193
  Rhineland (1936), 205–6
  Anschluss (1938), 210
  Czechoslovakia (1938–9), 212–15, 217, 220, 223–4
  in Second World War (1939–40), 227–8, 243–5
  armistice with France (June 1940), 248–9
Hoare, Sir Samuel, 176, 178, 193–4, 196
Hoare-Laval Pact (Dec. 1935), 194, 196–7, 201
Hoover, President Herbert, 168, 178
Hugo, Victor, 7
Huguet, General Victor, 46–7, 61, 95, 101, 103, 111
  views of the British, 104–6

Huguenot exiles in Britain, 15
Humanité, L', 218
Hundred Years' War, 5–6, 11
Hussein, Sherif of Mecca, 87–8, 126
Huxley, Thomas, 51

Illustration, L', 10
Imperial federation, 27, 176
Imperial preference, 86, 169
Indo-China, 30
International Steel Agreement (Sept. 1926), 152
Iraq, see Mesopotamia
Ironside, General Sir Edmund, 235
Italy,
    in First World War, 65, 74
    in 1930s, 182–3, 192, 221
    in 1940, 237
    armistice with France (24 June 1940), 249

James, Robert Rhodes, 179
Japan, 184, 191, 194
Joan of Arc, 6, 202
Joffre, Marshal Joseph, 49, 58, 62–3, 66–9, 101, 104
Johnson, Paul, 111
Journal des Débats, 17

Kapp *putsch*, 135
Keynes, John Maynard, 136
Kipling, Rudyard, 12, 41, 177–8
Kitchener, Field Marshal Lord, 9, 60, 62, 65, 68, 78
Kruger, President Paul, 10, 26

Lafayette, Marquis de, 90, 113
La Gloire (French ironclad), 8
Lanrezac, General, 61–2, 102
Lansdowne, Lord, 25, 27–30, 32, 34, 36, 38, 52
    Lansdowne letter (1917), 89
Larès, Maurice, 129
Laval, Pierre, 182, 187, 189–92, 194–7, 231
Law, Andrew Bonar, 140, 142, 157

Lawrence, T.E. (Lawrence of Arabia), 126, 128–9, 202
League of Nations, 110–11, 119, 122, 126, 128, 134, 172–3, 181, 186–7
    importance in British opinion, 176–7
    Ethiopian crisis, 191–7, 202
League of Nations Union, 176, 196
Lebanon, 87–8, 126, 128
Lebrun, President Albert, 236
Lerner, Henri, 128
'Limited liability', British strategy, 221–2
Lloyd George, David,
    before 1914, 44–5
    First World War, 65–6, 69–71, 73–4, 77, 85, 89–90, 103
    Paris Peace Conference (1919), 113–27, 130–1
        Fontainebleau Memorandum (25 March 1919), 117–19, 123, 146
    1920s, 135, 138–9, 142, 151
    Channel Tunnel, 157–8, 162–4
    mentioned, 199
Lloyd, George (Lord Lloyd), 57
Locarno, Treaty (1925), 150–2, 164–5, 179, 181, 204
London conference (July-Aug. 1924), 148
Loti, Pierre, 165
Loubet, President Emile, 28
Loucheur, Louis, 124, 137
Louis XIV, 6, 11, 54
Louis-Philippe, King, 7

McCallum, R.B., 252
MacDonald, Ramsay, 144–7, 149–50, 172–5, 178–9, 186–7, 193, 199
McKenna, Reginald, 79–80, 86
Maclean, Caid, 24
McMahon, Sir Henry, 87
Madagascar, 23, 30
Maginot Line, 205, 227, 230, 236

Malraux, André, 165
Manchuria, 184
Mandel, Georges, 206, 213
Mantoux, Paul, 90
Marandon, Sylvaine, 21
Marchand, Commandant
    Jean-Baptiste, 9, 24
Margerie, Roland de, 233
Maritime Transport Council (1918),
    81–2
Marlborough, Duke of, 6
Marne, battle (Sept. 1914), 63, 102
Martello towers, 8
Marxism, influence in France, 154–5
Mary, Queen, 50
Mathieu, Albert, 51
Maurois, André (Herzog, Emile),
    106–7, 201
Maurras, Charles, 181
Mayrisch, Emile (industrialist,
    precursor of ECSC), 152
Mesopotamia (later Iraq), 65, 87–8
Messimy, Adolphe, 61
Michelet, Jules, 1–2
Middle East, 121–6
Military conversations,
    Franco-British,
    before 1914, 45–6, 48–9, 56, 59,
        111, 179
    1930s, 185, 222
Millerand, Alexandre, 62, 65
Milner, Lord, 76
Monnet, Jean, 80–1, 228, 247
Mons, battle (Aug. 1914), 6, 62
Morand, Paul, 16
Morel, E.D., 161
Morgan, J.P. (bankers), 144
Morley, Lord, 58
Morocco, 23–5, 27–9, 32, 39,
    42–6
    Morocco crisis, 1905–6, 33–8, 54
    Morocco crisis, 1911, see Agadir
Mortimer, Raymond, 252
Morton, Desmond, 247
Mosley, Sir Oswald, 170
Mosul, 87–8, 131

Munich conference (29 Sept. 1938),
    217, 220, 223, 225
Mussolini, Benito, 182, 190–1,
    193–6, 225, 237
Mustafa Kemal, 129–31
Mutinies, French Army (1917), 70,
    72, 89

Napoleon I, 3, 7, 11, 20, 54, 105,
    131, 161, 202
Napoleon III, 8
Naval conversations, Franco-British
    before 1914, 47–8, 57
    1930s, 194–5
Nazi-Soviet Pact (Aug. 1939), 225
Nelson, Admiral Horatio, 3, 253
New Hebrides, 23, 28, 30
New Zealand, 176
Netherlands, The, 222
Newfoundland, fisheries, 14, 23,
    27–8, 30–2
Nicolson, Sir Arthur (Lord
    Carnock), 40, 57
Nicolson, Harold, 130
Nigeria, 30
Nineteenth Century, 51
Nivelle, General Robert, 63–4,
    69–72
Nivelle offensive (1917), 71, 103
'No separate peace' agreement (28
    March 1940), 228, 236–7, 245–6
North Africa, 1940, 233, 244, 246
Norway, 229
Nyon conference (Sept. 1937), 209

Ode à l'Angleterre, 219
Orlando, Vittorio, 114, 117
Osborne, Charles, 16
Ottoman Empire, see Turkey
Ottawa conference (1932), 169, 176

Painlevé, Paul, 73–4
Paléologue, Maurice, 32
Palestine, 65, 88
Palmerston, Lord, 7, 163
Panther (German gunboat), 43–4

Paris Commune, 15
Parti Populaire Français, 224
Passchendaele, battle (1917), 72,
    110, 180
Paul-Boncour, Joseph, 172, 210–1
'Peace Ballot' (1935), 176, 193
Pedroncini, Guy, 68, 75
Peel, Sir Robert, 7
Perfidious Albion, 11, 20, 106, 199
Pershing, General John, 76, 115
Pétain, Marshal Philippe, 75–6, 107,
    235–6, 240, 242–5, 248–9, 251–3
Petitbon, Colonel Jean, 221
Phipps, Sir Eric, 175, 186, 211, 231
Phoney War (1939–40), 227–31
Piétri, François, 189
Poincaré, Raymond, 49–50, 56, 74,
    76, 99, 124, 130, 132, 136,
    138–40, 142–5, 149, 182, 190
Poland, 124–5, 182, 207, 210, 223–5
    British guarantee, March 1939,
        224
    invaded by Germany, Sept. 1939,
        225, 227–8
Popular Front in France, 1935–36,
    207
Pownall, General Sir Henry, 206
Prague, German occupation (March
    1939), 223
Punch, 20

Quarterly Review, 20
Queux, William le, 41

Rathenau, Walther, 137
Réau, Elisabeth du, 209, 211
Religion, importance in English life,
    17–18, 200–1
Reparations, 119, 122–3, 135–9,
    168
Reparations Commission, 123, 135,
    137–40, 143
Repington, Colonel Charles, 52
Rethondes, 248
Reynaud, Paul, 213, 231, 233–7,
    242, 244–8

Rhineland, 85, 118–21, 140, 150,
    185
    German occupation (1936), 179,
        192, 204–7
Ribbentrop, Joachim, 188, 220
Ribot, Alexandre, 79
Rights of Man, 10, 20
Rire, Le, 10
Roberts, Field Marshal Lord, 60
Robertson, Field Marshal Sir
    William, 71, 74, 103
Robbins, Keith, 38
Rocque, Colonel de la, 181, 223
Romains, Jules, 200–1
Rome, Treaty (1957), 229
Rosebery, Lord, 31
Rouvier, Maurice, 35–6, 38
Royal Air Force: fighters in France,
    1940, 234, 243, 254
Royal Sugar Commission
    (1914–18), 80
Royal visit to Paris (July 1938),
    218–19
Ruhr, French occupation (1923),
    132, 135–6, 139–43, 149, 205
    British attitude, 140–2
Rumania, 182, 220, 225
Runciman, Lord, 86, 214, 217
Russo-Japanese War (1904–5), 29,
    34

St. Helena, 3, 7, 11, 202
St. Jean de Maurienne, Treaty
    (1917), 88
St. Pierre and Miquelon, 30
Salisbury, Lord, 9, 13, 25–7
Salisbury Committee on Home and
    Imperial Defence (1923), 161–2
Salonika campaign (1915–18), 65, 67
Salter, Arthur, 80
Samoa, 26
San Remo, conference (April 1920),
    135
Sarajevo, 55
Sargent, Sir Orme, 211, 220
Sarraut, Albert, 205

Sartiaux, Albert, 51, 155–6
Schlieffen Plan, 47, 55
Scotland, 16, 22
Sembat, Marcel, 85
Serbia, 55
Sèvres, Treaty (Aug. 1920), 129–30
Sheriff, R.C., 155
Siam, 9, 14, 23, 28, 30
Siegfried, André, 16, 198–200
Simon, Sir John, 16, 172–4, 176,
  178, 185–7, 216, 226
Smuts, General Jan, 116, 119, 123
Smyrna, 129–30
Somme, battle (1916), 65, 68–70,
  110, 180, 183
Somme-Aisne line (1940), 236,
  240–1, 244
Soviet Union (USSR), 182, 212,
  229
  Franco-British negotiations with,
    1939, 224–5
Spa conference (July 1920), 135
Spanish Civil War (1936–39), 207–9
  British policy, 208–9
  French policy, 207–8
  Non-Intervention Committee,
    208–9
Spears, General Sir Edward, 62,
  95–6, 98, 100–1, 128, 160, 247
  views of the French in First
    World War, 101–3
'Splendid isolation', 12–13, 25–6
Stalin, Joseph, 182
Stavisky scandal and riots (1934),
  180–1, 203
Steed, Wickham, 57
Steiner, Zara, 32
Stockholm peace conference (1917),
  89
Strasbourg, statue, 14, 120
Stresa conference (1935), 187, 189
Stresemann, Gustav, 141–2, 148,
  150–1
Suarez, Georges, 146
Sudetenland, Sudeten Germans,
  212, 214, 216–17

Supreme War Council:
  1917–18, 73–5, 77, 81–2, 114
  1939–40, 228–9, 233, 238, 242–3,
    245
Sykes-Picot Agreement (1916),
  87–8, 130
Sweden, iron ore, 229
Switzerland, 222
Syria, 87–8, 126–8, 130–1

Talleyrand, Charles-Maurice de, 7, 25
Tangier, 33, 43
Tardieu, André, 178
Taylor, A.J.P., 161
Temps, Le, 118, 221
Ten-Year Rule, 184
Tennyson, Alfred Lord, 8, 51
Terraine, John, 60
Thoiry conference (Sept. 1926), 151–2
Tilman, H.W., 155
Times, The, 240
  on 'ever closer union', 229
'Tipperary', 95
Tocqueville, Alexis de, 15
Toulon, 194–5
Trafalgar, battle (1805), 7
Transvaal, 10
Turkey, Ottoman Empire, 65,
  87–8, 90, 126–31

U-boat warfare, 79, 81, 89
Union of Democratic Control, 144,
  161, 179
Union between Britain and France,
  1940:
  discussed, 229
  British offer, 16 June 1940, 246–8
United States,
  First World War, 70, 79, 87, 90,
    113
    loans, 79–80
  Paris Peace Conference, 1919,
    114–26
  1920s, 144, 154
    loans, 133–4
  Second World War, 242, 251

Vansittart, Sir Robert, 177–9, 193, 247
Verdun, battle (1916), 65–8, 107, 183
Verne, Jules, 15
Versailles Treaty (1919), 87, 121–6, 132, 204
'War guilt' clause, 123–4, 136
Vichy government, regime, 240
Victoria, Queen, 2, 8, 11–12
Viviani, René, 66, 84–5
Voroshilov, Marshal Kliment, 225
Vuillemin, General Joseph, 221

War aims, French and British:
First World War, 82–91
1939–40, 227–8
War crisis (July 1914), 54–9
War memorials, 109, 218
War poets, 108, 155
Warrior, HMS, 8
Waterloo, battle (1815), 6–7
Weather, effect on English character, 18
Wellington, Duke of, 3, 7–8
Werth, Alexander, 180, 203, 218

Weygand, General Maxime, 235–6, 238, 240, 243–6
Wheat Executive (1917), 80
Wiesbaden agreements (Oct. 1921), 137–8
Wilhelm II, Kaiser, 26, 33–4, 43, 86, 91
Wilhelmina, Queen, 232–3, 244
William III, King, 6
Winter War, USSR-Finland (1939–40), 229–30
Wilson, Field Marshal Sir Henry, 45–7, 52, 63–4, 76, 158
Wilson, Sir Horace, 216
Wilson, President Woodrow, 83, 88, 113–14, 117–23, 125, 151, 162
Fourteen Points, 113, 115–16
Winter, Denis, 97
Winter, Jay, 94
Wolfe, General James, 6
Wolseley, Field Marshal Sir Garnet, 51, 53

Yeats, W.B., 204
Yugoslavia, 182